STUDIES IN BIOLOGY, ECONOMY AND SOCIETY
General Editor: Robert Chester, Department of Social Policy and Professional Studies, University of Hull

The study of eugenics today has the aim of increasing understanding of our own species and of the rich complexity of the biosocial fabric, so that professional workers, decision-makers in the community and the public at large may be well informed in areas of concern to the whole society. The Eugenics Society promotes and supports inter-disciplinary research into the biological, genetic, economic, social and cultural factors relating to human reproduction, development and health in the broadest sense. The Society has a wide range of interdisciplinary interests which include the description and measure-ment of human qualities, human heredity, the influence of environ-ment and the causes of disease, genetic counselling, the family unit, marriage guidance, birth control, differential fertility, infecundity, artificial insemination, voluntary sterilisation, termination of preg-nancy, population problems and migration. As a registered charity, the Society does not act as an advocate of particular political views, but it does seek to foster respect for human variety and to encourage circumstances in which the fullest achievement of individual human potential can be realised.

Amongst its activities the Eugenics Society supports original research via its Stopes Research Fund, co-sponsors the annual Darwin Lecture in Human Biology and the biennial Caradog Jones Lecture, and publishes the quarterly journal *Biology and Society*. In addition, the Society holds each year a two-day symposium in which a topic of current importance is explored from a number of different stand-points, and during which the Galton Lecture is delivered by a distinguished guest. The proceedings of each symposium from 1985 constitute the successive volumes of this series, *Studies in Biology, Economy and Society*. Although the balance between different disciplines varies with the nature of the topic, each volume contains authoritative contributions from diverse biological and social sciences together with an editorial introduction.

Information about the Society, its aims and activities, and earlier symposium proceedings may be obtained from: The General Sec-retary, The Eugenics Society, 19 Northfields Prospect, Northfields, London, SW18 1PE.

STUDIES IN BIOLOGY, ECONOMY AND SOCIETY
General Editor: Robert Chester, Department of Social Policy and Professional Studies, University of Hull

Published
Milo Keynes, David A. Coleman and Nicholas H. Dimsdale (*editors*)
THE POLITICAL ECONOMY OF HEALTH AND WELFARE

Peter Diggory, Malcolm Potts and Sue Teper (*editors*)
NATURAL HUMAN FERTILITY

Milo Keynes and G. Ainsworth Harrison (*editors*)
EVOLUTIONARY STUDIES: A Centenary Celebration of the Life of Julian Huxley

David Robinson, Alan Maynard and Robert Chester (*editors*)
CONTROLLING LEGAL ADDICTIONS

Series Standing Order
If you would like to receive future titles in this series as they are published, you can make use of our standing order facility. To place a standing order please contact your bookseller or, in case of difficulty, write to us at the address below with your name and address and the name of the series. Please state with which title you wish to begin your standing order. (If you live outside the UK we may not have the rights for your area, in which case we will forward your order to the publisher concerned.)

Standing Order Service, Macmillan Distribution Ltd, Houndmills, Basingstoke, Hampshire, RG21 2XS, England.

Controlling Legal Addictions

Proceedings of the twenty-fifth annual symposium of the Eugenics Society, London, 1988

Edited by

David Robinson
Institute for Health Studies
University of Hull

Alan Maynard
Centre for Health Economics
University of York

Robert Chester
Department of Social Policy and Professional Studies
University of Hull

MACMILLAN

in association with
THE EUGENICS SOCIETY

First published 1989

Published by
THE MACMILLAN PRESS LTD
Houndmills, Basingstoke, Hampshire RG21 2XS
and London
Companies and representatives
throughout the world

Printed and bound in Great Britain at
The Camelot Press Ltd, Southampton

Typeset by TecSet Ltd, Wallington, Surrey

British Library Cataloguing in Publication Data
Eugenics Society, *Symposium* (25th:1988:London
England)
Controlling legal addictions: proceedings of the
twenty-fifth annual symposium of the Eugenics
Society, London 1988.   (Studies in biology, economy
and society)
1. Great Britain. Alcoholism. Tobacco smoking.
Control measures
I. Title   II. Robinson, David, *1946*–   III. Maynard,
Alan, *1941*–   IV. Chester, Robert, 1929–   V. Series
362.2'9
ISBN 0–333–49252–8 (hardcover)
ISBN 0–333–51740–7 (paperback)

Contents

List of Tables

Notes on the Contributors

Rob Baggott is Lecturer in Politics, Polytechnic of Leicester, and was Research Fellow, ESRC Addiction Research Centre, University of Hull, 1983–6.

Virginia Berridge is Deputy Director, AIDS Social History Group, Department of Public Health and Policy, London School of Hygiene and Tropical Medicine, University of London.

Marcus Grant is Senior Scientist, Division of Mental Health, World Health Organisation, Geneva.

Christine Godfrey is Research Fellow, Centre for Health Economics, University of York, and was Research Fellow, ESRC Addiction Research Centre, University of York, 1983–8.

Michael Gossop is Director of Research, Drug Dependence Unit, Bethlem Royal Hospital, Beckenham, Kent.

Larry Harrison is Lecturer in Social Work and Addictions, Department of Social Policy and Professional Studies, University of Hull, and was Research Fellow, ESRC Addiction Research Centre, University of Hull, 1983–8.

Keith Hartley is Professor of Economics and Director of the Institute for Research in the Social Sciences, University of York, and was Associate, ESRC Addiction Research Centre, University of York, 1983–8.

Ray J. Hodgson is Head of the Clinical Psychology Service, South Glamorgan Health Authority, and Honorary Professor of Clinical Psychology, University of Wales Institution of Science and Technology, Cardiff.

Alan Maynard is Professor of Economics and Director of the Centre for Health Economics, University of York, and was Co-Director of the ESRC Addiction Research Centre, University of York, 1983–8.

Melanie Powell is Lecturer in Economics, Polytechnic of Leeds, and was Research Fellow, ESRC Addiction Research Centre, University of York, 1987–8.

David Robinson is Professor of Health Studies and Director of the Institute for Health Studies, University of Hull, and was Co-Director of the ESRC Addiction Research Centre, University of Hull, 1983–8.

Philip Tether is Senior Research Fellow, Institute for Health Studies, University of Hull, and was Senior Research Fellow, ESRC Addiction Research Centre, University of Hull, 1985–8.

Editors' Preface

In an increasing number of countries, those who are concerned with the drug issue are giving much greater emphasis than in the past to prevention rather than to treatment, and to legal as opposed to illegal substances. Recent resolutions, reports and activities of the World Health Organization have, in no small measure, stimulated this refocusing of attention and effort on controlling legal addictions.

The Eugenics Society's symposium on Controlling Legal Addictions, held at the Zoological Society of London, brought together some of the latest policy research relevant to the question of how best to respond to the increasing number of legal addiction problems. The symposium, organised with the assistance of the ESRC Addiction Research Centre at the Universities of Hull and York, addressed four key issues: the extent and cost of addiction; the addiction market; international responses; and UK control policy. With eight out of the twelve papers being presented by members of the ESRC Addiction Research Centre, much of the thrust of the symposium was concerned with the Centre's own key concern: the identification of impediments to co-ordinated national approaches to the control of alcohol and tobacco-related problems. For those seeking to 'do something about' legal addictions, that has been the main research task of the 1980s.

In many countries, both developed and developing, the increasing attention given to controlling legal addictions is part of a broader shift over recent years towards a concern with healthy public policy. In the UK, during the first two decades of the National Health Service, the efforts of successive governments were devoted, understandably, to ensuring that specialist services and facilities were distributed throughout the country, to carrying out the hospital building programme and to restructuring primary health care. During the 1970s, the lack of sufficient attention to prevention was highlighted and a series of reports and recommendations from, among others, the Department of Health, the Royal Colleges and the Social Services and Employment Sub-Committees of the House of Commons, stressed that over the coming decades the emphasis must be on the prevention as much as on the management of most of the common health and social problems of our time, and also that prevention is not merely a matter for the government, the DHSS and the caring professions but is 'everybody's business'.

As far as controlling the large number of alcohol and tobacco-related problems is concerned there is now widespread agreement among medical and other health workers, many government departments, the media and large sections of the general public that 'something must be done'. Unfortunately, people have not found it quite so easy to reach agreement about what is the best preventive approach. Their disagreements have revolved around what they mean by 'the problem'. For some people, those who are addicted are the real problem, for others the problem is contemporary behaviour patterns and attitudes in relation to alcohol and tobacco, while yet others see the problem as the level of availability of the substances themselves. More recently, however, there have been more constructive discussions about how to establish coherent, co-ordinated national prevention policies which encompass the early identification of those in need of help, the modification of unhealthy attitudes and behaviour, and control over the amount of alcohol and tobacco available in the community.

Many countries are beginning to develop national alcohol and tobacco policies. For example, the draft Australian National Health Policy on Alcohol contains objectives in relation to availability, price and taxation, advertising and marketing, and other legal controls, together with policies in relation to education, treatment, the non-governmental sector and research. Strategies for achieving those objectives are set out, as are evaluation indices. The good sense of such objectives, strategies for action and indices for judging progress is undeniable. But the trick, of course, is to turn policy statements into policy practice, as Australia is starting to do under its National Campaign Against Drug Abuse (NCADA).

In spite of some interesting developments in many Western nations, much discussion and debate about the control of legal addiction problems still concludes with little more than a statement to the effect that the desired goals of policy will be achieved if only there is sufficient 'political will'. This is not to say that the political will issue is not important. It is, of course, a vital aspect of the policy complex. But the core question is 'why is there insufficient political will?' And in order to begin to answer that question a realistic understanding of the policy terrain and the policy-making process is needed. Because, as David Robinson stressed in his Galton Lecture at the symposium, only when you know what is there can you 'take advantage of what's there'.

Every presentation at the symposium made clear that in the drive to control legal addictions there is an urgent need for a much greater understanding of the complexity of the policy world, without which much policy debate will continue to be little more than the exchange of slogans under the guise of 'recommendations'. Virginia Berridge reminds us in her chapter on 'History and Addiction Control' that many contemporary socio-political and economic debates have been live for over a hundred years, while Michael Gossop illustrated the basic nature of the legal addictions world which must be accommodated by anyone concerned with control, namely the simple fact that there are 'Many Problems in Many Forms'. Alan Maynard stresses the need for very much better data in order to even begin to address the issue of 'The Costs of Addiction and the Costs of Control' and, in particular, that we have very poor knowledge of the costs and benefits *at the margin* of alternative control devices. Marcus Grant places the debate about 'Controlling Alcohol Abuse' within not only an international-organisational perspective but within the broad sweep of cultural differences, with particular emphasis on the problems and concerns of developing countries.

Just as there are many legal addiction problems in many forms, so there are many types and levels of control. Ray Hodgson in his discussion reveals the increasing amount of evidence for the effectiveness of 'Low Cost Responses' and their place in an overall control strategy. But, of course, the total population interventions such as those concerned with availability, taxation and price will continue to dominate much of the discussion about controlling legal addictions. In relation to these, Christine Godfrey reviews the complexity of the 'Price Regulation' debate and the impediments to a health based tax policy. Melanie Powell amplifies one particular impediment 'Tax Harmonisation in the European Community' and makes clear that in relation to legal addiction control, no less than many other policy concerns, no island is an island. In similar vein, Larry Harrison shows how both political and technological changes are making it much less possible for governments to manipulate the 'Information Component' of any national control strategy. This has, he says, made a fundamental reassessment of government information policy long overdue.

Both Rob Baggott and Keith Hartley in their respective discussions of 'The Politics of the Market' and 'Industry, Employment and Prevention Policy' make clear that the nature of the industrial market-place within which legal addiction substances are created and traded is not nearly as straightforward as the sloganisers would have us believe. In discussion of control measures it cannot be assumed that alcohol and tobacco-related firms are passive or that their responses will be predictable. Higher taxes, for example, might not be passed on to the consumers through higher prices. The burden might be shifted to workers, shareholders or suppliers either at home or abroad. An expected reduction in home market sales might be responded to by greater advertising or sponsorship, by acquiring rivals or by diversification. Similarly, the apparently clear relationship between control policies and employment in the legal addiction substance industries is by no means simple. The same point is made by Philip Tether in relation to the relative utility of 'Legal Controls and Voluntary Agreements'.

The symposium on Controlling Legal Addictions may have been unusual in that it did not rehearse familiar debates about, for example, whether or not addictions are diseases, whether or not there should be a combined approach to alcoholics and drug addicts, whether or not there is a fetal alcohol syndrome, whether or not women are more susceptible than men to liver cirrhosis, whether or not the children of drug addicts become addicts themselves, and whether or not there is an addictive personality. The symposium was based on the premise that no amount of biomedical, social-psychological, and treatment research can begin to make an impact on the world of legal addictions unless it is complemented by a real understanding of the socio-political and economic realities of the legal addictions market and the processes of policy formation and policy implementation. The aim of the symposium was to move the control debate one step forward and to set an outline agenda for policy research and action during the 1990s.

DAVID ROBINSON
ALAN MAYNARD
ROBERT CHESTER

1 Controlling Legal Addictions: 'Taking Advantage of What's There'

David Robinson

INTRODUCTION

With the ubiquity of tobacco and alcohol and the increasing availability and use of so many other legal drugs, it has become widely recognised that there is no such things as *the* addiction problem. There are many legal addiction problems, and there are many health and social problems in which the use of alcohol or some other legal drug is a contributory factor. Not surprisingly, and particularly over the last decade, there has developed a general consensus that 'something must be done'.

But in spite of the wide-ranging activities and sound guidance of the World Health Organization, and the publication in many countries of a wide array of well thought out reports and policy proposals by government departments, expert committees, professional bodies and concerned individuals, there has been no noticeable decrease in the number and range of legal addiction problems. Why? And is it possible to develop better policies?

In this chapter I shall:

- place the discussion of legal addiction control policies within the broader context of healthy public policy,
- stress the importance of understanding the policy climate and the policy terrain, and
- indicate how legal addiction control policy might be better cultivated, not least, by 'taking advantage of what's there'.

THE HEALTHY PUBLIC POLICY CONTEXT OF
ADDICTION CONTROL

The formulation of policies and strategies to combat legal addictions takes place within the broader context of health and social policy. Policy here is a larger concept than mere legislation. It represents, in addition, the dominant beliefs, attitudes, aspirations and expected behaviours which make up our view of what contemporary life ought to be like. And among the manifestations of an increasingly important component of the current health and social policy context have been the 1986 Ottawa Charter and, before that, the 1978 Declaration of Alma Ata.

The magnitude of the world's health problems and the inadequate and inequitable distribution of health resources both between and within countries have made it imperative to construct a new approach to health and health care. The International Conference on Primary Health Care, organised by WHO and UNICEF, reaffirmed in its *Declaration of Alma Ata* (1978) that health is a fundamental human right. It also stressed that the attainment of the highest possible level of health requires the action of many other social and economic sectors in addition to the health sector and then, echoing the Thirtieth World Health Assembly (WHO, 1977), set as a target for governments, international organisations and the whole world community; 'the attainment by all the peoples of the world by the year 2000 of a level of health that will permit them to lead a socially and economically productive life'.

Primary health care, within comprehensive national health care systems, is seen as the vehicle for achieving that target of 'health for all' by the year 2000. It was expected that each country would interpret and adapt primary health care within its own social, political and developmental context. Already, in many parts of the world, the content and organisation of primary health care is changing as more and more people come to recognise and respond to the fact that this 'front line of activity' is, in the words of Dr Mahler the recently retired Director-General (Mahler, 1977) 'the cornerstone to ensure health for all'.

The Declaration of Alma Ata (Section V) emphasises that 'governments have a responsibility for the health of their people'. But just as governments must provide 'adequate health and social measures' so the people of any country have the 'right and duty to participate individually and collectively in the planning and implementation of their health care' (Section IV).

As part of the development of the policy context designed to make more likely both that government action and that public participation, the *Ottawa Charter* was adopted in 1986 at the First International Conference on Health Promotion. The Charter recognised the increasing attention being given to what has become known as the 'new public health' and also re-emphasised the key thrust of the Declaration of Alma Ata by stressing the need for health promotion to put health 'on the agenda of all policy makers in all sectors and at all levels'. The Charter saw the role of health promotion as combining:

> diverse but complementary approaches including legislation, fiscal measures, taxation and organisational change. It is coordinated action that leads to health, income and social policies that foster greater equity. Joint action contributes to ensuring safer and healthier goods and services, healthier public services, and cleaner, more enjoyable environments.

> Health promotion requires the identification of obstacles to the adoption of healthy public policies in non-health sectors, and ways of removing them. The aim must be to make the healthier choice the easier choice for policy makers as well.

The Ottawa Charter identified five key aspects of effective health promotion action:

- building healthy public policy,
- creating environments that support health,
- strengthening community action,
- helping people to develop skills, and
- re-orienting health services.

The first of these concerns 'Healthy Public Policy' was the subject of the Second International Conference on Health Promotion, from which came the *Adelaide Recommendations* (1988) which attempted to put some policy infrastructural flesh on the bare Ottawa bones.

The main aim of healthy public policy is:

> to create a supportive environment to enable people to lead healthy lives. Healthy choices are thereby [to be] made possible and easier for citizens. Social and physical environments are [to be] made health enhancing. In the pursuit of healthy public policy,

government sectors concerned with agriculture, trade, education, industry and communications need to take account of health as an essential factor during policy formulation. These sectors should be accountable for the health consequences of their policy decisions. As much attention should be paid to health as to the economic considerations.

The 1988 Adelaide Recommendations further stress that, since health is a fundamental right as well as a sound social investment, governments:

need to invest resources in healthy public policy and health promotion in order to raise the health status of all their citizens, [and] . . . New efforts must be made to link economic, social and health policies into integrated action.

The Recommendations also underline the fact that while government plays an important role in health:

health is also influenced greatly by corporate and business interests, non-governmental bodies, and community organisations. Their potential for preserving and promoting people's health should be positively encouraged. [and] . . . New alliances must be forged to provide the impetus for health action.

I have taken time to outline the main thrust of the Ottawa and Adelaide deliberations since they neatly represent an increasingly influential way of talking about health and health issues not merely in international organisations, but in many countries – both developed and developing. In relation to any health issue the challenge has always been to recognise not merely the interrelatedness of 'host, agent and environment' in the traditional epidemiological terminology – now rephrased in healthy-public-policy-speak as 'people, products and settings' – but to take seriously the interrelatedness of policies and, in particular, the surrounding, the consequential, the non-direct, the non-centrally-defined effects of policy which might make more likely the development of health problems or impede the recognition of those problems or their alleviation.

One value of the recent healthy public policy debate has been to re-emphasise the legitimacy and necessity of taking this broader view. In fact, healthy public policy is a useful rephrasing of the familiar injunction for prevention to be 'everybody's business'. It is everybody's business not just in the sense of everybody being susceptible to health problems. Nor is it everybody's business just as private individuals responsible for making life decisions which affect their own health. But it is everybody's business as public citizens involved in everyday social action which affects the lives of others. Healthy public policy, therefore, is:

> an integral part of policy making in every appropriate sector and sphere of activity . . . It is not a separate or isolated body of policy. (WHO, 1988a, p. 2)

The focus of healthy public policy concern is not just at national level, although that is the level which has received most attention. The WHO Healthy Cities programme involving over one hundred cities in Europe, North America and Australasia is concerned with moving toward 'health for all' through healthy public policy at the local level. Philip Tether and I have been concerned with local policy in relation to alcohol for many years (Tether and Robinson, 1986; Robinson *et al.*, 1989) But, in addition to national and local action, healthy public policy has an important international dimension which can be illustrated by considering some of the outline features of the tobacco story.

The links are well known between smoking and cancer of the lung, mouth, larynx, pharynx, oesophagus and elsewhere; heart and circulatory diseases; respiratory malfunction and other disorders. It is estimated that in Western Europe four out of five premature deaths are smoking related and that as Alan Maynard points out in Chapter 5 in the UK alone 100 000 people each year die directly as a result of their smoking. Their smoking, however, is merely the last link in a chain of international activity which is itself not always quite what it seems.

If you pop your head round the door of the local street corner tobacconist you are confronted by a bewildering array of cigarettes and cigars, varying in strength and length, taste and tar level. You may well think to yourself that here is the famous market economy, supply and demand, capital and competition playing itself out before your eyes. You would be quite wrong. Today, the world manufacture of tobacco products outside Eastern Europe is controlled by a handful of multinational companies, sometimes called transnational tobacco conglomerates or TTCs; British American Tobacco, and

Imperial, with a combined annual tobacco turnover of approximately fifty thousand million pounds.

But vast though this turnover is, the manufacture of cigarettes and cigars is as Keith Hartley in Chapter 10 reminds us, only the tip of the iceberg of the TTC's operations. For together, in combination and co-operation, they effectively control every aspect of tobacco-related business from leaf production to the distribution of the finished product. For instance, over 90 per cent of the tobacco that enters into international trade is under the control of six transnational leaf-buying corporations, all of which are either TTC subsidiaries or very much more closely linked with the TTCs than with the leaf producers.

TTCs have bought up shipping companies to transport their leaf tobacco and then bought oil companies to ensure fuel for those ships. They control the companies that make the machines that make the cigarettes, and the paper mills and printing companies that produce the packaging. When it comes to outlets, the TTCs have bought leisure, food, supermarket, store, hotel and other chains that will take their products. They own the cigarette vending machine companies and, where they do not actually own the outlet, have a tight system of controlling bonuses to ensure that retailers display the correct products in the correct place in their windows at the correct non-discount price.

TTCs have now achieved a position which makes it quite impossible for any new company to even contemplate entering the 'competition'. Normal market forces are almost totally irrelevant including, crucially, the pricing of the product. As the United Nations report on 'The Marketing and Distribution of Tobacco' (1978) revealed, a feature of the tobacco market is a seller-determined price:

> The oligopoly [it said] sets the price and sells at that price whatever quantity the market will take . . . Price leadership (price fixing) implies that not only must pricing policies be coordinated, but that the price, once agreed upon, must be sustained until a further change is required by the oligopoly collectively.

The direct impact of smoking on health in developed countries is still considerable, even though consumption in many is declining and smokers are becoming an ever smaller minority of the population. But at the same time, as we know, the prime targets for the TTCs have become the 'new smokers' in the developing world where the most dangerous, high tar level, products are being sold, without health warnings, to the least informed consumers and where, not surprisingly, the indicators of smoking-related diseases are rising sharply. In countries like Thailand, Zambia, Malawi and Brazil the impact on health is not merely from the smoking, but is from the working of the tobacco market itself. For more and more millions of acres of what could be food-growing land and thousands of millions of working days are given over to the cultivation, for barely subsistence level returns to the land worker, of something which eventually goes up in smoke at risk to health and life.

Any problem which arises in the context of an international market, whether legitimate like most tobacco or illegitimate like most narcotics, calls for an international response. But such a response may not always be entirely helpful. Some years ago, for example, Britain and Pakistan concluded an agreement of co-operation to fight the trade in heroin and, in particular, to attempt to eradicate opium poppy cultivation in the wild and remote areas of the north-west frontier which alone was quite able to flood all the world's heroin markets. Britain has now contributed several million pounds to support rural development programmes with the principal aim of replacing the poppy with other crops, such as wheat, maize, tea – and tobacco!

Clearly, there is a need for a healthy public policy approach to the political economy of tobacco and health. For the tobacco issue could be substituted, of course, food, pharmaceuticals, water, alcohol and other substances. Or the focus may be on appropriate technology, or systems of care or the international regulation of pollutants or carcinogens.

UNDERSTANDING THE CLIMATE AND TERRAIN OF CONTROL POLICY

It is within this broad healthy public policy context that much contemporary debate about how to combat legal addiction problems is taking place.

As we know, the vast amount of alcohol, tobacco, and prescription drugs consumed – and their contribution to so many health and social problems – has led to a widespread recognition that treatment alone, no matter how successful it is judged to be for specific individuals, is unlikely to make much impact on any nation's legal addiction problem.

We also know that, as a consequence, in an increasing number of countries the question of how to control the development of legal addiction problems is assuming much greater importance. For many people, this emphasis on control and prevention has been stimulated in no small measure by WHO in the ways which Marcus Grant outlines in Chapter 4. In relation to alcohol, for example, the Thirty-Second World Health Assembly recognised that 'the problems related to alcohol, and particularly its excessive consumption, rank among the world's major public health problems' (resolution WHO 32.40). Three years later the technical discussion at the Thirty-Fifth World Health Assembly brought together participants from over a hundred countries to discuss 'the development of national policies and programmes'. In the following year a resolution (WHO 36.12) at the Thirty-Sixth World Health Assembly requested the Director-General to 'continue and intensify WHO's programme on alcohol related problems as an integral part of the strategy for health for all'.

Paralleling these and other resolutions concerning alcohol have been similar statements about tobacco and prescription drugs, while WHO has produced a series of strategic publications. Taken together these WHO resolutions, reports and associated activities over the past decade have contributed greatly to the general shift in prime international concern away from legal addiction problems – their classification, identification and management – to prevention and the construction of national control policies.

National alcohol and tobacco policies are increasingly being developed in the form of overall strategic objectives with in addition, in some cases, action plans to achieve these objectives and, in just a few cases, indicators of how to evaluate those actions. For example, in the draft National Health Policy on Alcohol (1986) in Australia presented to the Ministerial Council on Drug Strategy objectives were set in relation to availability, price and taxation, advertising and marketing, and other legal controls, together with policies in relation to education, treatment, the non-governmental sector and research. Strategies for achieving those objectives were set out and followed by evaluation indices. The indices on advertising, included:

• the restriction of direct advertising of alcohol on television to those periods scheduled for adult viewing,
• the reduction of tax deductibility of expenditure on alcohol advertising to 0 per cent,

- the elimination of direct advertising of alcohol beverages, as distinct from corporate identification of sponsorship, in conjunction with sporting and cultural activities. (1.3)

The good sense of such objectives, strategies for action and indices for judging progress is undeniable. But the trick, of course, is to turn them from policy statements into policy practice. To date, however, much discussion and debate about the control of legal addiction problems has concluded with little more than a statement to the effect that the desired goals of policy will be achieved if there is sufficient 'political will'. An example of this can be found at the end of the final chapter of Don Cahalan's recent book *Understanding America's Drug Problem: How to Combat the Hazards of Alcohol* (1987) where he concludes:

> In relation to alcohol policy: obviously our state, local, and national governments are the agencies we should hold responsible for bringing about equitable relationships between the general consuming and tax-paying public, the sellers of the alcoholic beverages, the sufferers from alcoholism and their families, and those who treat alcoholics . . . Our country has solved even worse problems before. With a little *political backbone* [my emphasis], we should be able to reduce drinking to a livable level without a return to prohibition. (p. 196)

In the policy arena, this call for more political backbone is the equivalent of the therapeutic demand to 'pull yourself together'; namely, the last resort of those with nothing more useful to suggest. The call as you will remember in the 1960s used to be for 'relevance', then in the 1970s it became 'more education', now in the 1980s it has been – in various guises – 'political will'. If only, runs the assertion, we could make our work relevant/have more education/mobilise political will we would be on the right track to prevent/minimise/solve some of those awful social/health/addiction problems which plague our organisation/locality/nation.

This is not to say that the political will issue is not important. It is, of course, as Rob Baggot makes clear in Chapter 9, a vital aspect of the policy complex. But it is a matter to be considered in relation to the following core questions: 'why don't we do what all right thinking people know ought to be done to combat alcohol-related and other

legal addiction problems?' This then becomes: 'why is there insufficient political will?' And in order to begin to answer that question we
need to know something of the policy terrain.

Some of those who call for national control policies do not appear
to appreciate the range and complexity of existing policies and
activities. In fact they sometimes seem to be suggesting that there is
no national policy at all. But, of course, every country in which there
is any alcohol or other legal drug has its *de facto* national policy. We
may or may not like that policy, but that is a separate matter.

A detailed map of the current policy terrain in any country would
reveal a wide range of statutory, commercial, voluntary, professional, service sector and other agencies, groups and organisations
involved in some way with alcohol, tobacco, prescription drugs and
related problems. At government level alone, for example, there will
be many ministries or departments of state that play some role in
relation to some aspect of regulation, taxation and legislation,
importation and exportation, production and distribution, promotion
and sale, or the consequences of consumption. The laws, regulations
and activities of these governmental and many other organisations
constitute that country's national policies. The question now arises of
what then actually constitutes the policy terrain in any particular
country. In most countries it might helpfully be thought of in terms of
policy issues, and policy organisations.

Much debate, however, about how best to combat alcohol and
tobacco problems is over-simple in relation to both issues and
organisations. The issues, for instance, are often no more firmly
delineated in policy debate than in calls for 'something to be done'
about some small combination of high profile problems or target
groups such as: young people, advertising, road safety, taxes,
customs controls, pregnant women, and so on. All of these are
important issues. But since the list could be extended endlessly it
helps if they are grouped for purposes of both policy statement and
policy practice. When matters are more systematically considered it is
usually found that most discussion of legal addiction issues tend to be
primarily concerned with either:

- employment and the market,
- education,
- advertising and the media,
- health and safety, or
- law and order.

Within these constellations of issues there are, of course, numerous specifics. Within 'law and order', for example, there are, among many other things, matters to do with:

- illegal possession,
- illicit production,
- illegal sale or purchase,
- product and purchase-related theft,
- importation, trade and tax offences,
- public drunkenness and public disorder,
- liquor licensing,
- drinking and driving, etc.

Yet even this is too simple a level for mapping the real terrain of policy issues. Within the 'drinking and driving' issue, for example, there is a multitude of policy strands such as:

- motorists' rights,
- apprehension procedures,
- adequacy of breath test apparatus,
- police records,
- court practice,
- sentencing policy, etc.

together with once-removed contextual concerns such as:

- highway construction,
- surface markings and lighting,
- car design,
- learner driver education,
- general public safety education, etc.

In any policy issue constellation, then, there are these levels of policy specifics and policy strands which go to make up the real policy terrain. All this is obvious. But does it matter? In particular, does it matter for those concerned with policy development? In order to answer that question we need to consider the second major area of common over-simplification in the legal addictions policy debate: organisations.

As with issues, much discussion of policy organisations is restricted to dominant groupings; often little more than:

- the government
- the (helping) professions

- the trade
- the law
- the general public

All these are, of course, important sets of offices and people. But in any policy debate it is unhelpful if they are not disaggregated. There is no such thing as *a* trade or *a* professional view on alcohol or tobacco. Similarly no 'government' is an entity in relation to legal addictions any more than it is in relation to anything else. Governments each have many addiction relevant policies, which will be more or less explicit and more or less compatible with each other.

In their recent analysis of *Alcohol Policies: Responsibilities and Relationships in British Government*, Tether and Harrison (1988) have mapped out the policy complexity within sixteen government departments. They fascinatingly outline the departmental alcohol responsibilities and then describe where these responsibilities are located within departmental structures, trace out the principal intra and inter-departmental policy-making links and, finally, indicate each department's contacts with the most important non-departmental organisations which may contribute to the alcohol policy process.

The Department of Transport (DOT) will here serve as a small case example. Within the DOT various aspects of policy are divided between policy Directorates, four of which have alcohol responsibilities. These four Directorates are: Road and Vehicle Safety, Marine and Ports, Railways, and Civil Aviation. In addition there is the Accident Investigation Branch.

In relation to alcohol the DOT has a concern with, among many other things, consumption in the Merchant Navy. This is a matter, therefore, for the Marine and Ports Directorate. The following is a brief extract from Tether and Harrison's account.

The (Marine and Ports) Directorate has two sections concerned with alcohol-related problems: the Occupational Health and Safety Section, which is part of the Marine Survey Service and comes under a Deputy Surveyor; and Section B in Marine Division 1, which is concerned with employment conditions and discipline in the Merchant Navy.

The Occupational Health and Safety Section has only a limited role in relation to alcohol and work policies. Guidelines on alcohol and work policies were issued in 1981 by a joint employers and trades

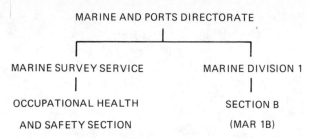

MARINE AND PORTS DIRECTORATE

MARINE SURVEY SERVICE

OCCUPATIONAL HEALTH
AND SAFETY SECTION

MARINE DIVISION 1

SECTION B
(MAR 1B)

union body, the National Maritime Board, which is now a limited company, British Maritime Technology Limited. These guidelines went to the 80–90 shipping companies which are members of the General Council of British Shipping (GCBS). Over half of these companies have now adopted an alcohol and work policy. The Department of Transport's Occupational Health and Safety Section distributes copies of a booklet *Don't Drink and Sink*, which was produced by the now disbanded Alcohol Education Centre. The Section is also concerned with environmental safety measures, such as the regulations governing the size and use of gang planks. Since most alcohol-related drownings occur in ports, when seafarers are leaving or returning to their vessels, environment safety measures are an important part of any prevention strategy. However, alcohol-related issues have been the province of the Marine Division 1 historically, and the Survey Service do not seem to have realised that many of their activities have an alcohol dimension.

In Marine Division 1, Section MAR1B deals with the discipline and medical fitness of merchant seamen. The disciplinary function is bound up with the Department's responsibility for issuing a certificate of competence to all prospective Merchant Navy Officers who pass the Nautical College examination. In cases of serious misconduct, the Department convenes an enquiry under Section 52 of the Merchant Shipping Act. This enquiry, which can take away an officer's certificate of competence, is run along legal lines, chaired by a legally qualified person. The Department of Transport acts as the prosecution in such cases. The person appointed to run the enquiry adjudicates, assisted by professional assessors. There are only a few Section 52 cases each year, and of these, just under half involve alcohol-related offences.

MAR1B is also concerned with alcohol and medical fitness. Under the Merchant Shipping (Medical Examination) Regulations, 1983, it is an offence to employ a seafarer on a UK registered seagoing ship of 1600 gross tonnage or over without a medical examination. The statutory medical examinations take place very five years for seafarers under 40, and every two for those who are older. The medical standards are laid out in the Department of Transport's Merchant Shipping Notice No. M1144. 'Alcohol abuse' is covered in Section V. If alcohol consumption is causing a 'physical or behavioural disorder' the examining physician must record a 'Category B' decision, indicating that the required standard has not been met and that the seaman must be judged permanently unfit. There are approximately 300 doctors, either retained or employed by the ship owners, who are authorised to conduct statutory medical examinations. A seaman who has lost his livelihood in this way can appeal to the Department of Transport, who have a panel of 12 independent doctors. The identification of alcohol dependency is a frequent concern for the appeal panel. (pp. 26–7).

I make no apology for quoting this extract from Tether and Harrison, since it gives some indication of the real complexity of the policy terrain in just one corner of one Directorate in one government department in the UK. Without such specifics and such detail, addiction control debate is just so much sloganising.

CULTIVATING CONTROL BY TAKING ADVANTAGE OF WHAT'S THERE

However conducive the policy climate, the complexity of the policy terrain means that legal addiction control policy can not possibly be cultivated by every relevant policy organisation being involved in every policy issue. In the real world of policy, activity takes place in networks where the issues and the organisations meet. For it is in the policy networks where the policy issues are the property of policy organisations. It is in policy networks where policy is developed.

Those who participate in any particular network may not all share the same view about the nature of any particular issue that they are addressing, or share the same view about who does or should do what, when, where, with whom in relation to it. For policy networks are not made up of organisations and groups which agree with each other. They are made up of those who need or choose or are required to be involved in some overlapping policy area of interest and concern.

In any country there will be, of course, a wide range of policy networks in relation to legal addictions. There may well be dominant clusters of networks concerned with policy action on major constellations of policy issues such as those mentioned earlier:

- employment and the market,
- education,
- advertising and the media,
- health and safety,
- law and order.

Taking 'alcohol and safety' in the UK as a small case example; in addition to the involved government departments such as Transport, Education and Employment there are over eighty occupational health and safety groups spread throughout the country whose membership includes health and safety at work officers, personnel officers, supervisors and managers. Most are affiliated to the Royal Society for the Prevention of Accidents and to that body's Occupational Health and Safety Group's Advisory Committee on which sit senior safety professionals from the Health and Safety Executive, the medical profession, trade unions, employers' organisations and insurance companies. And this is only one corner of the safety network. Add to it the Pedestrian's Association, the Guild of Experienced Motorists, the Cyclists' Touring Club, the Institution of Highway Engineers, the County Surveyors' Society, coroners with their statutory right to comment about and advise on the circumstances and conditions surrounding fatalities, local government home safety committees and road safety departments, the fire service, accident and emergency departments, and many, many more, and one gets some idea of the complexity of this one network area.

While sets of dominant issues may be readily identifiable clear boundaries cannot be drawn around the policy networks. Moreover, there will be sub-networks where specific issues are focused on and fought over. And, of course, network will interact with network because policy organisations may well be involved in more than one policy network. This also means that policy cultivation in one network may drag an organisation or part of an organisation in one direction which may conflict with the way it is being dragged in another network. This happens most obviously with the premier policy organisation, national government, where – as we know – an agriculture or trade ministry may be encouraging the further development of tobacco or whisky industry while the health, law and transport ministries may be attempting to cope with the consequences of increased consumption.

It is in response to this state of affairs that many people call for a national plan of action, a national committee or even a national supremo in the belief that these conflicting activities would then disappear, and coherent and co-ordinated national policy could be cultivated. But from what we know of the complex policy terrain this can never be. Not least because it would require the control of legal addiction problems to be universally agreed to be the highest good – that is, more important than anything else. It would have to be more important than tax and duty revenue, industrial production, employment in certain localities, and international treaty obligations, not to mention personal pleasure, civil liberty and individual freedom which are not unfamiliar components of the legal addiction debate.

The close understanding and appreciation of the policy climate and the policy terrain mean that there are no simple answers to the question 'how do we control legal addictions?'. But that does not mean nothing can be done. It is not a recipe for despair. The mistake which is often, and understandably, made is to equate the need to avoid over-simplification with the feeling that single issues are unimportant. In fact, of course, single issues are vital. Single issues are what control, in reality, is all about about. It is in relation to single issues that actual policy networks can be involved and mobilised. It is in relation to single issues that the general population can be mobilised, excited or, at least, interested. It is via single issues that resources can be sufficiently concentrated to move legal addiction matters up particular political agendas.

The inter-departmental Ministerial Group on Alcohol Misuse which was established (Home Office, 1987) to review and develop the Government's strategy for combating alcohol-related problems has been criticised by some for its concentration on a small number of high-profile issues: road safety, public disorder, young people, etc. To the extent that this criticism is aimed at an assumed unwillingness by the Ministerial Group to address those issues which confront dominant trade interests it may for that reason for some be justified. To criticise the group for taking on a small number of meaty sets of problems and making policy proposals for their alleviation is unjustified. It is certainly banal to criticise any organisation for not doing everything. So, the Ministerial Group is addressing some high profile issues and mobilising some cross-departmental action. But given the extensive list of other major legal addiction concerns all departments should keep explicitly rubbing up against the legal addiction components of the policies for which they have responsibility. The healthy public policy challenge for the rest of us is to ensure that they acknowledge those components and act.

This placing of the legal addiction debate within the everyday business of social and political activity is essential if any realistic progress is to be made toward the cultivation of better policies to control legal addiction problems. And within the real policy world – as opposed to the world of apolitical exhortation – things do change. And so they can change in the 'right' direction; as defined by those who wish to control legal addiction problems. Three current changes are particularly important.

First is the change in policy climate which was mentioned earlier. And here the movements for Health for All by the Year 2000 and for Healthy Public Policy are playing their part in trying to raise the issue of health higher up the political agenda. The aim is to make health less an unintended consequence of other policy action and less a residual category or second/third order concern and more a defining characteristic of public policy.

The second way in which things can change for the better is by the very nature of most social policy cultivation. Rather than pressing for a co-ordinated, supra departmental, national policy – under which all action is geared to securing some well defined objectives in a rational policy approach – the reality of the policy terrain demands that a desired national policy-in-action, rather than merely policy-on-paper, can only be cultivated through a process of what is often called 'partisan mutual adjustment' (Lindblom, 1965). As Harrison and Tether (1987) have succinctly described it:

> Agencies are 'partisan' in that they pursue their own interests but they are capable of 'mutual adjustment', in that they adapt to the decisions made by other agencies, or attempt to influence some through negotiation, bargaining and manipulation. The policy which emerges may not be the theoretical optimum, but it will be one over which agreement has been reached, and which therefore stands some chance of being implemented. [In Lindblom's analysis] 'partisan mutual adjustment' is both descriptive and pres-

criptive in that it purports not only to describe what happens but to recommend it as a 'democratic' way of making policy.

The strategic – and democratic – task then for those who want to push alcohol, tobacco and other legal drug policy in what they consider to be the 'right' direction is to get involved in the policy cultivation process. This is clearly possible in the complexity of organisations which make up the policy terrain. It is particularly important to do so when the policy climate, as now, is conducive to change.

The third positive sign for change, and closely related to the second, is that there has been a growing emphasis on things other than *national* policy in relation to legal addictions. Let us be quite clear; national control policies are certainly essential. But concentration on action at the national level to the exclusion of any serious consideration of anything else is mistaken. It implies, unhelpfully, that the only worthwhile response to contemporary health and social problems is global action by central government. Such a viewpoint diverts attention from the wealth of other – sectoral and local – prevention and control resources which are so often unrecognised and, therefore, untapped.

No local prevention policy package will, of course, be able directly to change such things as customs regulations, retailing law, the drink-driving law or the Chancellor of the Exchequor's taxation policies. Nevertheless, many effective and sensible meaures can be taken at the local level without the backing of legislation, massive funding or central government commitment (Tether and Robinson, 1986; Robinson *et al.*, 1989). What is required locally as Ray Hodgson makes clear in Chapter 6, is the careful identification and cataloguing of resources, together with specific intervention by interested people, at the right time, through appropriate organisations which will encourage, promote and co-ordinate minor, but important, changes in existing practices and procedures.

So those engaged in the identification, management and prevention of legal addiction problems in particular localities should not wait for national initiatives. They should create policy at the periphery where the problems and so many of the resources are located and where, moreover, developments serve as models for national policy-makers. For good practice at the local level today is often, as any political analyst knows, tomorrow's central policy.

Much national legal addictions policy is discussed and debated as though it existed in isolation not merely from local activities but from the activities and interests of other nations. The internationality of the illicit addictions market is, of course, well recognised and there is increasing effort being made to develop multinational agreements and programmes to deter and detect drug trafficking. The International Conference on Drug Abuse and Illicit Trafficking held in Vienna in 1987 called for active collaboration between intergovernmental organisations and member states. In the Australian National Campaign Against Drug Abuse (NCADA), which covers both legal and illegal drugs, one of the core principles of the Campaign is to control supply with particular emphasis in the Campaign document (Department of Health, 1985) put on the fact that:

drug abuse is a subject of growing significance in Australia's foreign relations, at the multinational, regional and bilateral level. (with Australia being) an active, concerned and cooperative member of United Nations bodies dealing with drug control. Australia has been a member of the United Nations Commission on Narcotic Drugs continuously since 1973 and continues to be actively involved in United Nations initiatives to combat drug abuse and drug trafficking. The Australian Federal Police has been actively involved in regional operations and will continue to pursue international drug law enforcement cooperation through participation in international liaison meetings and training. The Customs Service will pursue further opportunities for improving drug interception at the Customs barrier through the exchange of information and mutual assistance through Customs administrations. (p. 10)

The Australian NCADA addresses itself not just to supply reduction of illicit drugs through multinational activities of the kind just mentioned but to demand reduction within its own boundaries. The interrelation between these two sets of control strategies is obvious and itself international. As George Shultz, the American Secretary of State, acknowledged in 1987 on his visit to Bolivia, there is no point in criticising that country for not reducing the production and exportation of cocaine if the United States, the main market, does nothing to reduce the demand for its importation. All that is uncontentious in relation to illicit drugs.

But there are equally important international dimensions to the legal addictions debate which tend to be overlooked by those who call for and suggest possible components of national control policies. In particular, there are those who play down or do not acknowledge at all the implication of their own national actions for the development of problems in other countries. In the excellent Australian NCADA document there is no mention of the massively increasing export and internationalisation of their alcohol trade. And in relation to alcohol no less than illicit drugs 'no island is an island'. It is understandable and right for Australia to emphasise some of the early pointers to success in the NCADA. As the Minister of Health, Neil Blewett, modestly summed it up at the end of the 1987 Leonard Ball Oration, 'I am encouraged by some of the tentative indicators that we are on the right path' (Blewett, 1987, p. 14). But a fully rounded national approach would also pay attention to those activities of its citizens and organisations which exacerbate the legal addiction problems of other countries. In short the question to be addressed is 'how many problems are being exported with the products?'

The Australian NCADA provides the framework for such questions to be legitimately addressed since, as I mentioned earlier, the Campaign document emphasises a comprehensive approach to drug use and drug problems since as it says 'it is inappropriate to focus exclusively on one type of drug or on one group of drug users' (p. 3). This principle was also adopted by the WHO expert working group representing all WHO regions which drew up the Consensus Statement *Towards Healthy Public Policies on Alcohol and Other Drugs* (WHO, 1988b) which raises cross-substance multinational questions within the context of the call to formulate national policies and programmes. WHO has recently adopted as a target for 1995 the establishment of comprehensive national policies and programmes on alcohol and drugs in at least half the Member States.

Another weakness of much discussion on the construction of national policies is the assumption, usually implicit and, probably, unconsidered, that nations *can* control the aspects of their life which are focused on in the policy. The 1970s and early 1980s in the United Kingdom have seen many reports and recommendations from government departmental advisory committees, professional bodies and others which conclude that action needs to be taken to prevent the increase in alcohol and tobacco-related problems. There has been, as we know, the call in most reports for the manipulation of taxes and the need for more and better information and education.

Now the good sense of these suggestions may well be undeniable. But rarely is there any discussion of whether such policy components, even if agreed by everyone in the country, could actually be implemented. Melanie Powell has spelled out the lack of control which the UK government might have over the setting of excise duty levels in Chapter 8 and in her recent Data Note in the *British Journal of Addiction*:

> The European Commission has already tabled over 75% of the 300 White Paper proposals on the international market, including those required to achieve fiscal approximation. A report on the progress of Member States is due by 31 December 1988. There can be no doubt that substantial changes will occur in the taxation of alcohol and tobacco within the European Community. For countries like the UK which raise a larger proportion of revenue from excise, the Commission proposals will result in substantial reductions in the levels of excise duty charged on alcohol and tobacco (Powell, 1988, pp. 971–2).

It is unclear yet whether the UK Chancellor of the Exchequor will be able to persuade finance colleagues in other Community countries of his alternatives to fixed approximation. In relation to the advertising and information giving about alcohol, tobacco and prescription drugs Larry Harrison points in Chapter 11 to the many recent developments both political and technological which will curtail the ability of any nation to determine the information component of any legal addictions control policy.

CONCLUSION

The extent of the world's alcohol, tobacco and prescription drug consumption demands that serious consideration be given to how best to develop policies to combat associated problems. Over the past decade there has been a rapidly increasing recognition in many countries of the need for 'something to be done'. In many countries, this concern has taken the form of little more than exhortation and the identification of a number of desirable policy goals.

I have tried to place the debate about the control of legal addictions within the broader context of the drive toward healthy public policy, while at the same time bringing that currently fashionable way of talking about health issues down to the earth of the complexity of legal addiction specifics, the boundaries to the development of control policy, the competing interests and the other features of the real legal addictions world which are stressed in many other chapters. All of which has pointed to the need to:

• know what's there,
• use what's there,
• build on what's there, and
• prepare for what's going to be there.

The development of more effective policies in relation to legal addiction problems can only take place if there is:

• an appreciation of the healthy public policy climate,
• an understanding of the policy terrain, in particular the range of policy issues and the disposition of policy organisations, and
• a recognition of the impact of climate and terrain on the process of policy cultivation, in particular the nature and role of national and international policy networks and the need to take seriously the development of policy at the local level.

In short, we need to 'take advantage of what's there'. And as the other chapters in this book make clear, that is not a soft option.

References

Adelaide Recommendations (1988) *Report of the Second International Conference on Health Promotion*. WHO/Australian Department of Community Services and Health.
Blewett, N. (1987) *National Campaign Against Drug Abuse: Assumptions, Arguments and Aspirations*. 19th Leonard Ball Oration, 11 March 1987. NCADA Monog Series, 1, Australian Government Publishing Service.
Cahalan, D. (1987) *Understanding America's Drinking Problem: How to Combat the Hazards of Alcohol* (London: Jossey-Bass).
Declaration of Alma Ata (1978) *Report of the International Conference on Health Care*, WHO/UNICEF, ICPHC/PRA/70.10.
Department of Health (1985) *National Campaign against Drug Abuse*. Campaign document issued following the Special Premiers' Conference, Canberra 2 April 1985, Australian Government Publishing Service.
Harrison, L. and Tether, P. (1987) 'The Coordination of UK Policy on Alcohol and Tobacco: the Significance of Organisational Networks', *Policy and Politics*, 15.2, 77–90.
Home Office (1987) Home Secretary Announces Ministerial Group on Alcohol Misuse, *News Release*, 18 September.
Lindblom, C. (1965) *The Intelligence of Democracy* (New York: Free Press).

Mahler, H. (1977) *Blueprint for Health for All*, WHO Chronicle 31. 491.

National Health Policy on Alcohol (1986) Draft presented to the Ministerial Council on Drug Strategy, Canberra.

Ottawa Charter for Health Promotion (1986) *Report of the Interntional Conference on Health Promotion* (WHO/Health and Welfare Canada/ Canadian Public Health Association).

Powell, M. (1988) Data Note 15, 'Alcohol and Tobacco Tax in the European Community', *British Journal of Addiction*, vol. 83, pp. 971–8.

Robinson, D., Tether, P and Teller, J. (1989) *Local Action on Alcohol Problems* (London: Routledge).

Tether, P. and Harrison, L. (1988) *Alcohol Policies: Responsibilities and Relationships in British Government*, Addiction Research Centre Monograph, Universities of Hull and York.

Tether, P. and Robinson, D. (1986) *Preventing Alcohol Problems: A Guide to Local Action* (London: Tavistock).

United Nations (1978) *Marketing and Distribution of Tobacco*. A study by the UN Conference on Trade and Development.

WHO (1977) Resolution WHO 30.43 *WHO Official Record*.

WHO (1979) Resolution WHO 32.40 *WHO Official Record*.

WHO (1983) Resolution WHO 36.12 *WHO Official Record*.

WHO (1988a) *Healthy Public Policy: Issues and Options*. Conference working paper for the Second International Conference on Health Promotion, Adelaide.

WHO (1988b) *Towards Healthy Public Policies on Alcohol and Other Drugs*. Consensus Statement proposed by a WHO Expert Working Group, Sydney–Canberra, 24–31 March 1988.

2 History and Addiction Control: The Case of Alcohol

Virginia Berridge

There is a richness and diversity of alcohol history. At the international level, alcohol historians are animated by an *esprit de corps* which helps facilitate the development of cross-national trends and comparisons. The work of the Social History of Alcohol Conference at Berkeley in 1984, the alcohol epidemology section of ICAA and now the Kettil Bruun Society should be mentioned. The US and Scandinavian traditions of work are notable. Why is this so? The names and places mentioned above give a clue.

Much alcohol history has been conceived and written, if not from the perspective of the present, at least with the explicit aim of analysing and illuminating contemporary tensions and perceptions. The 'manifesto' for the Social History of Alcohol Conference saw the function of history in this way. The conference was 'planned to bring different historical experiences to bear on a number of substantial and practical theoretical issues concerning the cultural positioning of alcohol and the nature and prevalence of alcohol problems in complex societies'. It was also aimed 'to have practical implications for alcohol policy and alcohol problems prevention' (Alcohol and Temperance History Group Newsletter, 1983). There is less of a tradition in alcohol history of relating alcohol to the concerns of the parent discipline–history or social policy.

But Britain seems to be an exception. Alcohol was an early example of the 'relevant' history now much in demand from politicians and which animates discussions of health policy in particular. But because much work on alcohol here is of a relatively older vintage, the role of alcohol has been related in this country more to non-alcohol debates. Harrisons's *Drink and the Victorians* (1971) was really concerned with the role of temperance as part of the reformist post-Chartist labour movement: Michael Rose's and John Turner's work on drink in the First World War contributes to the debate on war and social change; Dingle's concern for drink in the late nineteenth century was part of the consideration of working-class living standards (Dingle, 1972; Rose, 1973; Turner, 1980). One could comment similarly on work by Peter Clark or Peter McCandless (Clark, 1983; McCandless 1984).

In this chapter, I draw on both traditions; and of course they are not mutually exclusive. 'Controlling Legal Addictions' is the overall theme; and the role of medical theories of addiction and of the practices of medical control which have accompanied them will be my central focus. I make no apologies for an exclusively British approach, nor can I lay any claim to comprehensiveness. In looking at my main themes – the ideology of disease; the idea of treatment; the role of public health; the advent of psychology; and the resurgence of many of these themes post-Second World War, perhaps a primary conclusion will be the need for more historical and policy research. Like much social history of medicine, the twentieth century in particular awaits analysis.

THE IDEOLOGY OF DISEASE

Controlling legal addictions requires some notion of a definable condition to be controlled. How – and when – did this come about? Such an apparently simple historical question at once brings forth a host of theories and perspectives, closely allied with recent debates on insanity in the eighteenth and early nineteenth centuries. What one can call the 'traditional-progressive' view of alcohol history saw the development of the disease concept of addiction as part of the general era of progress in psychiatry. Pinel struck the chains from the mad at the Bicetre in Paris. In England, the Tuke family at the York Retreat initiated 'moral therapy'. Alcohol's counterpart was Thomas Trotter, who published his *Essay Medical Philosophical and Chemical on Drunkenness* in 1804. Trotter stated at the outset that the 'habit of drunkenness is a disease of the mind'. Moralists and parsons had, he thought, been well-meaning in exposés of it as vice or sin, but at last the disease had been set within its rightful domain, to be managed by the 'discerning physician'. Like Rush in America, Trotter was hailed as the 'discoverer' of disease.

But the social history of medicine in general and insanity in particular has largely overthrown such Whiggish notions in favour of a desire to see medical developments in their social and intellectual context. Foucault, for example, saw the new rationalist mentalities associated with the Enlightenment and the bureaucratic and police powers associated with the modern absolutist state combining to confine 'irrational' elements of society; insanity was fundamentally reconceptualised as both moral and mental. The disease view of alcoholism was part of this broader paradigm shift, or new discourse. Harry Levine has been the chief protagonist of this view for alcohol (Levine, 1978).

Such revisionism has, in its turn, been subject to revision. Roy Porter, in his alternative interpretation of eighteenth-century developments in insanity sees institutional developments as part of the rise of a consumer society and emphasises the eighteenth-century roots of the ideology of care and cure (Porter, 1985). Alcohol theories have their place in this context. The language of disease in relation to alcohol was common in that century; and before Trotter, John Coakley Lettsom and others had grasped the full cycle of addiction. There were differences; the eighteenth-century accounts were based on an associationist psychology of habituation, the nineteenth drew on Esquirol and Prichard's theories of moral insanity as paralysis of the will. Trotter was distinct from the eighteenth-century writers too in favouring abrupt and immediate, rather than gradual, withdrawal from alcohol.

Certainly disease theories were not that new; but their social and political significance was much greater in the nineteenth century. The temperance movement and teetotalism with its emphasis on total abstinence combined with the developing medical profession to make disease theory the central interpretation of chronic drunkenness. This *rapprochement* took place in the last three decades of the nineteenth century; until then the temperance approach had stressed more general social and environmental reform rather than a strictly medical paradigm. In fact, as Brian Harrison (1971) has noted, because of the strength of temperance in Britain, scientific studies of alcohol were largely confined to continental Europe in the earlier decades of the nineteenth century. In Britain, the *rapprochement* was symbolised by the formation in 1884 by the Society for the Study of Inebriety (briefly and optimistically the Society for the Study and Cure of Inebriety). Its president, Norman Kerr, forcefully advanced the disease position.

'What is inebriety?' he proclaimed, at the inaugural meeting of the Society, 'We may define it as a diseased state of the brain and nerve centres, characterised by an irresistible impulse to indulge in intoxicating liquor or other narcotic, for the relief which these afford, at any peril. This ungovernable, uncontrollable over-powering impulse may hurry on the diseased dipsomaniac to his destruction, even when he has no relish for the toxic agent, but on the contrary loathes and detests it.

In such cases the power of self control has been so weakened, and the desire to resort to intoxicants has become so ungovernable, that the abjectness of the bondage under which the shiftless and helpless victims of dipsomania groan is indeed most piteous.' (Kerr, 1884)

The medical members of the Society saw themselves as scientific and objective observers of an area which had previously been marked only by moral and penal judgements. But teetotal (and anti-opium) views were inextricably entwined in the concept of inebriety. Many of the Society's medical members (and its non-medical associates) were themselves temperance supporters; and moral judgements about loss of control (which were also founded on contemporary psychiatric theory) were transferred into the medical arena. Inebriety, like theories of insanity, saw a conjuncture between somatic and moral approaches.

Disease was, at the end of the nineteenth century, a physical hereditarian concept. But William Bynum has shown that degenera-tionism as a means of explanation of alcoholism was in decline before the First World War (Bynum, 1984). The purely physicalist concept of disease also came under attack. Sir William Collins, Liberal MP and President of the SSI during the First World War, noted that the belief in a physical cause of addiction tended to 'flounder in the quicksands of responsibility and irresponsibility'. He subscribed to the term 'addiction', with its origins in the Latin word describing those who by debt had become slaves of their creditors. But Collins drew on the same combination of the somatic and the moral. Addiction was a

disease of the will – if one may couple terms derived from the opposite poles of the material and the volitional – and assuredly a disease in which the individual possessed has in many instances a most essential co-operative influence in his own worsement or betterment. (Collins, 1919)

But the concept of disease as a physical entity remained strong in the inter-war years. Edward Mapother, superintendent of the Maudsley Hospital in the 1930s, saw alcoholism as 'commonly seen in those whose psychopathic tendency is of generalised and endogenous origin needing explanation in terms of biochemistry rather than psychology'. Korsakov's psychosis, which saw alcoholism as a vitamin deficiency was then in favour; hormone therapy and insulin treatment offered physical models of treatment. The removal of hidden foci of infection, bad teeth in particular, contributed to the concept of alcoholism as a physical disorder of the system. Mapother commented, 'I am more hopeful of results from physical than from any psychological methods yet invented' (Mapother, 1939).

TREATMENT AND THE INEBRIATES ACTS

The natural corollary of disease was treatment; it is to this preferred medical control of inebriety which we must now turn. It was ironic that, as the failure of the asylum became apparent towards the end of the century, optimism revived about the curative potential of compulsory institutional confinement for the inebriate. The medical reformers envisaged an extensive institutional system to which drunkards could be transferred from within the criminal justice system. Medicine would be the policeman. But the legislative and practical reality never lived up to the ideal. Even the most extensive (and last) inebriates act to be passed, that of 1898, only committed criminal inebriates who had pleaded guilty to drunkenness or who had been tried and convicted four times in one year. Conflict about financing of reformatories between central government and local authorities ensured that few were established. Only twelve were ever built; during their existence they dealt with 4590 inmates (compared with 250 000 prison committals annually in the UK for drunkenness) (Radzinowicz and Hood, 1986).

But medical optimism remained undimmed. Given compulsion, there appears to have been no doubt in medical minds that the inebriate could be cured. Cure was seen as the automatic result of treatment. But little specific evidence was produced to prove the case. The Home Office appointed inspector of retreats simply reiterated in his report the information provided by the retreat owners; in general, there was remarkably little concern on the part of most superintendents as to what happened to their patients when they left. Robert Welsh Branthwaite, medical superintendent of the Dalrymple Home, the first inebriates home to be established (in 1883) and later Home Office Inspector under the inebriates acts did produce regular audits of patients admitted. When cure rates were discussed, it was a generally accepted rule of thumb that around 30 per cent could be cured if treated early enough. But in general, after-care rehabilitation and relapse had little place in the general optimism about cure.

One reason why this was so was the secular but ultimately moral reading of human behaviour which lay behind discussions of inebriety. If the patient did not get well, that was a matter of volition and individual responsibility. Thus the inculcation of acceptable social values and behaviour, of self-control and self-help was a major part of what was seen as 'scientific' treatment. Behind it lay that mixture of humanitarianism and social control which had also animated the moral treatment of insanity. Treatment was differentiated according to class; this was underlined by the retreat/reformatory distinction in the 1898 Act. Some drug treatment was given at this time, but not much.

In general, the scientific concept of inebriety provided the rationale for a regime which, for better off patients, provided little more than a religiously inclined health farm, and, for the poorer, also included the benefits of work therapy. Dr F. J. Gray, superintendent of Old Park Hall retreat in Staffordshire, described his methods (1888):

I have adopted the mode of having two classes of patient, first and second, the fees ranging for the former according to bedroom accommodation; and the latter somewhat according to the amount of assistance than can be rendered by the patient. The first class live with me in front of the Home, the second in the back part of the Home with male attendants, these latter are taken at 35/- per week, and they have to render services about the grounds morning and afternoon, or in the workshop, and the evening they have for recreation.

Treatment was a mixture of muscular Christianity and good food.

In the cricket season we have a half-day's match every week. I get a surgeon or school master to bring a team from the town, and often some medical men and clergymen come up for tennis, so that there are plenty of means both for exercise and amusement on the premises . . . we begin the day with prayers read from the Book of Common Prayer, and finish the day with prayers. Breakfast at nine o'clock, which consists of porridge (to which I attach a great importance), bacon and fried fish, varied with eggs, sausages, bread, butter, jam and marmalade.

Gray's retreat obviously catered for male patients. But over 80 per cent of those committed to reformatories were in fact women (although the majority of drinking offences were committed by men). Work by Hunt, Mellor and Turner on the LCC's Farmfield Reformatory and by Patrick McLaughlin on Scottish inebriate reformatories has uniformly stressed the preponderant role of women (Hunt, Mellor and Turner, 1987; McLaughlin, 1987). This was a notable point of similarity with the late nineteenth century insane asylum. By the end of the nineteenth century 'women had decisively taken the lead in the career of psychiatric patient'. The tightening up of Poor Law administration increased stress on poor women; for others, the asylum offered a more tolerant and interesting life than they could expect outside.

THE ROLE OF PUBLIC HEALTH: MENTAL HYGIENE AND NATIONAL EFFICIENCY

The nature of inebriety treatment both expressed and reinforced prevailing social values and attitudes towards the poor and working-class women, in particular. Ideas of disease and treatment were also expressions of the dominant late nineteenth-century clinical and bacteriological approach in medicine. Roy Macleod has pointed out that the initial strategy of the Society for the Study of Inebriety placed it in the medico-political rather than the social medicine camp (Macleod, 1967). But variants of the ideology of public health did have a role to play. This section will consider how the mental hygiene movement in particular influenced ideas of national and industrial efficiency in the pre- and post-First World War decades.

The early medical advocates of disease came from two broad camps – the alienist tradition, represented by the superintendents of asylums and nursing homes for inebriates, and the public health strand, represented by those with a public health qualification (the DPH) often working as a local Medical Officer of Health. Both

Norman Kerr and W. Wynn Westcott, his successor as President of the Society, were from the latter camp. But the environmentalist, social reforming tradition of the early stages of public health activity had little impact on medical views of alcohol. The inebriates acts bore more of a relationship to the latter tradition of quarantine and isolation exemplified in the 1889 Notification of Infectious Diseases Act. It is notable how often this public health model was cited by advocates of compulsory treatment, even down to the 'socially infectious' disease of the Brain Committee's definition in 1965.

The demonstrable failure of insane asylums to do much to cure insanity and the unwelcome professional consequences this entailed led to a shift in medical strategy in the early decades of the twentieth century. There emerged in many areas of social and welfare policy a complex meshing of hereditarian ideas of the late nineteenth century and the ideology of the public health movement into what became known as 'social' or 'mental hygiene'. The existing alienist/public health alliance of medical forces advocating the extension of the inebriates acts already formed in embryo such an alliance and alcohol was of central importance in the new paradigm. Compulsory treatment of drinkers and drug takers still remained the ultimate and desirable goal; but prevention was also now seen as the remedy for inherited disease.

The need for preventive education about the dangers of alcohol was a strong theme too in temperance writing. Alcohol became part of the debate on degeneracy and national efficiency stimulated by Britain's poor performance, and the poor physical state of her recruits, in the Boer War. It fitted well into a paradigm in which concern about continuing high infant mortality was fuelled by concern about poor mothering; the stress was on individual failing rather than on social situation. Medical evidence presented to the key Edwardian enquiry, the inter-departmental committee on physical deterioration, made the connection. Drinking females were particularly at fault.

The compulsory introduction of hygiene and temperance teaching in the school curriculum was seen as the remedy. Despite medical efforts in this direction, temperance and hygiene teaching was permitted but not made compulsory; efforts were made at the local level, with local authorities developing hygiene and temperance classes (Taylor, 1905). Historical work on the theme of working class mothers and infant mortality in Edwardian England has stressed how the 'maternal ignorance and incompetence' school of thought (of which the debate on alcohol was part) continued its line of argument in the face of evidence which stressed environmental factors. The infant welfare movement placed its emphasis on instruction for motherhood rather than the provision of material aid, such as dinners or subsidised dried milk (Lewis, 1980). The medical response to alcohol was also to place emphasis on instruction – in this case temperance teaching – and a stress on the individual drinking mother.

The mental hygiene debates on alcohol also developed a strong economic dimension. The economic arguments had their roots in the temperance movement. A. E. Dingle has shown how, in the 1870s and 1880, temperance economics were widely accepted, enjoying an influence comparable to Henry George's single tax on land. Temperance reformers regularly drew up a 'National Drink Bill' showing the annual national expenditure on drink; drink appeared to be the primary cause of the economic problems of commercial depression and of poverty itself. In particular domestic under consumption could be remedied by the reduction of wasteful expenditure on drink. Dingle remarks, 'For temperance economists it was but a short step from offering prohibition as a solution to poverty, unemployment and commercial depression, to asserting that spending on drink had been the cause of these difficulties in the first place' (Dingle, 1977).

The connection between the eradication of ill-health and economic efficiency was a continuous theme in both public health and the later mental hygiene movements. Health was seen as an economic value. The conjuncture between public health, hereditarianism and temperance brought a shift in economic arguments, too. The stress was increasingly on the question of industrial performance, work discipline and its relationship to drink. The First World War alcohol control measures made this issue a central one; the researches of the Central Control Board's medical advisory committee published in 1918 as *Alcohol: its Action on the Human Organism* focused on the relationship between work performance and alcohol consumption.

Alcohol and work retained its importance in the inter-war years. In his Norman Kerr Memorial Lecture in 1929, Sir Josiah Stamp spoke on 'Alcohol as an Economic Factor' (Stamp, 1930). He ranged (in evidence he also gave to the Royal Commission on Liquor Licensing) on the dynamic effects of reduction of alcohol consumption by transfer to savings and to expenditure on other goods and to the second line effect on production, in particular efficiency in output. Stamp also analysed the economic costs of crime due to drink, and of poverty due to drink, along with the cost of sickness, accident and greater mortality due to alcohol. He pointed to the need to distinguish between the economic effects of alcohol as a general problem and the economic effects of alcoholism. The other side of the balance was the economic gains to be made from alcohol as a taxing medium. Increasingly discussions of the economics of the alcohol question focused on this question of taxation.

An emphasis on alcohol research was another significant sideshoot from the mental hygiene and industrial efficiency movements. The history and politics of alcohol and drugs research deserves to be written: and a few points can be touched on here. Alcohol research in the early twentieth century was to be found primarily at the international alcohol congresses and was set within a temperance and hereditarian context. Babor and Rosencrantz, in a recent article on social science and liquor control in Massachusetts at this time have noted a more self-conscious reference to research and to statistics as social controls on alcohol, formerly the presence of temperance interests, became more closely associated with professional groups (Babor and Rosencrantz, 1987). In Britain, in-house production of follow-up statistics and statistical work on the relationship between alcohol and heredity, notably in the work of Pearson and Elderton at the Galton Laboratory for National Eugenics at University College, exemplified this tendency.

There was also a strand of physiological research on alcohol, given particular stress by the First World War and the ensuing stress on industrial efficiency. The wartime Medical Advisory Committee produced research by Edward Mellanby and H. M. Vernon which was published in the post-war Medical Research Council's Special Report series, and which, in 1918, appeared in book form as *Alcohol: its Action on the Human Organism*, a basic text in medical alcohol circles in the inter-war years. The focus was on the effect of alcohol on the central nervous system; Vernon examined significant variations in the speed and accuracy of typewriting under the effects of alcohol. Alcohol research was initially funded out of the concern for industrial efficiency; and in so far as it developed in the inter-war years it bore a close relation to the particular drink-driving issue. Courtenay Weekes, Director of the National Temperance League produced statistics, supported by further work by Vernon (1937) on the effects of alcohol on speeding and on accident frequency (Weekes, 1931; Vernon, 1937). The development of the blood-alcohol test in the 1930s stressed the tradition of biochemical research, one which the Society for the Study of Addiction also developed in the 1940s and 1950s at the Burden Institute in Bristol, with controversial funding from the brewers.

THE ADVENT OF PSYCHOLOGY

Research on alcohol and road accidents was connected with the work of the National Institute of Industrial Psychology; the concern for industrial efficiency had its roots in mental hygiene, but also in the significant development of 'applied psychology' in England during and after the First World War. The advent of psychology as a scientific expert discipline in relation to alcohol was of considerable importance.

Psychological medicine was, of course, not new in the early twentieth century. But discussion of the mind to physicians in the nineteenth century was still a medical and biological topic, and notions of psychopathology underpinned Victorian degeneration theory. By the end of the century, alienists, in attempts to move out of the backwater of late Victorian psychiatry, moved towards exploration of the subconscious mind as a conscious professional option. As Samuel Shortt (1986) comments,

> If mental illness was the result of the unconscious gone astray in an otherwise normal person, the focus of psychiatry was suddenly expanded beyond a concern for the overly mad and degenerate among the poor. And as the psychiatric gaze widened to encompass ostensibly sound and healthy middle-class citizens in the community, so too did the social authority of the profession escalate.

Although alienists, influenced by Freud and other European theorists had begun to explore the dynamic unconscious at the end of the nineteenth century, the crucial impact of psychology came in the First World War with the treatment of shell shock. Martin Stone's work (1985) has shown how Victorian theories of hereditary degeneration were significantly undermined as 'normal' and 'respectable' young men were reduced to mental wrecks by trench warfare (Stone, 1985). The existing medical and institutional structure of British psychiatry came under effective attack from the 'shell shock' doctors in the immediate post-war years.

The impact of psychology on conceptions of alcoholism and of alcohol treatment was noticeable in the inter-war years. The institutional option for alcoholism was effectively dead; the last inebriates bill fell on the outbreak of War in 1914 and only two institutions still provided treatment under the acts in the inter-war period. The emphasis on compulsion associated with treatment and with the mental hygiene movement was also less obvious in the inter-war years. Psychology had a clear impact on the conceptualisation of alcoholism.

Its claims were advanced to raise the standing of the profession as well as to enhance the understanding of the subject. J. R. Rees, Deputy Director of the Institute of Medical Psychology was of the opinion that the psychological imperative was the dominant factor:

One should, I believe, keep an open mind on the question of the degree in which chemical action helps in the formation of the drug habit. The effect of increasing tolerance upon the individual may also be important, but I cannot help feeling that beyond doubt the essential causative factor in these conditions is a habit of mind, an attitude towards life. Alcoholism and drug addiction are, in almost every case, the symptoms of a psychological maladjustment. (Rees, 1933)

But Rees also justified the psychological approach as a professional strategy. Psychiatry, he argued, was the 'Cinderella' of medicine and medical psychology offered a fruitful way forward in professional terms. 'We in the medical profession have constantly to widen our field of work', he concluded.

The role of drug addiction in mediating the acceptance of psychological approaches in the inter-war period was an important one. Drug addicts were then a mainly middle-class group small in number and often with some medical connection. Psychological concepts were seen as particularly appropriate in the treatment of this otherwise respectable group in the community.

Medical witnesses to the Rolleston Committee in the mid-1920s differed considerably on matters of policy and of treatment; but there was general acceptance of the addict's 'neurosis' (Rolleston Committee, 1926). Crichton Miller, Director of the Tavistock Clinic, commented in 1922 that 'the morphia addict is merely the psychoneurotic who has lighted upon a chemical solution of his problem . . . '. Psychology enabled doctors to claim this group of addicts as suitable for treatment (Crichton Miller, 1923).

It provided the theoretical rationale for what was treatment practice in the inter-war period. For drugs this meant, post-Rolleston, a continuance of the possibility of maintenance prescribing by general practitioners, or other forms of mainly out-patient treatment. For alcohol, it justified the virtual abandonment of institutionalisation. Alcohol treatment shifted to out-patient clinics, part of the contemporary emphasis on voluntary out-patient treatment which found expression in the 1930 Mental Treatment Act. But the bulk of alcoholism treatment whether psychotherapeutic or physicalist was mainly located in private practice at this time. In 1931 the Maudsley had only 29 alcoholic out-patients.

POST SECOND WORLD WAR

Many of the themes touched on above – in particular the ideology of disease and of institutional treatment and also the role of public health – underwent a resurgence post Second World War. In fact, for many years alcoholism as a concept and in terms of treatment structures was seen as originating in the 1940s and 1950s. The focus was on E. M. Jellinek, the work of the Yale Center for Alcohol Studies, and the *Quarterly Journal of Studies on Alcohol*.

The earlier British history of disease and of treatment was over-looked. In part this was because many British alcohol doctors themselves appeared to forget their own history. In a discussion at the AGM of the Society for the Study of Addiction in 1951, Dr Lincoln Williams referred with optimism to 'the dawning of this new humanitarian conception that addiction is an illness and not a moral failing' (Williams, 1952). British doctors looked to American example; the enthusiasm of the 1880s was renewed.

The physical version of disease also enjoyed a resurgence. In a sense this had never died away, as discussions of insulin coma and the other physical treatments have shown. Also important in Britain in the immediate post-war years was the apomorphine treatment of alcoholism, publicised since the 1930s by Dr John Yerbury Dent, editor of the *British Journal of Addiction*, a doctor with a large private practice specialising in the treatment of alcoholics. Dent was resolutely hostile to anything but a physical explanation of alcoholism and its treatment. In his *Anxiety and its Treatment* (1941), he wrote:

Recently there has been a plethora of psychological schools striving to explain the action of the mind by forcing it to fit every conceivable theory. Psycho-analysts have ceased to be concerned with the slow investigation of the anatomy and physiology of the brain and have irresponsibly postulated not only the soul and will, but have invented every kind of attribute for them – complexes, fixations, repressions, libidos. Let us cut out all this and consider what a man's brain actually is: it is a mass of nerve-cells and fibres whose function is to co-ordinate the response of the individual to alterations in his surroundings and maintain the chemical and physical balance of his blood linking up the behaviour of every part of his mechanism with every other part.

Alcoholism was thus to be seen 'not as a sin nor as weakness of character but as a chemical disease'. It was a physical disease like any other

asthma, but most surely diabetes and alcoholism, are diseases with a chemical foundation and must be treated chemically. Sufferers from them should be encouraged to face the necessity for such treatment and the altered habits it entails. This encouragement is psychological treatment and, in my opinion, all the psychological treatment necessary (Dent, 1941)

Dent was only an extreme example of a general tendency in approaches to alcoholism at this time. Antabuse, used in Denmark, was introduced in Britain in the late 1940s. Convulsive therapy, even leucotomy, had their advocates in cases of alcoholism. At a broader level, the resurgence of biochemical modes of explanation and of treatment, the avoidance of social or environmental explanation can be related to the political direction of the late 1940s and 1950s and its effects on medical research.

A more fruitful development post-war was a *rapprochement* between psychology and biochemistry which had been foreshadowed in the inter-war years. Professor D. K. Henderson of Edinburgh, in his Norman Kerr Lecture for 1936, stated that it would be unwise to divorce psychology and physiology (Henderson, 1937). The *rapprochement* between the two came in the 1950s and early 1960s and was consolidated by international action. Pre-war the Health Committee of the League of Nations had not been willing to consider alcohol; and international discussions of drug addictions had more to do with control of supply than with definitions.

Post-war the role of the newly established World Health Organization in establishing internationally applicable medical concepts was significant. The WHO's definitions of alcoholism in the 1950s and drug addiction in 1964 incorporated both physical and psychological parameters. In Britain, Lincoln Williams saw the necessity for an alliance both in terms of theory and of practice. 'It is surely high time we cease being fanatically intolerant of any approach other than the one which happens to take our particular fancy from among the 5 As – Apomorphine, Aversion therapy, Antabuse, Analysis and Alcoholics Anonymous' he wrote in 1954 (Williams, 1954).

Such a synthesis gave scientific authority to the new psychiatric and alcohol treatment policies under the National Health Service. This had again been foreshadowed pre-war. Henderson in his Kerr Lecture (entitled Alcoholism and Psychiatry) urged the integration of alcoholism into the mainstream of psychiatry and envisaged the creation of 'a mental health service which would cater for all groups of nervous and mental illness of whatsoever type of grade – for alcoholics, drug addicts, sexual offenders, and other types of delinquent, attempted suicides, psychoneurotics, and psychotics . . . ' (Henderson, 1937). Alcoholism treatment was part of the new structure of the National Health Service psychiatry. But the form that treatment initially took, the specialist alcoholism treatment unit, has remained controversial.

It is not the place in this chapter to rehearse its history; despite an excellent introduction by Robinson and Ettorre (1980) the history of post-war alcohol treatment policy remains to be written. Certain features are, however, clear. The NHS was a hospital dominated service from the start; and alcoholism treatment found its place as part of that structure. The 1962 Ministry of Health Memorandum *The Hospital Treatment of Alcoholism* was in one sense all of a piece with a general focus in the new service on specialist hospital treatment. It also had specific roots in the demand for compulsory institutional treatment under the inebriates acts and the mental hygiene and eugenic desire to segregate drunkards. But the post-war agitation by alcohol doctors for NHS provision did not focus exclusively on specialist rather than out-patient facilities. Dr Pullar-Strecker, a friend of Jellinek and Secretary of the Society for the Study of Addiction, in a paper in 1951 entitled 'The Problem of Alcoholism and its Treatment as it concerns or should concern the medical profession' envisaged both in- and out-patient facilities. The need as he saw it was to provide beds and treatment (Pullar-Strecker, 1952). In a letter of the *Spectator* in 1953, he wrote:

> The 252 Hospitals listed in the current time-table of out patient clinics available in Greater London alone run between them 2,257 clinics for every form of sickness except alcoholism. In the whole of London there is not one clinic specifically devoted to the needs of the alcoholic patient . . . they should be able to find a clinic devoted to their needs, as is provided for every other form of sickness.

Beresford Davies founded an out-patient clinic in Cambridge; and Pullar-Strecker himself was involved in the establishment of a clinic to be jointly run by the Church of England Temperance Society, the National Association for Mental Health and the Society for the Study of Addiction (Society for the Study of Addiction, 1955). The specialist model does not appear to have been necessarily an automatic choice for alcohol doctors; and further research is needed to analyse why policy took the direction it did.

The post-war role of public health in relation to alcohol remains to be considered. In the 1970s and 1980s, behaviourally-orientated psychologists and psychiatrists have offered a counter-conception to disease. In the sociological literature, a 'post-addiction model' has emerged, alcoholism disaggregated into its consistent alcohol-related problems (Room, 1983). As Harry Levine has pointed out, this concept is as vague and ambiguous, as riven with opinions and with ideology as the disease concept (Levine, 1984). The genealogy of alcohol and drug problems can be traced to the 'social problem group' which so concerned the social hygienists of the 1930s. Geoffrey Searle has shown how the 1930s social problem perspective made those problems appear the result of scientific laws rather than of defective economic and social relationships (Searle, 1979).

In the 1980s the problem perspective is widely credited with marking a transformation from a medical to a social and community based response. Perhaps, on the model of the 1930s, we are witnessing a more complex symbiosis whereby the medical model is transferred into the social arena. In the 1980s problem drug and alcohol use are part of the 'new public health' with its emphasis on primary care, individual lifestyle, health planning, indicators and information. Planners, epidemiologists and health economists, as in the inter-war years, play their part in defining problem use; psychologists and clinicians still retain the basic core of dependence.

CONCLUSION

The conclusion that 'more research is needed' is, as a historian once remarked, 'the last refuge of a scoundrel' (Summers, 1986). Yet this indeed remains a justified response at the end of a brief and imperfect survey of theories and influences on alcoholism and of twentieth-century policy on alcohol treatment. The inter-war and post-war history of alcoholism in theory and in treatment practice, like that of insanity in general, remains to be written. Despite some promising work, the development of alcohol research, the politics of alcohol at the international level, also await historians. Largely unknown, too, is the formulation and role of public understanding of medical theories in the post-temperance period. Robin Room has commented that the 1980 WHO Expert Committee Report 'relies more on technocratic and professionalised strategies for managing and preventing problems, not moral fervour and popular movements' (Room, 1981). Archer Tongue, Director of ICAA, in a 1984 interview, regretted the decline of the disease concept precisely because it had attracted public support and understanding (Tongue, 1984). The relationship between medical and popular perceptions also needs to be explored. Both from the 'relevant' perspective of the present and from the disciplinary angle, we need more alcohol history.

Acknowledgements

I am grateful to the Society for the Study of Addiction for funding part of the research on which this chapter is based. My thanks are also due to Liz Dillon and Ingrid Maynard for secretarial assistance.

References

Alcohol and Temperance History Group Newsletter (1983) *Berkeley Conference on the Social History of Alcohol*, vol. 7, pp. 8–9.
Babor, T. and Rosencrantz, B. (1987) 'Public Health, Public Morals and Public Order: Social Science and Liquor Control in Massachusetts 1880–1916', in Barrows, S. Room, R. and Verbey, J. (eds), *The Social History of Alcohol* (Berkeley: Alcohol Research Group).

Bynum, W. (1984) 'Alcoholism and Degeneration in 19th Century European Medicine and Psychiatry'. *British Journal of Addiction*, vol. 79, pp. 59–70.

Clark, P. (1983) *The English Alehouse: A Social History 1200–1830* (London: Longman).

Collins, W. (1919) 'Drink and Drugs of Addiction', *British Journal of Inebriety*, vol. 16, pp. 85–9.

Crichton Miller, H. (1923) 'Contribution to a Society for the Study of Inebriety Discussion', *British Journal of Inebriety*, vol. 20, pp. 147–61.

Dent, J. Y. (1941) *Anxiety and its Treatment with Special Reference to Alcoholism* (London: Skeffington).

Dingle, A. E. (1972) 'Drink and Working Class Living Standards in Britain, 1820–1914', *Economic History Review*, vol. 25, pp. 608–622.

Dingle, A. E. (1977) 'The Rise and Fall of Temperance Economics', *Monash Papers in Economic History*, vol. 3.

Gray, F. J. (1888). 'The Classes of Inebriates and Their Treatment', *Proceedings of the Society for the Study of Inebriety*, vol. 18, pp. 1–11.

Harrison, B. (1971) *Drink and the Victorians* (London: Faber).

Henderson, D. K. (1937) 'Alcoholism and Psychiatry', *British Journal of Inebriety*, vol. 34, pp. 99–123.

Hunt, G., Mellor, J. and Turner, J. (1987) 'Wretched, Hatless and Miserably Clad: Women and the Inebriate Reformatories from 1900–1913' (unpublished paper).

Kerr, N. (1884) 'Presidential Address', *Proceedings of the Society for the Study and Cure of Inebriety*, vol. 1, pp. 1–16.

Kerr, N. (1887) 'The Pathology of Inebriety', *Proceedings of the Society for the Study and Cure of Inebriety*, vol. 12, pp. 1–12.

Levine, H. (1978) 'The Discovery of Addiction: Changing Conceptions of Habitual Drunkenness in America', *Journal of Studies on Alcohol*, vol. 39, pp. 143–74.

Levine, H. (1984) 'What is an Alcohol Related Problem? (or, what are People Talking about when they Refer to Alcohol Problems)', *Journal of Drug Issues*, pp. 45–60.

Lewis, J. (1980) *The Politics of Motherhood. Child and Maternal Welfare in England, 1900–1939* (London: Croom Helm).

McCandless, P. (1984) 'Curses of Civilisation': Insanity and Drunkenness in Victorian Britain', *British Journal of Addiction*, vol. 79, pp. 49–58.

McLaughlin, P. M. (1987) 'Inebriate Reformatories in Scotland, 1902–1921; an Institutional History', in Barrows, S., Room, R. and Verbey, J. (eds), *The Social History of Alcohol* (Berkeley: Alcohol Research Group).

Macleod, R. (1967) 'The Edge of Hope: Social Policy and Chronic Alcoholism 1870–1900', *Journal of the History of Medicine and Allied Sciences*, vol. 22, pp. 215–45.

Mapother, E. (1939) 'The Physical Basis of Alcoholic Mental Disorders', *British Journal of Inebriety*, vol. 36, pp. 103–32.

Porter, R. (1985) 'The Drinking Man's Disease: The Pre-history of Alcoholism in Georgian Britain', *British Journal of Addiction*, vol. 80, pp. 385–96.

Pullar-Strecker, H. (1951) 'The Problem of Alcoholism as it Concerns or

Should Concern the Medical Profession', *British Journal of Addiction*, vol. 49, pp. 21–32.

Radzinowicz, L. and Hood, R. (1986) *A History of English Criminal Law. Volume 5. The Emergence of Penal Policy* (London: Stevens) pp. 288–315.

Rees, J. R. (1933) 'Psychological Factors in the Prevention and Treatment of Alcohol and Drug Addiction', *British Journal of Inebriety*, vol. 30, pp. 91–103.

Robinson, D. and Ettorre, B. (1980) 'Special Units for Common Problems: Alcoholism Treatment Units in England and Wales', in Edwards, G. and Grant, M. (eds), *Alcoholism Treatment in Transition* (London: Croom Helm), pp. 234–47.

Rolleston Committee (1926) *Report of the Departmental Committee on Morphine and Heroin Addiction* (London: HMSO).

Room, R. (1981) 'A Farewell to Alcoholism? A commentary on the WHO 1980 Committee Report', *British Journal of Addiction*, vol. 76, pp. 115–23.

Room, R. (1983) 'Sociological Aspects of the Disease Concept of Alcoholism', *Research Advances in Alcohol and Drug Problems*, vol. 7, pp. 47–91 (New York: Plenum Press).

Rose, M. E. (1973) 'The Success of Social Reform? The Central Control Board (Liquor Traffic) 1915–21', in Foot, M. R. D. (ed.), *War and Society* (London: Elek).

Searle, G. (1979) 'Eugenics and Politics in Britain in the 1930s', *Annals of Science*, vol. 36, pp. 159–69.

Shortt, S. E. d. (1986) *Victorian Lunacy: Richard M. Bucke and the Practice of Late Nineteenth-Century Psychiatry* (Cambridge: Cambridge University Press).

Society for the Study of Addiction (1955) Manuscript minutes.

Stamp, J. (1930) 'Alcohol as an Economic Factor', *British Journal of Inebriety*, vol. 27, pp. 129–66.

Stone, M. (1985) 'Shellshock, the Psychologists', in Bynum, W, Porter, R. and Shepherd, M. (eds), *The Anatomy of Madness: Essays in the History of Psychiatry*, Vol II (London: Tavistock).

Summers, A. (1986) 'Review', *Bulletin of the Society for the Social History of Medicine*, vol. 38, pp. 101–2.

Taylor, E. C. (1905) 'The Teaching of Temperance in Elementary Schools', *British Journal of Inebriety*, vol. 3, pp. 36–9.

Tongue, A. (1984) 'Interview', *British Journal of Addiction*, vol. 79, pp. 245–9.

Turner, J. (1980) 'State Purchase of the Liquor Trade in the First World War', *Historical Journal*, vol. 23, pp. 589–615.

Vernon, H. M. (1937) 'Alcohol and Motor Accidents', *British Journal of Inebriety*, vol. 34, pp. 153–65.

Weekes, C. (1931) 'Alcoholic Indulgence in Relation to Motor Transport', *British Journal of Inebriety*, vol. 28, pp. 163–82.

Williams, L. (1952) Contribution to Discussion, *British Journal of Addiction*, vol. 49, pp. 16–20.

Williams, L. (1954) Contribution to Discussion, *British Journal of Addiction*, vol. 51, pp. 39–50.

3 Many Problems in Many Forms

Michael Gossop

There has been much concern with something called 'the drug problem' in recent years. What is this thing? Perhaps the first and most important point to make is that it is not an 'it' but a 'them'. The phrase 'the drug problem' obscures more than it reveals, and it can mislead us into thinking of a wide range of different problems as if they were some relatively fixed and unitary issue. Perhaps we might ask which drugs cause problems? Or, to start with, ask what looks like an even simpler question, 'what is a drug?'

The answer to this would certainly encompass such drugs as heroin and cocaine. It is increasingly common to recognise such prescribed drugs as the benzodiazepine tranquillisers (of which Valium is perhaps the best known) as capable to being misused and of leading to many problems including dependence. There are other prescribed drugs which can also be misused in various ways. Certain slimming tablets can create interesting altered states of consciousness. And what of the array of drugs that can be found on display at your local chemist's shop? Any knowledgeable street addict will inform you that amongst these well-stocked shelves are many drugs which can take you up, bring you down or turn your head around.

Although the over-the-counter preparations are not usually seen as worthy of inclusion in any discussion of the drug problem, there clearly are a number of drug problems here. Non-opiate analgesics (that is, drugs of the aspirin, paracetamol type) are the most widely consumed medicines in Western countries, and all sorts of unfounded pharmacological and medical actions are regularly attributed to them. As with most forms of drug misuse, it is difficult to obtain clear figures about incidence, but one estimate suggested that as many as 250 000 people in the UK are taking five or more analgesics every day without any medical reason (cited in Murray, 1974). The range of damage that can be caused by the excessive use of such drugs may include stomach upsets, including gastric bleeding and peptic ulceration, various anaemias, and damage to the liver and kidneys.

Over-the-counter drugs are also responsible for the majority of acute overdoses that occur in the UK every year. There are a number of easily obtained preparations which are liable to be abused, among them Gee's linctus, codeine linctus, Actifed, Collis-Browne's compound and Feminax. Collis-Browne's compound, for example, dates back to the Victorian days of patent medicines. It contains a quite literally staggering combination of opium, alcohol and chloroform, and these contents make it a candidate for abuse. Among heroin addicts it is widely known as a last resort drug when other opiates cannot be obtained.

Then we move on to our more familiar and domestic drugs. We know that some people can become hooked on alcohol. Such people have been known to stagger over to us when we leave the theatre asking if we can spare some money for 'a cup of tea'. But there has been greater resistance to seeing alcohol as a 'real' drug, in the same sense that heroin is a drug. But alcohol certainly is a drug, and a very powerful one at that. In high enough doses alcohol can kill. In lower doses it produces sufficient impairment of judgement and skills to lead to road traffic accidents, acts of aggression and other assorted but more minor misjudgements that may, none the less, be regretted the morning after.

Alcohol is a central nervous system depressant which, in some ways is very similar to the benzodiazepine tranquillisers and the barbiturate sedatives. As the blood alcohol level rises, brain functions change and deteriorate. The first consistent changes in mood and behaviour occur at about 50 mg/dl, at which level most people tend to feel carefree and relaxed. Complex skills such as driving may be affected at 30 mg/dl and emotional behaviour is impaired. These effects become more marked as blood alcohol levels increase further. By 300 mg/dl confusion, inability to stand or to walk and unconsciousness are evident, and the fatal concentration lies between 500–800 mg/dl (Royal College of Psychiatrists Report, 1986).

Tobacco should be included in any list of problematic drugs. Tobacco smoke contains hundreds of different chemicals, but there is little doubt that the most important drug ingredient is nicotine. In its pure state, nicotine is a colourless, volatile, strongly alkaline liquid which turns brown on exposure to air and which gives off a characteristic tobacco smell. It is so powerfully toxic that one drop of the free substance placed on the tongue or skin is capable of killing within minutes (Larson, *et al.*, 1961). When cigarette smoke is inhaled, the drug effects reach the brain within a matter of seconds, and blood nicotine levels rise very rapidly, probably peaking at roughly the time that the cigarette is extinguished.

But the list of domestic drugs does not stop there. Caffeine is probably the world's most popular drug. Tea, coffee, chocolate, cocoa and cola drinks all contain caffeine, and in these forms it is used by most of the population throughout their lives. Caffeine is another central nervous system stimulant which, in moderate doses, can lift mood and improve concentration. But in higher doses it can produce anxiety-type symptoms including irritability, tremor, insomnia and headache. And among heavy chronic users (12 or more cups of tea or coffee per day) it shows every sign of being a drug of dependence.

With regard to the question of which drugs cause problems, it is probably safest to assume that any substance which has drug effects can also cause problems. But an analysis of drug problems should look beyond the specific substances to the manner in which they are used. In the case of such illegal drugs as heroin or cocaine there is a temptation to consider any use as problematic. This temptation should be avoided. If we return to a drug such as alcohol and ask 'what problems are caused by alcohol?', the answer is likely to take account of such factors as who was doing the drinking, the different styles of drinking and the different circumstances in which drinking occurs. A single episode on which a person drinks rather too much might not cause problems under certain circumstances, for instance, if it occurs at home at a Friday night dinner party. On the other hand, if the individual had been drinking heavily prior to driving home, it could cause very serious problems. Equally, one could easily see how problems could arise if the person drinks heavily on most nights or, indeed, if they were heavily drunk on a Sunday night, this could cause the familiar sort of problems at work the next morning.

But even the dinner party example is not entirely without risk. Alcohol reduces inhibitions. It may lead the drinker to make amorous advances to the wife of his friend, or to offer some vigorous opinions to his boss. The lowered inhibitions that reliably follow drinking also lead to an increased likelihood of aggression. If the dinner party conversation strays into some contentious area or if there is some disagreement about who should do the washing up after the guests have gone, it is not impossible that the alcohol may increase the risks of verbal or physical aggression. The unpleasant scenes that are so common at certain pubs at closing time are a vivid illustration of this effect of alcohol.

In most considerations of drug problems there is a tendency for the discussion to be drawn toward illicit drugs, and a tendency also to exaggerate the risks and dangers of those drugs. I have argued elsewhere (Gossop, 1987) that a perspective which focuses so strongly upon illicit drugs can be unhelpful. It can divert our attention from the many problems that are associated with the legal drugs, and it creates a climate for discussion in which 'drugs' are seen as massively dangerous, alien substances, as something quite separate from our own lives. Yet, one way or another, we are all drug takers. Every society has its own drugs and whether we wish they existed or not, we must learn to live with them since they are not going to go away.

Let us return to what the Royal College of Psychiatrists (1986) has called 'our favourite drug' – alcohol. In the last twenty years or so, the annual *per capita* consumption of alcohol has doubled in the UK. The problems that we must face in the wake of this trend are many and various.

ALCOHOL AND PROBLEMS FOR SOCIETY

Crime

The *per capita* consumption of alcohol in the UK is rising, and, as might be expected, the number of offences of drunkenness has also been steadily increasing since 1950. Alcohol has been found to be involved in a wide range of criminal acts. The consumption of alcohol and high blood alcohol levels have been linked to petty crime, home quarrels and minor outbreaks of public disorder. This link has been reported for 80 per cent of cases of breach of the peace, and in 88 per cent of cases of criminal damage. In a study of delinquency, 63 per cent of prisoners in a young offender's institution in Scotland claimed that they had been intoxicated at the time they committed the offence for which they were imprisoned (Heather, 1981). The same link can be made for much more serious offences. A large proportion of assaults, rapes and murders have involved the offender drinking shortly before the crime took place. In one study of 365 men accused of murder, 58 per cent were drunk at the time of the offence. Many of these offences occurred at weekends or on other occasions when heavy drinking was more likely (Lester and Lester, 1975). Violent crimes are more often associated with alcohol than are non-violent ones, and alcohol-related crimes are less likely to be premeditated. In a number of studies it was found that between 30–50 per cent of rapists had been drinking shortly before their assaults.

There are certain problems involved in the interpretation of these sort of statistics. For example, a rate of drinking of 30 per cent among offenders may be of no significance if it merely reflected the proportion of people of that age, sex and social grouping who might be expected to have a raised blood alcohol level at the time of the offence (Evans, 1986). It seems unlikely, however, that the alcohol–crime relationship can be entirely accounted for in this way.

Family problems

In its more serious manifestations, regular excessive drinking has been found in one third of cases of child abuse, and about a third of divorce petitions cite alcohol as a contributory factor. In one study, of the marital assaults reported to the police, half occurred after the husband had been drinking (Gerson, 1978). In a great many cases, the damage done within a family is not easily detectable since the family may, through shame, hide their difficulties from outside view, and the consequences of the drinking problem will not necessarily show themselves in the official statistics. Instead, the family may quietly suffer the drunken arguments, verbal and physical abuse that are linked to alcohol problems. It has been reported that the likelihood of violence is more than doubled in families with alcohol problems.

Road traffic and other accidents

At the legal limit in the UK (80 mg/dl) the chances of having an accident are twice as high as when sober. A study carried out by the Transport and Road Research Laboratory showed that in 1974 one in three drivers killed in road traffic accidents had blood alcohol levels above the legal limit. On Saturday night this figure rose to 71 per cent. Every year about 46 000 people die on the roads in the USA. Over half of all deaths on the road are alcohol related, and this is a problem which particularly affects young people. At the legal limit, the risk of being involved in a road traffic accident is about four times greater for young drivers.

There is also the matter of industrial accidents, but although there has been a great deal of speculation about the involvement of alcohol in accidents at work, there is little reliable information available. Maynard *et al*. (1987) comment that the costs to industry have not been properly identified much less measured. There is, however, sufficient information to cause concern. Several studies have shown that the incidence of industrial accidents is higher during the hours immediately after lunch than at any other time during the working day, and alcohol consumption has also been found more often among workers who have had accidents than among a non-accident group. Since the economic costs of alcohol to society are being addressed elsewhere in this volume I will not dwell upon this point except to note briefly that each year motor vehicle accidents involving alcohol have been estimated to cost more than £1 billion in property damage, medical and insurance costs, and it is even harder to guess at the costs to industry.

INTOXICATION, HEALTH DAMAGE AND ADDICTION

These alcohol-related problems are serious and extremely damaging. However, it is more often the case that drug problems affect both the individual and society simultaneously, and to a considerable extent, this distinction between the way that drugs may cause problems for the individual and for society may be artificial. A slightly different way of classifying the various problems that are associated with drug taking might look at them in terms of intoxication, damage to health, and addiction.

A general classification of the major drugs of dependence might include the opiate-type drugs such as heroin, stimulants such as cocaine and the amphetamines, sedative and tranquillising drugs including sleeping tablets and the widely used benzodiazepine tran-quillisers such as Valium and, of course, alcohol, and finally, in a category of its own, tobacco/nicotine.

Consider one drug from each of the categories in the table at the top of p. 49 in terms of the problems of intoxication, health damage, and addictive use.

Intoxication

Some of the problems associated with intoxication have already been mentioned. Many or even most of the commonly abused drugs produce powerful alterations in normal states of consciousness. Intoxication, by definition, is likely to interfere with concentration

	Intoxication	Damage to health	Addiction
Alcohol	Yes	Yes	Yes
Heroin	Yes	???	Yes
Cocaine	Yes	Yes	Yes
Tobacco	No	Yes	Yes

and judgement, and one of the main problems resulting from this is road traffic and other accidents. Alcohol is an obvious villain here, though there is an enormous potential problem associated with the widespread use of tranquillisers which may also be expected to produce similar impairment.

It has been suggested that as many as 5 per cent of men and 12 per cent of women in the UK are using tranquillisers daily for at least one month during the year. Since many of these people will drive while taking such drugs and many will also drink alcohol as well as using tranquillisers, thereby increasing the risk of intoxication and disinhibition, this must pose a very serious potential threat to their own safety and to that of others on the roads. It is disturbing therefore, that almost nothing is known about the damage that is done because of such drug effects. There are other problems that should be considered such as the increased risk of aggressive or violent behaviour that is associated with intoxication with the sedative drugs. Barbiturates and alcohol can both produce such effects, and even the tranquillisers (despite their name) may lower the threshold for such behaviour.

Of the four drugs listed, the only one that does not obviously produce intoxication is nicotine. Nicotine has many powerful drug effects. It increases heart rate, blood pressure, and produces a stimulating effect upon the electrical activity of the brain. In experimental studies of the effects of intravenous injections of nicotine it has been found to produce effects described as 'light-headedness or muzziness'. This was described as being pleasant by smokers and unpleasant by non-smokers and it is, presumably, similar to the effects of the first cigarette of the day. The importance of the drug effects are emphasised by those workers who regard smoking dependence primarily in terms of addiction to nicotine. However, nicotine does not produce states of intoxication that are comparable to those produced by alcohol, heroin or cocaine.

Health problems

In any discussion of the health risks associated with particular drugs it is worth trying to distinguish between direct and indirect relationships. When the cigarette smoker gets lung cancer this may be seen as directly related to many years of inhaling the various carcinogens that are present in tobacco smoke. Equally, when the heavy drinker gets cirrhosis, this may be seen as a relatively direct consequence of many years of heavy drinking. Even here, the link is not a simple cause and effect relationship. Not all smokers get lung cancer and only about 10 per cent of alcoholics develop cirrhosis. But these instances must count as among the more direct effects. There are other much less direct forms of health damage that can be related to drug taking.

One of the more important indirect forms of harm is caused by the method of administration. There are a number of serious health risks which are associated with drug abuse because of the manner in which the drug is used. Any drug which is injected puts the user at risk of a number of complications. These include vein damage, accidentally hitting an artery instead of a vein, as well as the risk of introducing a whole range of infections into the bloodstream, the most serious of which are hepatitis B and HIV. When sniffed, cocaine can damage the nasal membrane leading to bleeding and ulceration. The inhalation of drugs such as smoking 'crack', freebasing cocaine, or 'chasing the (heroin) dragon' are also hazardous procedures, not least because of the very high temperature of the drug vapours.

Although it can be misleading to attempt a comparison of the relative dangers of different drugs, the health risks associated with the legal drugs are, in many respects, just as great and in some areas greater than those linked even to illegal drugs such as heroin. It is widely believed that heroin is the most dangerous of all the drugs. In terms of *direct* damage, this is probably untrue. Most of the health problems that are associated with heroin are due to indirect factors. For example, the risk of HIV infection which is linked to drug addiction is a consequence of using infected needles or syringes and is not itself caused by the drug being used.

This should not be regarded as a trivial point. There are a number of important implications which follow from distinguishing between the harm done by heroin and the harm done by injecting. To the extent that prevention campaigns against AIDS and HIV infection depend upon accurately targeting the appropriate high risk groups it should be recognised that those drug takers who are at risk are those who inject their drugs. There are many amphetamine abusers who inject drugs who would be missed by a campaign targeted at heroin users alone. And there are also large numbers of heroin users who take their drug by inhalation, and who would not, therefore, be at immediate risk of HIV infection through shared needles or syringes. Despite its popular reputation as the most dangerous of all the drugs, heroin has not been shown to cause direct damage to the brain or the heart (although this should not be taken to imply that it has been shown that heroin does not cause such forms of harm). There must also be good reason to worry about the potential for harm to the liver associated with chronic use of this drug.

However, it is worth emphasising that long-term and high dose alcohol use have been directly linked to liver damage and brain damage and cigarette smoking is directly linked to lung cancer and to a variety of other serious and sometimes life-threatening illnesses.

A recent review of the various forms of harm associated with the misuse of alcohol (excluding the central nervous system) dealt separately with the mouth, the oesophagus, the stomach, the small bowel, the large bowel, the pancreas, the liver, the heart muscle, the skeletal muscles, bone marrow, vitamin deficiency, white blood cells, coagulation and platelet disorder, kidney disease, pulmonary disease, the endocrine system and sexual functioning, as well as several other sites and systems which may be damaged by alcohol. The author concluded that the abuse of alcohol 'adversely affects all of the organs of the body', and that alcohol 'is not only toxic *per se* but its metabolism may produce toxic metabolites such as acetaldehyde and accetate' (van Thiel, 1983).

Similarly, one might point to the undoubted health risks associated with cigarette smoking. Smokers are twice as likely as non-smokers to die before the age of sixty-five. In the Royal College of Physicians' (1983) report *Health or Smoking?* it was suggested that for every 1000 young men who smoke cigarettes:

1 will be murdered
8 will die in road traffic accidents
250 will die prematurely because of smoking.

It is generally agreed that the incidence of deaths from lung cancer in Britain is one of the highest in the world. The World Health Organization's figures for (male) deaths from lung cancer in 1955 and 1975 show that for every 100 000 men the death rate increased from 52 to 72 in England and Wales, and from 50 to 83 in Scotland. These

1975 figures compare with rates of 24 deaths per 100 000 in Sweden, 44 in the Irish Republic, or 35 in France.

Cocaine was once complacently regarded as a relatively harmless drug. Sigmund Freud wrote a song of praise to this 'magical drug' and described it as a 'wonderful remedy'. This is not the current appraisal of cocaine. It causes a rapid but shortlived intoxication when sniffed or smoked. This initial 'high' is followed by an equally marked 'down' state which is often relieved by further repeated doses of cocaine. It can cause a powerful dependence and one of the common patterns of cocaine abuse is through 'binges' in which the user will compulsively take cocaine over a period of many hours or even days until either the supply of cocaine is exhausted or they are. The binge typically ends with the person falling into a disturbed sleep.

The drug has a number of adverse effects on health, some of which are minor, but the drug can be a killer. Cocaine increases blood pressure and people who are otherwise at low risk of a cardiovascular accident are exposed to a greatly increased risk when using it (Gossop, 1988). Death may result from cardiac or, more often, respiratory arrest, and cocaine has precipitated death through heart attacks. High doses may also cause seizures, and among the hundreds of cocaine users who telephoned an American 'cocaine hotline', 14 per cent described having had seizures with loss of consciousness. Like the amphetamines, cocaine stimulates the central nervous system and persistent or high-dose use can produce serious psychological disturbances. This is dramatically illustrated in the drug induced psychosis in which the user experiences powerful delusions, hallucinations and paranoia.

Damage to others

There are certain special circumstances in which the drug taking of one person may have an effect upon another. One of these is when drugs are used during pregnancy. For many years there has been concern about the effects of heavy drinking upon the fetus. During the gin epidemic of 1720–1750 birthrates dropped and there was a sharp rise in the mortality of children under five years of age. As a result of research done in Seattle during the late 1970s the term 'fetal alcohol syndrome' was coined to describe the characteristic cluster of problems caused to the baby by drinking during pregnancy (Rosett and Weiner, 1984). Although this syndrome in its fully fledged form may be comparatively rare, it has been suggested that less severe forms of damage may be more common than was once thought, and the problem most commonly reported has been growth retardation. There is currently a debate about the extent to which such problems may be attributed to lower levels of alcohol consumption, and it remains a matter of controversy as to what advice should be given to pregnant women with regard to such risks. The advice offered by the Royal College of Psychiatrists (1986) is 'to minimise their use of . . . alcohol . . . never to become intoxicated, and never consume more than one or two standard units of alcohol more than once or twice a week'.

Similar risks can be attributed to most forms of drug taking. As with alcohol, there have long been suspicions that smoking may cause prenatal harm. By far the most common adverse effect of smoking during pregnancy is reduced birthweight. The first scientific studies to document this were done during the 1950s, and these showed that the effect was dose-related. Among the other forms of harm to the baby related to smoking are a higher incidence of pneumonia and bronchitis, a higher incidence of spontaneous abortion, and increased neonatal mortality. A recent bibliography of studies addressing these issues included more than 1200 entries (Abel, 1982). The same is true of almost all forms of drug taking. It is well established that women who abuse heroin and other illicit drugs also put the baby at risk (Green and Gossop, 1988).

One of the problems that is peculiar to cigarette smoking is that the act of smoking may itself harm others who are not involved in this form of drug taking. This effect, sometimes called passive smoking or involuntary smoking, is due to the exposure of the non-smoker to tobacco smoke in the air, and environmental tobacco smoke is itself a product of the sidestream smoke that burns off from the cigarette between puffs and the smoke exhaled by the smoker. One of the most complete and authoritative reviews of this subject, by the US Surgeon General (1986) concluded that involuntary smoking can cause disease, including lung cancer in non-smokers, that the children of parents who smoke have increased frequency of respiratory infections and other respiratory problems when compared to the children of non-smoking parents, and that although the simple separation of smokers and non-smokers within the same air space may reduce the risks of involuntary smoking, it does not eliminate them.

The problem of addiction

One of the ways in which drug problems have a powerful impact both at the individual level and upon society is through the addictive use of drugs. This is certainly one of the more serious of the many problems linked with drug taking but it often receives such a disproportionate share of attention that it is possible to be misled into believing that this was somehow more important or more threatening than any of the others. In 1985 the British Government suggested that this was 'one of the most worrying problems facing our society today' (Home Office, 1985).

It is surprisingly difficult to define precisely what we mean by 'addictive behaviour'. However, it is generally agreed that the following are important or essential elements of what we mean by an addiction.

- A strong desire or sense of compulsion to engage in the particular behaviour (particularly when the opportunity to engage in such behaviour is not available).
- Impaired capacity to control the behaviour (notably in terms of controlling its onset, staying off or controlling the level at which the behaviour occurs).
- Discomfort and distress when the behaviour is prevented or stops.
- Persisting with the behaviour despite clear evidence that it is leading to problems.

Not all of these features will be found in every instance of addictive behaviour, but most of them are usually evident, and the first element, the sense of compulsion, would seem to be an essential ingredient. It contradicts our understanding of what we mean by an 'addiction' that someone could be said to be addicted to something but not experience a strong need for it. Together these four features provide a good picture of addictive behaviour with its sense of compulsion, the difficulty of maintaining control over the behaviour, the distress associated with withdrawal, and the persistence that such behaviours show once they have become established.

For many years the notion of 'addiction' has been virtually synonymous with drug addiction. And of the various forms of drug addiction, one in particular has had a quite disproportionate influence upon thinking about the problem, namely addiction to heroin and to the other opiates. Certainly the behaviour of the heroin addict meets all the defining characteristics stated above. There is a strong compulsion to take the drug (craving). There is impaired control, most conspicuously shown by the repeated failures to give up the drug based on will-power alone. There is the discomfort and distress caused by withdrawal symptoms; and there is the continued use of the drug despite the many and various problems caused by the habit (the financial costs, the criminal risks, the dangers of infection and ill-health).

The fact that heroin has always been linked to such clear cases of addictive behaviour has undoubtedly helped to mislead many people into the belief that addictiveness could be understood as being a property that was intrinsic to certain drugs. This produced futile arguments along the lines of whether this or that drug was 'really addictive'. Also, because of the stigma that surrounds heroin addiction, there has been a popular tendency to link addiction to illegal and prohibited substances. However, addictive behaviour is not just a problem related to the use of certain illegal drugs. Indeed, in many respects it needs to be emphasised that some of the most prevalent and most damaging forms of addiction are not linked to the illicit drugs at all.

There has never been much doubt that alcohol leads many people into an addictive pattern of use though it is only comparatively recently that the significance of this has been acknowledged. As late as the 1950s the World Health Organization suggested that alcohol did not qualify as an addictive drug in the full sense of the term. However, both the Bible and the Hindu *Ayurveda* (dating from about 1000 BC) refer to the perils of intoxication and habitual drinking. The prophet Isaiah complained that 'Priests and prophets are addicted to strong drink and bemused with wine; clamouring in their cups, confirmed topers, hiccuping in drunken stupor; every table is covered with vomit.'

None the less, the fact that alcohol is such a familiar intoxicant (and possibly because there are so many economic vested interests in its production and distribution) there is a tendency to underplay the enormous damage that it can do to individuals and to societies. A 1978 survey of drinking in England and Wales (Wilson, 1970) suggested that 5 per cent of men and 2 per cent of women reported alcohol-related problems, and at a conservative estimate, there may be as many as half a million people in Britain with problems of such severity that they could be regarded as addicted to alcohol. One measure of the scale of the problem can be taken from recent research in general hospitals which has showed that approximately 25 per cent of acute male admissions to medical wards are directly or indirectly due to alcohol: an even higher proportion of surgical emergencies are related to alcohol.

Until quite recently there was a similar tendency to underrate the addictive potential of smoking and to under-play the damage done by this habit. However, the habit of cigarette smoking has also demonstrated its own powerful addictive capacity to trap and to harm smokers. It is somewhat surprising that this was so slow to be fully acknowledged. When the first Spanish settlers in the New World were reproached for their indulgence in 'such a disgusting habit' as smoking they replied that they found it impossible to give up. During the four and a half centuries since then, smoking has continued to cause dependence, though it is only in recent years that it has been possible to take it seriously in this respect. Earlier this century it was possible for Sir Humphrey Rolleston, one of the leading medical figures in public health matters to state that 'To regard tobacco as a drug of addiction may be all very well in a humorous state, but it is hardly accurate' (Rolleston, 1926).

As the evidence for the health hazards of smoking has strengthened and people have continued to find it so difficult to give up, the humour of its addictiveness has lessened somewhat. Another authoritative view from earlier this century, this time from Louis Lewin (sometimes called the father of psychopharmacology) was that the compulsion to use tobacco was very much less than that for drugs like the opiates, and that 'If the use of tobacco has to be stopped for medical or other reasons, no suffering of the body or morbid desire for the drug appears' (cited by Jaffe and Kanzler, 1981). The degree to which views about smoking as an addictive behaviour have changed can be gauged by measuring these earlier expert opinions against a more recent one that cigarette smoking is probably 'the most addictive and dependence producing' form of drug taking known to man (Russell, 1976). One study reported that of those teenagers who smoke more than a single cigarette, only 15 per cent manage to avoid going on to become regular dependent smokers (McKennell and Thomas, 1967). It is interesting that some heroin addicts have suggested that it would be easier for them to give up heroin than to give up smoking, and in a survey of British opiate addicts it was found that addicts described their need for cigarettes as being at least as great as their need for heroin (Blumberg *et al.*, 1974).

But even a definition of drugs which is extended to include such legally available substances as alcoholic drinks or cigarettes is not sufficient to encompass the various forms of addictive behaviour. It is interesting to note that there are addictive behaviours which do not involve the taking of drugs at all. Compulsive gambling is one such activity. There are many people for whom gambling has passed beyond the occasional placing of bets into a realm of behaviour which can lay strong claims to being an 'addictive behaviour' with its associated implications of compulsion, preoccupation, difficulties of control, and persisting with it despite the obvious financial and social harm that it causes. One rough estimate of the number of people with compulsive gambling problems suggests that it may be a little under 1 per cent of the population, or, in the United States, about one million people (Dickerson, 1984).

Like drinking and drug taking, gambling is an ancient activity, and is a recorded part of ancient Egyptian, Chinese, Greek and Roman civilisations. One of the main influences upon Chinese thought has been Confucian philosophy, according to which alcohol, opium, womanising and gambling are identified as the four major vices (Singer, 1974). One way of coping with a problem like compulsive gambling, alcoholism or drug addiction could involve total abstinence. This is not possible for eating, an activity which for many people can cause similar problems to the other addictive behaviours. Orford in his book *Excessive Appetites* (1985) cites several such cases. Instances are given of people craving food, being unable to control their eating, stealing food or money to buy food, hiding and hoarding food, and lying about their eating. Such addictive behaviour is capable of leading to its own adverse consequences (often associated with obesity) and can be just as resistant to change as any other addiction.

The problem of addiction, however, should not be overstated. It is not, for example, an irreversible condition. This notion of progressive deterioration is a view of drug use that has considerable resonance with popular conceptions of addiction. In its crudest form it can be found in the 'dope fiend' myth of inevitable social, moral and physical decline that is assumed to accompany confirmed drug use. This view has been with us since at least the end of the last century, and it is a testimony to its staying power that a variation on this theme surfaced in the recent government anti-heroin campaign, which under the slogan 'heroin screws you up' depicted rapid decline in health and loss of control over intake. The market research evaluation of the campaign showed, among other things, that there was an increased belief among young people that death was an inevitable consequence of heroin use.

There is certainly a place for greater optimism about the eventual outcome even for severely addicted individuals. A recent study of relapse and abstinence among a group of opiate addicts after leaving treatment found that although there was a poor *immediate* outcome with the majority of the group using opiates on at least one occasion within the first few weeks of leaving the drug unit, this needed to be balanced against the finding that the proportion who were abstinent gradually increased throughout the next six months until at six-month follow-up 45 per cent were abstinent and living in the community (Gossop *et al.*, in press). In a ten-year follow-up study of a group of heroin addicts who approached London drug clinics in 1969, Stimson and Oppenheimer (1982) estimated that 38 per cent had become abstinent. There was considerable evidence for the stability of abstinence. Of the forty who had maintained abstinence for nine months or more at seven-year follow-up, only two relapsed to heroin use by the tenth year. It was also clear that those who became abstinent from heroin had not, for the most part, transferred their dependence to other substances. There is now no doubt that many addicts do become abstinent.

If we examine the behaviour of people during a phase of prolonged, regular drug use, we find an extraordinary diversity of lifestyles, coping strategies, and problems (or lack of them). There is no simple link between the prolonged ingestion of alcohol or drugs and behavioural outcome. Studies of the heroin addicts who were receiving prescriptions for heroin from drug clinics after they were first established (in the late 1960s), found a wide range of behavioural differences. Some addicts had chaotic lifestyles with high levels of crime, unemployment and high involvement with other drug users, whereas others led stable lives which might be indistinguishable from those of many who are not drug users. Although the drug doses used by these drug takers suggests that all were dependent, there was no obvious correlation between this and behaviour. There are also important differences in such basic factors as patterns of use within heroin users. In a recent sample of heroin addicts seen by the Maudsley Community Drugs Team a substantial number of heroin addicts were identified for whom the primary route of administration was by 'chasing the dragon'. This study (Gossop *et al.*, 1988) suggested that chasing was not simply a pre-injecting phase of heroin use and that many users persisted with this pattern of use for many years without moving into intravenous use. We know relatively little about this type of heroin use, about the social and psychological ways in which chasers may differ from injectors, and about how their different patterns of use may be associated with different 'careers'. The diversity that exists in such basic parameters as these may have an important influence upon outcome, but they have been largely neglected by existing natural history models.

Static descriptions of the individual at a single point in time are likely to be misleading, and are less useful than descriptions of processes and phases across time. When we look closely at the patterns of drug or alcohol use within any given period of time, we notice much more movement in and out of use, or from heavy to lighter use and vice versa. An early study of drug users living in the community conducted in Cambridge showed that of the heroin users who were identified in the first year of the study, less than half were regular daily users. A follow-up of the original sample and later recruits found that there was considerable variation in patterns of use over time. In particular, frequency of drug taking diminished over three years. For example, at one stage in the study 63 per cent were regular users, but two years later this had declined to 11 per cent. Even so-called 'regular' users rarely use for 365 days a year.

Although researchers and agency workers have drawn attention to patterns of use that differ from 'dependence', the direct research evidence is paltry. This neglect is related to the major sources of information in the UK which are usually based upon people who have come into contact with statutory services such as drug clinics, general medical practitioners or the prison service. Within this group it could be expected that there would be a high proportion of drug users who have experienced drug or drug-related problems and who have relatively well established and/or high dose habits.

THE DIVERSITY OF PROBLEMS

If the diversity of behaviour and of outcomes is so marked among confirmed addicts or alcoholics, the degree of variation is even more marked when we look at drinkers and drug takers who have stopped short of dependent use. The problems related to non-dependent use deserve attention if for no other reason than that they are the more common. The survey evidence on patterns of use indicates that problematic dependent use is a statistical rarity (one might say the same about surveys of drug use). A good example of the sort of evidence that is found in such surveys is work by Plant *et al.* (1985) on Scottish schoolchildren. This showed that levels of illicit drug use were quite high (37 per cent of males and 23 per cent of females reported at some time having used illicit drugs) but that the majority of this group who had tried drugs were not regular users. Opiate use was understandably quite rare (1 per cent) in this population of schoolchildren, and in all cases, frequency of use was less than weekly. However, alcohol was very widely used.

In an investigation of 15 and 16-year-old schoolchildren, Plant *et al.* (1984) selected six items which indicated relatively serious consequences of drinking: having had four or more hangovers in the previous six months; having had a drink in the morning to steady nerves or get rid of the hangover; having been advised by a doctor to drink less; having had an alcohol-related accident or injury; having had a shaky hand in the morning after drinking; and having missed a day at school due to drinking. Twenty per cent of the males and 13 per cent of the females indicated that they had experienced one or more of these problems.

The theme of many problems in many forms can also be found in the way that they vary throughout the population. There are regional variations in the types of illicit drugs that are used and in the ways in which they are abused. The same is true of cigarette smoking and drinking. The rates of officially recorded drinking problems, for example, are generally higher in Scotland, Northern Ireland, and Northern England than they are further south. This applies to the three areas of intoxication (drunkenness offences), health damage (liver cirrhosis deaths), and addiction (hospital admissions for alcohol dependence). Men are more likely to drink heavily and the rates of alcohol-related problems are consequently higher than for women, though there is a national trend towards increased drinking among women which contrasts with a more or less static level for men.

The importance of recognising that many problems may occur in many forms can be seen in this issue of sex differences. The level of 'safe' drinking for women is lower than for men. Current estimates from the Royal College of Psychiatrists (1986) suggest that, the potential for harm increases greatly when drinking exceeds 50 units/week for men (a standard unit of alcohol is one half pint of beer or one glass of wine) and 35 units for women. For regular drinkers the report recommends that drinking be kept well below these levels.

Such factors must be taken into account in an understanding of and response to the many forms of addiction problems.

References

Abel, E. (1982) *Smoking and Reproduction: A Comprehensive Bibliography* (London: Greenwood Press).
Ashton, H. and Stepney, R. (1982) *Smoking: Psychology and Pharmacology* (London: Tavistock).
Blumberg, H., Cohens, S., Dronfield, B., Mordecai, E., Roberts, J. and Marks, D. (1974) 'British Opiate Users: I. People approaching London Treatment Centres', *International Journal of the Addictions*, vol. 9, pp. 1–23.
Dickerson, M. (1984) *Compulsive Gamblers* (London: Longman).
Edwards, G. (1984) 'Drinking in Longitudinal Perspective: Career and Natural History', *British Journal of Addiction*, vol. 79, pp. 175–83.
Evans, C. (1986) 'Alcohol and Violence: Problems Relating to Methodology, Statistics and Causation', in P. Brain (ed.) *Alcohol and Aggression* (Beckenham: Croom Helm).
Gerson, L. W. (1978) 'Alcohol-related Acts of Violence: Who was Drinking and Where the Acts Occurred', *Journal of Studies on Alcohol*, vol. 39, pp. 1294–6.
Gossop, M. (1987) *Living with Drugs* (Aldershot: Wildwood House).
Gossop, M. (1988) 'Beware Cocaine', *British Medical Journal*, vol. 295, p. 945.
Gossop, M., Green, L., Phillips, G. and Bradley, B. (in press) 'Lapse, Relapse and Survival among Opiate Addicts after Treatment: a Prospective Follow-up Study', *British Journal of Psychiatry*.
Gossop, M., Griffiths, P. and Strang, J. (1988) 'Chasing the Dragon: Characteristics of Heroin Chasers', *British Journal of Addiction*, vol. 83, pp. 1159–62.
Green, L. and Gossop, M. (1988) 'The Management of Pregnancy in Opiate Addicts', *Journal of Reproduction and Infant Psychology*, vol. 6, pp. 51–7.
Heather, N. (1981) 'Relationships between Delinquency and Drunkenness among Scottish Young Offenders', *British Journal on Alcohol and Alcoholism*, vol. 16, pp. 150–61.
Home Office (1985) *Tackling Drug Misuse: A Summary of the Government's Strategy* (London: HMSO).
Jaffe, J. J. and Kanzler, M. (1981) 'Nicotine: Tobacco Use, Abuse, and Dependence', in J. Lowinson, P. Ruiz (eds), *Substance Abuse: Clinical Problems and Perspectives*, (Baltimore: Williams & Wilkins).
Larson, P. S., Haag, H. B. and Silvette, H. (1961) *Tobacco: Experimental and Clinical Studies* (Baltimore: Williams & Wilkins).
Lester, D. and Lester, G. (1975) *Crime of Passion: Murder and the Murderer* (Chicago: Nelson Hall).
McKennell, A. C. and Thomas, R. K. (1967) *Adults' and Adolescents' Smoking Habits and Attitudes* (London: HMSO).
Maynard, A., Hardman, H. and Whelan, A. (1987) 'Measuring the Social

Costs of Addictive Substances', *British Journal of Addiction*, vol. 82, pp. 703–6.

Murray, R. (1974) 'Analgesic Abuse', *British Journal of Hospital Medicine*, vol. 2, pp. 772–80.

Orford, J. (1985) *Excessive Appetites: A Psychological View of Addictions* (Chichester: Wiley).

Plant, M., Peck, D. and Samuel, E. (1985) *Alcohol, Drugs and School Leavers* (London: Tavistock).

Plant, M., Peck, D. and Stuart, R. (1984) 'The Correlates of Serious Alcohol Related Consequences and Illicit Drug Use amongst a Cohort of Scottish Teenagers', *British Journal of Addiction*, vol. 79, pp. 197–200.

Rolleston, H. (1926) 'Medical Aspects of Tobacco', *Lancet*, vol. 1, p. 961.

Rosett, H. and Weiner, L. (1984) *Alcohol and the Fetus* (Oxford: Oxford University Press.

Royal College of Physicians (1983) *Health or Smoking* (London: Pitman).

Royal College of Psychiatrists (1986) *Alcohol: Our Favourite Drug*, (London: Tavistock).

Russell, M. A. H. (1976) 'Tobacco Smoking and Nicotine Dependence', in R. Gibbins *et al.* (eds) *Research Advances in Alcohol and Drug Problems*, vol. 3. (New York: Wiley).

Singer, K. (1974) 'The Choice of Intoxicant amongst the Chinese', *British Journal of Addiction*, vol. 69, pp. 257–68.

Stimson, G. and Oppenheimer, E. (1982) *Heroin Addiction* (London: Tavistock).

Surgeon General (1986) *The Health Consequences of Involuntary Smoking* (US Department of Health and Human Services, Maryland).

van Thiel, D. (1983) 'Effects of Ethanol upon Organ Systems other than the Central Nervous System', in B. Tabakoff, P. Sutker and C. Randall (eds), *Medical and Social Aspects of Alcohol Abuse* (New York: Plenum).

Wilson, P. (1970) *Drinking in England and Wales*, OPCS (London: HMSO).

4 Controlling Alcohol Abuse

Marcus Grant

INTRODUCTION

Ever since the First World Health Assembly in 1948, the World Health Organization (WHO) has recognised that it has a role as the focus for international concern about alcohol-related health problems, where health is defined not merely as the absence of disease but as a state of complete physical, mental and social wellbeing. Since alcohol-related problems affect virtually every area of psychosocial functioning, it is evident that WHO's mandate implies a clear commitment to the alleviation of these problems. It is important to emphasise at the outset that WHO's concern is therefore with the prevention of a very wide range of alcohol-related health problems.

In setting about the task, WHO's aim is to investigate and develop technologies that will enable individuals suffering from the alcohol-dependence syndrome and from its associated problems to be more rapidly identified. A further challenge for WHO is to develop preventive strategies that will reduce alcohol-related mortality and morbidity and to promote these strategies to Member States. WHO is also investigating treatment approaches, focusing particularly on simple interventions.

Another reason why WHO takes a particular interest in the question of alcohol-related problems is that such problems are now being reported in increasing frequency from countries that had previously been relatively free from them. While alcohol consumption and alcohol-related problems are beginning to level off in some developed countries in Europe, for example, they are showing signs of increasing in a number of developing countries in Africa, the Americas, and the Western Pacific. Certainly, representatives from many countries in those regions of the world are expressing growing concern at the extent to which such problems are increasing there. WHO has particular responsibility to prevent disease and to promote health in developing countries, so that such expressions of concern require to be taken very seriously indeed. Nor is it sufficient to recommend improvements in the provision of treatment services. In view of its global responsibility to work with countries to prevent alcohol-related problems, it is essential that WHO should be in a position to offer advice on all relevant aspects of alcohol policies, including the question of availability.

In keeping with the expressed concerns and priorities of the World Health Assembly, WHO supports member states in their efforts to reach decisions on prevention of alcohol-related problems which are consistent with their national needs and circumstances. In recent years, for example, it has conducted a series of studies and workshops relating to development of national alcohol policy. These efforts have been carried out at headquarters and regional levels, with collaborating governments and research institutions, and have produced a valuable body of reports and publications (Moser, 1985).

CURRENT TRENDS IN WORLD ALCOHOL CONSUMPTION AND ALCOHOL PROBLEMS

The most important lesson to emerge from recent research is that trends in alcohol-related problems are generally positively associated with those in alcohol consumption. In the report of the WHO Expert Committee on Problems Related to Alcohol Consumption (WHO Expert Committee, 1980), it is pointed out that, while the association between consumption and problems cannot be described in precise mathematical terms, a considerable body of empirical evidence supports such an association. Studies of individual countries over time and comparative studies of different countries and regions have demonstrated this association most convincingly for liver cirrhosis, but there is also evidence relating both to other alcohol-related diseases and to indirect indices, such as arrests for drunkenness.

After reviewing a number of qualifying variables that have to be taken into account in assessing the validity of this association, the Expert Committee concludes that 'in spite of all these considerations, the available evidence suggests that, in a given cultural setting, an increase in consumption tends to be accompanied by an increase in potentially harmful drinking, whatever the specific consequences for each country and each drinking culture'.

Heavy consumption of alcoholic beverages (above 15 litres per adult) is mainly a feature of certain western and southern European countries. The consumption levels of most of the other developed regions of the world, namely Northern America, the remainder of Europe, Australia and New Zealand, are also comparatively high (10–15 litres of pure alcohol per adult each year). With few exceptions, the average consumption levels of Central and South America and the Caribbean countries are considerably lower than those of the developed countries (less than 10 litres per adult). The adult populations of Asia, Africa and Oceania typically have a very low intake of alcohol (less than 5 litres per adult).

Looking at the rate of increase in beer consumption *per capita* between 1960 and 1981 in selected regions of the world, it appears that the regions with low consumption show extremely high growth rates (over 600 per cent), whereas the countries with high consumption show comparatively moderate increases (about 40 per cent). In the case of central African countries, this increase brought their consumption level relatively close to that of Europe and Northern America in 1960.

CONSIDERATIONS RELEVANT TO PREVENTIVE POLICY WITH PARTICULAR REFERENCE TO DEVELOPING COUNTRIES

It is clear that Member States wishing to prevent alcohol-related problems face many difficulties – among them, diffusion of relevant governmental authorities, opposition of economic interests, and uncertain public support. These considerations are relevant in both developed and developing countries, but it is important to emphasise those which are especially relevant to developing countries.

Alcohol-related problems manifest themselves differently in different cultures (in part, because drinking practices differ) and at different stages of socio-economic development. None the less, in many of the forms they take, across many cultures, they tend to increase as *per capita* consumption of alcohol increases. In many developing countries, the general outlines of such problems are already apparent, such as:

In Swaziland, where

our outpatient departments are filled on Monday by victims of weekend drinking, our wards are filled with cases of cirrhosis of the liver, hemorrhaging gastric varicosities, ataxias and peripheral neuritides . . . We also know the loss to industry and the civil service of young middle-aged men who drop out because of addiction. The mental hospital figures of psychoses directly due to alcoholism are fairly constant, at 20 to 25 per cent of admissions . . . The figures from the High Court . . . are also striking. Of the 97 cases of murder or culpable homicide heard during 1978 and during 1979 till November, drink played an important role in 58, that is, about 60 per cent. Drunken driving cases are frequent in the subordinate courts and are assuming alarming proportions. (Reinhold, 1980)

The 'long gestation of many of the chronic physiological consequences of drinking does not make these problems less important to developing countries; even where overall life expectancy is low, the life expectancy of those who survive to 'drinking age' is quite high' (Room, unpublished draft, 1982). Thus, developing countries in which *per capita* consumption of alcohol has increased greatly over the last 20 years – and whose experience of alcohol-related problems to date may have consisted largely of traffic accidents, accidents in the workplace, violence, and malnutrition of children – can anticipate, in addition, a 'substantial "epidemic" ' of the long-term physiological consequences of alcohol consumption in the near future (Room, unpublished draft, 1982). The additional strain on scarce economic and social resources will be considerable and, in the absence of vigorous efforts to prevent alcohol-related problems, will continue to grow.

Many developing countries are themselves eager to encourage the growth of domestic alcohol industries. Brewing, in particular, can seem an attractive proposition in the early phases of industrialisation. The technology is relatively simple, the required capital investment is not large, it uses agricultural inputs, it provides a base for other industries (for example, glass and packaging). It also 'serve[s] as a source of state revenue and obviate[s] the use of foreign exchange for imported beverages' (Room, unpublished draft, 1982). This occurred for example:

In Zambia, between 1969 and 1980, where recurrent revenue to the government from the alcohol industry increased more than five-fold (as a result of annual increases in the price of alcoholic beverages) while total recurrent revenue to the government less than doubled. By 1980, revenue from the alcohol industry comprised 15 per cent of total government recurrent revenue (up from about 5 per cent in 1969, having peaked at about 19 per cent in 1979). In 1979–1980, the turnover of the Breweries Division comprised an estimated 41 per cent of the total turnover of the Industrial Development Corporation of Zambia, Ltd. (up from 23 per cent in 1970–1971). Employment in the Breweries Division is nearly one-quarter of total employment of the companies owned by this government holding company, which produces more than half of the manufactured output of the nation (Serpell, 1982).

Retailing of alcoholic beverages also offers attractive investment opportunities, such as:

In Botswana, where '10 per cent of the medium-sized loans made by the National Development Bank are for bottle stores and bars' (Report of a Meeting on Community and National Response to Alcohol-Related Problems, 16–21 November 1981, Lusaka, Zambia, Part II).

In Zimbabwe, where in 1983 alone, the number of liquor licenses issued increased 'nearly 50 per cent for Harare District and 20 per cent and over in 13 other districts. In one district only . . . was the increase under 10 per cent' (Zimbabwe MOH, 1984).

Domestic production of alcoholic beverages, whether commercial or non-commercial, requires agricultural products and water, which in many developing countries are in very short supply. Such countries will want to consider the implications for nutrition and health status of devoting scarce agricultural land, foodstuffs, and water to the production of alcoholic beverages. For example:

In India, 'the moral question of wastefulness with foodstuffs has played a large part when alcohol has been debated publicly. To use the inadequate production of cereals and other foodstuffs for the manufacture of alcoholic beverages is regarded as a mark of civic irresponsibility' (Armyr *et al.*, 1982).

Undernourished persons may be more vulnerable to alcohol-related problems than those with an adequate diet; this may reinforce the harmful effects of alcohol consumption in developing countries in which malnutrition is prevalent (WHO Expert Committee, 1980).

In developing as well as developed countries, measures which affect the price, production, distribution and sale of alcholic beverages can be difficult to enforce. Examples of this can be found in:

In Mexico, a 'law prohibiting the opening of liquor stores near industrial parks, health facilities, or schools has been rendered moot by the explosive growth of Mexico City and the proliferation of these facilities' (Medina-Mora, 1982).

'In most Caribbean countries, there is a legal age limit, but children walk into supermarkets and buy alcohol without being questioned' (Beaubrun, 1982).

In 'many developing countries . . . centralized price policies have little bearing on the considerable non-commercial production of alcoholic beverages' (Mäkelä *et al.*, 1981).

In many developing countries, it is possible to identify traditional cultural, religious, and social norms which will support efforts to prevent alcohol-related problems. Recognition that alcohol-related problems interfere with desired social and economic development can also encourage public support.

In developing as well as developed countries, the possibilities for effective community action to prevent alcohol-related problems, independent of measures taken by government, should not be overlooked. For example:

In Honduras, in the *barrio* of Santa Eduviges, 'by a community decision, the local food store no longer sells alcohol. [Santa Eduviges, a *barrio* of 60 houses and 300 people, is located in a district of high unemployment and low wages marked by family instability, violence, and alcoholism]. Although alcohol is still readily available from nearby outlets, the insistence that it should not be sold locally reflects a change in community values [which evolved in the course of its participation in a mental health/ community development project initiated in 1975] that has been accompanied by a decrease in the frequency and severity of alcohol-related problems' (World Health Organization, 1984).

INTERNATIONAL EVIDENCE ON THE EFFECTIVENESS OF PREVENTIVE MEASURES

Many measures which might prevent alcohol-related problems have never been systematically evaluated, and current knowledge is insufficient to permit detailed advice on a great many technical points important to the development of effective national policies. However, the scientific evidence summarised here does support two confident – and hopeful – conclusions:

- Alcohol-related problems *can* be prevented.
- They can be prevented by measures which governments can take.

In fact, history offers ample evidence that alcohol-related problems not only rise but also fall, often very rapidly. Such changes have occurred in both developing and developed countries, in many historical periods. In recent times, national trends in alcohol-related problems have been largely upward. However, there are also clear recent instances in which they have been halted or even reversed. For example in France between 1956 and 1982, per capita consumption of alcohol declined nearly 27 per cent: from more than 26 litres of ethanol per person aged 15 years or more to just over 19 litres. And decreases in significant alcohol-related health problems have followed. Between 1975 and 1982, the death rate from cirrhosis of the liver declined 21 per cent for both men and women. Between 1960 and 1982, the death rate from alcoholism/alcoholic psychosis declined 43 per cent for men, 53 per cent for women.

Measures for which there is reasonably good evidence of effectiveness

Increasing the relative price of alcoholic beverages

The sum of scientific evidence and historical experience affirms that, other factors being constant, an increase in the price of alcoholic beverages relative to other commodities generally reduces *per capita* consumption.

More recently, there is also explicit evidence that the price of alcohol, acting through its effects on consumption, influences the level of alcohol-related problems. This has happened, among other countries, in Trinidad and Tobago, where between 1966 and 1975 the number of road traffic accidents per year 'rose and fell predictably . . . with changes in the price of rum relative to *per capita* income' (Kendell *et al.*, 1983).

In Scotland, in 1981, a combination of tax and price increases caused the price of alcoholic beverages to increase faster than the retail price index and average disposable income. Unemployment rose simultaneously. Surveys of 'regular drinkers' conducted in Edinburgh and the surrounding area in 1978–9 and again in 1981–2 indicate that, between surveys, total alcohol consumption fell by 18 per cent and associated adverse effects by 16 per cent. Although rising unemployment was responsible for up to one-fifth of the reduction in consumption, 'the increased price of alcohol was the major influence. Heavy drinkers and dependent drinkers both reduced their consumption at least as much as light or moderate drinkers and suffered fewer adverse effects as a result' (Kendell *et al.*, 1983).

Increasing the price of alcoholic beverages *may* deprive the families of some drinkers who are poor. However, there is little reason to believe that poor drinkers are less likely than other drinkers to reduce their alcohol consumption in response to price increases. And, to the extent that consumption does decline in response to higher prices, both family income and the health of the drinker may improve (Moore and Gerstein, 1981).

In sum, increasing the price of alcoholic beverages relative to other commodities can be expected to reduce consumption (by heavy drinkers as well as others in the drinking population), and, thus, to prevent alcohol-related problems.

Sharp restrictions on the distribution of alcoholic beverages

Sharp restrictions on the distribution of alcoholic beverages (as illustrated by periods of rationing, prohibition, and strikes in the distribution system) significantly reduce alcohol-related problems. For example:

In Canada, Finland and the United States during the first few years of prohibition, with the exception of automobile accidents, 'all indicators of alcohol consumption and alcohol problems reached the lowest level yet achieved in any period for which there are relevant data' (Bruun *et al.*, 1975). It is estimated that, in the United States, total alcohol consumption declined sharply during the early years of prohibition, then rose somewhat toward the end of the 1920s (Aaron and Musto, 1981).

In Norway, in 1978, a nine-week strike of production, storing, and transport workers at the Norwegian Wine and Spirits Monopoly stopped deliveries of wine and spirits to all retail outlets and licensed premises. However, retail sales of wine and spirits continued until stocks were exhausted and beer was on sale as usual. Sales of beer, imports of wine and spirits, home production of wine, and illegal home distilling all increased during the strike period. The estimated decrease in total alcohol supply was approximately 10–15 per cent; the estimated decrease in total alcohol consumption was 5–10 per cent. None the less,

> most measures strongly influenced by skid-row alcoholics, i.e., admission to detoxification centres, the use of detoxification rooms at the so-called protection homes, reports of drunkenness, drunkenness arrests, offenses called 'home quarrels', number of drunkards in the street, and injuries caused by falling, showed a marked decrease (Horverak, 1983).

In Poland, in 1981, the rationing of alcohol 'involving a 20 per cent overall drop in consumption, was accompanied by declines of 11 per cent in cirrhosis deaths, 39 per cent in admissions to sobering up stations, and 40 per cent in first hospital admissions for alcoholic psychoses' (Room, 1984).

Moreover, as the examples indicate, it is not simply moderate drinkers whose consumption is influenced by such general changes in the availability of alcoholic beverages. In fact, 'it is precisely the heavy drinkers most likely to appear in . . . casualty and crime statistics whose behaviour often seems most strongly affected' (Room, 1984).

Increasing the minimum legal 'drinking age'

Lowering the minimum age at which a person may legally purchase alcoholic beverages (or at which alcoholic beverages may legally be sold to him) frequently increases the rate of automobile accidents among young people, sometimes including young people not yet of legal 'drinking age' (Wagenaar, 1983).

Although these findings are limited to Canada and the United States, they are relevant to many countries in which motor bicycles are widely used by the young and/or in which alcohol-related motor vehicle accidents are a major cause of death and injury among young people. They may be relevant also to countries which have very low minimum age requirements or none at all.

It should be noted that minimum age requirements are often seen as expressing and communicating society's view of appropriate conduct – and, for that reason, as having important symbolic effects in addition to their demonstrated impact on automobile accident rates.

Increasing the probability of detection and punishment

Increasing the probability of detection and punishment for drinking and driving reduces deaths and injuries in traffic accidents. Both the actual probability of detection and punishment and the public's perception of that probability are crucial to sustained effectiveness. The critical elements of action to this end include:

- making driving with a blood alcohol concentration (BAC) higher than a specific level a legal offence *in itself*;
- requiring that BAC be established by chemical tests (for example, of blood, breath or urine);
- requiring police to test BAC at roadside if a driver is involved in an accident or a traffic violation *or* permitting police to stop drivers and test for BAC at roadside without any prior evidence of possible drinking; and
- imposing punishment considered 'severe and depriving' for driving with a BAC above the legal limit (for example, mandatory suspension of driver's licence) and applying it also for refusal to submit to the tests.

These conclusions emerge from the cumulative experience of several countries. In particular:

In the United Kingdom, in 1967, the law was amended to define driving with a blood alcohol concentration of 80 mg/100 ml or higher as an offence and to permit police to demand a roadside breath-test (to screen for blood-alcohol concentration) if a driver was involved in an accident or a 'moving' violation of traffic law or gave reasonable cause to the police to suspect he had been drinking. 'Refusal to take part in the tests was punishable as though the tests had been failed'. (Since 1962, the law had required a year's suspension of driver's licence for serious motoring offences, including drinking and driving.) Enactment and implementation of the 1967 law were accompanied by substantial controversy and resulting publicity and 'road casualties declined impressively' in the months subsequent to its implementation. In particular, fatal and serious injury crashes on weekend nights ('in which alcohol is much more commonly involved . . . than at other times') dropped 66 per cent in the first month, 'an unprecedented and highly significant decline'. 'For the three months following the passage of the act, casualties from traffic accidents were reduced 16 per cent from the same period the previous year, and fatalities were reduced 23 per cent'. The percentage of all drivers killed in England and Wales who had illegal blood alcohol concentrations declined from 25 per cent in December 1966 – September 1967, prior to the implementation of the law, to 15 per cent in the corresponding period of 1967–8 (Ross, 1981).

Similar measures were subsequently adopted in France, the Netherlands, Canada, and New Zealand – with some impact initially (though less than in the United Kingdom) and a similar decline in effectiveness over time. The initial effectiveness of these laws has been attributed to 'overestimation of the probability of punishment' for drinking and driving, 'produced by the publicity and newsworthiness of the new laws'. The eventual decline of their effectiveness, to drivers 'learning through experience' that the actual probability of punishment, even if much increased, was considerably lower than they had originally estimated, in some cases remaining 'negligible'.

In sum, '[t]here is good evidence that if drivers in general perceive a high risk of being arrested if they drive drunk they will be deterred from doing so, and alcohol-related traffic accidents will decrease substantially' (Reed, 1981).

Measures widely believed to be effective, though little scientific evidence is currently available

Education of school children and the general public

Neither individual school-based alcohol education programmes nor public education campaigns via the mass media have proved effective in reducing alcohol-related problems – though, in the short term, they not infrequently increase knowledge and sometimes change attitudes. These findings are generally attributed to methodological weakness in evaluations of the programmes and/or in the programmes themselves (for example, failure to define objectives or target groups with sufficient precision).

A few experimental efforts to encourage and support behavioural change in a health-enhancing direction have succeeded in reducing health risks. These programmes had several critical elements in common – among them, the following:

- They attempted to change *several* types of behaviours associated with adverse health effects.
- They combined mass media campaigns with other measures.
- They were based in and involved the community.

The implications of the literature on school-based alcohol education (whether it conveys information about alcohol and alcohol-related problems, teaches decision-making skills or attempts to 'clarify values') are less clear. However, teaching and counselling by peers (rather than adults) is thought to increase impact. One recent United States review argues that school programmes should focus on *current* alcohol problems of young drinkers (for example, traffic accidents, fights, diminished school performance) rather than trying to shape drinking practices over a lifetime (Moore and Gerstein, 1981). This would be consistent with findings that efforts to prevent onset of smoking among young people are 'most successful' when they emphasise 'social and immediate consequences of smoking rather than long-term health consequences' (USDHHS, 1982). There have also been promising initial results from experimental efforts to teach children skills for recognising and resisting 'social pressures' toward tobacco, alcohol and drug use.

The *cumulative* effect of 'forces that alert, motivate, instruct, and maintain changes in public attitudes and practices' (Farquhar *et al.*, 1981) may well be substantial, especially when they are sustained and highly visible over the course of a generation or more.

This experience suggests that, over time, sustained public education by a wide range of public and private organisations might, for example, reduce social pressures to drink, sharply discourage drunkenness and drinking in high-risk situations, and offer support to individuals who wish to drink little, if at all.

Education of health professionals and other primary health care workers

Education and training of persons who provide health care might be expected to prevent or reduce a variety of specific alcohol-related problems – among them, the following:

- adverse alcohol-drug interactions;
- combined dependence on alcohol and drugs;
- adverse effects of alcohol consumption during pregnancy; and
- widespread alcohol-related problems, including the alcohol dependence syndrome, among health professionals themselves.

Early studies of the attitudes of physicians and other health professionals toward alcoholics found these attitudes 'to be pervasively negative and to limit diagnostic and therapeutic abilities' (Fisher *et al.*, 1976). Attempts to change attitudes were not generally successful, perhaps because 'many of the programs were based on the assumption that attitudes would be favourably influenced merely by an increase in knowledge' (Ewan and Whaite, 1983).

More recent studies suggest that attitudes can be improved by training which emphasises clinical problems and provides considerable time for small group discussion; opportunities to meet recovering alcoholics and visit alcoholism treatment programmes are also considered helpful. One study, concurring that 'formal education is of limited value in changing attitudes', indicates 'these deficiencies may be overcome if courses are combined with opportunities to gain support and experience' (Cartwright, 1980).

The importance of improving the attitudes of health professionals towards alcoholics is weighed differently by different observers. It is argued by some that, faced with a limited amount of time in which to teach about alcoholism (for example, to medical students), the emphasis is best placed on acknowledging and exploring negative attitudes toward alcoholism and alcohol-dependent patients; the conviction is that such efforts are 'important prerequisites of positive educational outcome, particularly . . . augmented clinical skills' (Grant, 1984).

Measures for which evidence of effectiveness is mixed

Other restrictions on the distribution of alcoholic beverages

Statistical analyses of relationships between alcohol consumption, alcohol-related problems and various measures of the physical availability of alcoholic beverages (for example, density of different types of sales outlets) have produced widely varying results.

For example, there is a 'major effect on consumption and problems of intoxication' if outlets for alcoholic beverages are closed for a whole day each week (Smart, 1982).

In 1977, State-owned stores for the off-premise sale of spirits and wines in a region of Finland were closed on Saturdays for eight months (though light and medium beer continued to be available at grocery stores). 'The closure reduced public drunkenness and alcohol-related violence, as well as total consumption.' There was no evidence of an increase in consumption of illicit alcohol (Smart, 1982).

In Mexico, 'in the month of December 1981, a decrease in the number of accidents, arrests, etc., occurred in one state that carried out an experiment to see if alcohol consumption would drop when sale of liquor was limited to certain hours and days of the week' (Medina-Mora, 1982).

However, individual small changes in merchandising practices, hours of sale, and type, location, and frequency of outlets are generally found to have 'small or insignificant effects' on total alcohol consumption and alcohol-related problems (Smart, 1982). For example:

In Scotland, in 1976, the law was amended to permit 'licensed premises' to remain open for an extra hour in the evening on weekdays. Surveys to monitor the effects of this change found 'no statistically reliable evidence of overall increase (or decrease) in [average] consumption' subsequent to the change. Furthermore,

> examination of statistics of drink-related offences known to the police provides no evidence of increased numbers as a result of the extra permitted hour's drinking and there is some evidence of a decrease possibly associated with the change. The distribution of the timing of offences shows substantial decreases between 10 p.m. and 1 p.m. with corresponding later increases. Very similar results are found from an examination of road accident statistics (Bruce, 1980).

Regulation of advertising and other promotion of alcoholic beverages

It is not known whether or to what extent advertising for alcoholic beverages influences *per capita* consumption of alcohol or the nature and level of alcohol-related problems.

Econometric studies (which usually consider the effects of marginal changes in advertising volume as measured by marginal changes in expenditures for advertising) usually conclude there is no significant relationship between advertising and *per capita* consumption. Where relationships are observed, they are generally small and often contradictory (van Iwaarden, 1983). In brief, neither the existence nor the direction of a causal link between advertising and *per capita* consumption has been established.

Indeed, many studies find it 'just as likely that increased sales will stimulate advertising expenditures as that advertising will stimulate sales'. Some note that 'in a fairly stable market the advertising budget of a certain product in general is a fixed percentage of the sales volume' (van Iwaarden, 1983). And there is no lack of empirical support for the alcoholic beverage industry's argument that brand advertising simply shifts the distribution of market shares, without increasing total demand.

Other studies, however, point out that under certain conditions advertising *may* increase total demand – for example, when social, economic and technological forces are 'favourable to the spontaneous expansion of demand' (Whitehead, 1983). For developing countries in which a large proportion of the population does not presently drink alcoholic beverages, disposable income is rising (or the relative price of alcohol falling), and transportation and distribution networks developing rapidly, these findings may warrant special attention.

It should also be noted that regulation of advertising for alcoholic beverages is often seen as relevant to accomplishing purposes other than reduction of alcohol-related problems – among them, the following:

- signalling the government's conviction that alcohol consumption poses serious risks to health and social well-being;
- increasing the credibility of other governmental actions to prevent alcohol-related problems;
- creating an environment in which public education about risks associated with alcohol consumption has greater opportunity to be effective; and
- reducing the possible influence of advertising revenues on editorials and news reports about alcohol-related problems.

In addition, it is often seen as having important symbolic effects.

*Encouraging consumption of beverages with lower alcohol content
or no alcohol content at all*

Sharp price differentials have been known to shift consumption from
distilled spirits to beer, with consequent reductions in total alcohol
consumption and in some alcohol-related problems. For example:

In Denmark

> during World War I, the price of . . . akvavit was raised from 0.9
> Kronor to 11 Kronor per litre; the corresponding increase for beer
> was from 0.15 to 0.24 Kronor. This drastic measure reduced the
> rate of per capita alcohol consumption from 6.7 to 1.6 litres of
> absolute alcohol within two years. The decrease was mostly due to
> the diminished consumption of akvavit . . . Denmark was thereby
> transformed from a primarily distilled spirits drinking country to a
> beer drinking country. Not only was consumption affected, but the
> rate of registered cases of delirium tremens declined from 27 to 2
> per 100 000 inhabitants, and there was a corresponding decrease
> from 12 to 2 in the death rate from [chronic alcoholism]. (Bruun *et
> al.*, 1975)

The effects on alcohol consumption and alcohol-related problems of
increasing the availability of non-alcoholic beverages have not been
systematically evaluated. However, in some countries, alcoholic
beverages are less expensive than fruit juices and soft drinks and
non-alcoholic beverages (including water) are not always easily
available.

Although the risks of some alcohol-related problems may be
greater with the consumption of one alcoholic beverage than another,
it must be remembered that consumption of low-alcohol beverages is
no protection against development of alcohol-related problems; the
more significant factor is total amount of alcohol consumed.

**Measures for which there is virtually no evidence of effectiveness,
though they seem promising**

There are a number of measures which might prevent specific
alcohol-related problems for which very little evidence of effectiveness currently exists, though the logical argument for their value is
strong and/or efforts to date have shown promise. These include
efforts: (1) to reduce alcohol-related accidents in the workplace; (2)

to prevent physical and psychological problems among children whose parents are alcoholics; and (3) to modify physical and social environments so that when drinking and drunkenness do occur certain harmful consequences will not also occur.

CONCLUSIONS

The continuation of current trends in alcohol production and consumption has far-reaching public health implications. Awareness of these implications can create the opportunity for countries to take the action necessary to halt or reverse adverse trends. Since governments have the capacity through legislation to control the supply of alcoholic beverages and thus to influence the rates of associated health and social problems, there is an urgent need for action to be taken now in those countries where *per capita* consumption rates are high or where the increase in *per capita* consumption is particularly steep.

WHO has already conducted a review of the relative effectiveness of various policy measures designed to reduce alcohol-related problems. Looking forward, there are two targets which have been agreed on for the Eighth General Programme of Work (1990–1995) for the WHO Programme on the prevention and control of alcohol and drug abuse. They are:

- Policies and programmes for the prevention and control of health problems related to alcohol and drug abuse will have been incorporated into the national mental health, health and, as far as possible, development planning in at least half of the countries in each WHO region.
- Health problems related to alcohol and drug abuse will have been reduced in at least one-quarter of the affected countries in each WHO region and the current unfavourable trends arrested in most of the other countries.

If these ambitious targets are to be achieved, it can only be through the active involvement of Member States in responding to the trends described in this report.

It is certainly not the function of international bodies like WHO to tell countries what they must and must not do. This is as true in the area of preventing alcohol abuse as it is in any other. What they can do is to assemble previous relevant experience from countries that have, one way or another, attempted to introduce national alcohol policies. They can then draw up guidelines from those examples and, through appropriate advice and support, assist those countries that request it. It is important to recognise, however, that some countries may well choose not to develop preventive policies at all and that others may choose to develop them without seeking advice from international organisations. In maintaining their ability to respond to a range of different requests from different countries, but mindful of the danger inherent in clinging to concepts that are rusting away through lack of use, international organisations can legitimately act in two ways. They can, through their advocacy role, encourage countries to develop their own national alcohol policies and programmes, and they can, in promoting appropriate technology, offer advice that will enable countries that do decide to act, to make their programmes as effective as possible.

All that, however, presumes a serious sustained commitment from the countries concerned. It requires both imagination and a great deal of hard work. The delicate act of balancing economic interests and public health interests is perhaps the central obstacle, but it is certainly not the only one. Co-operation among many different interest groups, within and outside government, will be necessary. Ministers with responsibility for education, agriculture, trade, employment and social affairs, among others, will need to be involved. The ministry of finance cannot but be deeply involved in the implications of any suggested policy changes. Equally, however, interested bodies outside government will have a part to play. Treatment agencies, self-help organisations and other voluntary bodies, religious institutions and teachers and parent organisations, will be likely to want to contribute to the process of policy development, and in some countries the list will be longer still. In addition, not only the alcoholic drinks industry but other industries, including catering, tourism, advertising and the media generally, will have essential contributions to make. The exclusion of any significant interested party is likely to prejudice the subsequent successful implementation of the preventive programme.

It would be naive to suppose, however, that all the different interest groups will have compatible points of view. Even within government, there will be conflicts between some ministries, as well as agreements between others; nor will the areas of agreement or disagreement be the same in every country. Within this complex interplay of different forces within countries, it is clear that the role of any international guidelines or advice is likely to be of importance in two distinct ways. Essential principles, such as the need to balance economic interests and public health interests, can be established; basic agendas can be drawn up for the area in which decisions have to be made; but the substances of these decisions is and will remain the prerogative of the countries themselves.

Note

This text is drawn from the following WHO publications and documents:

Walsh, B. M. and Grant, M. (1985) *Public Health Implications of Alcohol Production and Trade* (Geneva: World Health Organization) (Offset Publication No. 88).
WHO (1987) *1987 World Health Statistics Annual* (Geneva: World Health Organization).
Grant, M. (ed.) (1985) *Alcohol Policies* (Copenhagen: World Health Organization, Regional Office for Europe). (European Series, No. 18).
Farrell, S. (1985) *Review of National Policy Measures to Prevent Alcohol-related Problems* (Geneva: World Health Organization) (unpublished document WHO/MNH/PAD/85.14).

References

Aaron, P. and Musto, D. (1981) 'Temperance and Prohibition in America: A Historical Overview', in Moore, M. H. and Gerstein, D. R. (eds), *Alcohol and Public Policy: Beyond the Shadow of Prohibition*. Report of the Panel on Alternative Policies Affecting the Prevention of Alcohol Abuse and Alcholism (National Research Council, Washington, DC: National Academy Press).
Armyr, G., Elmér, A. and Herz, V. (1982) *Alcohol in the World of the 80s: Habits, Attitudes, Preventive Policies and Voluntary Efforts* (Stockholm: Sober Förlags AB).
Beaubrun, M. H. (1982) 'Comments on Smart, R. G., The Impact of Prevention Legislation: An Examination of Research Findings', in *Legislative Approaches to Prevention of Alcohol-related Problems: An inter-American Workshop, Proceedings* (Washington, DC: National Academy Press).
Bruce, D. (1980) 'Changes in Scottish Drinking Habits and Behaviour Following the Extension of Permitted Evening Opening Hours', *Health Bulletin* (Edinburgh), vol. 38(3), pp. 133–7.
Bruun, K. *et al.* (1975) *Alcohol Control Policies in Public Health Perspective* (Helsinki: Finnish Foundation for Alcohol Studies) vol. 25.
Cartwright, A. K. J. (1980) 'The Attitudes of Helping Agents Towards the Alcoholic Client: The Influence of Experience Support, Training, and Self-esteem', *British Journal of Addiction*, vol. 75(4), pp. 413–31.

Ewan, C. E. and Whaite, A. (1983) 'Evaluation of Training Programmes for Health Professionals in Substance Misuse', *Journal of Studies on Alcohol*, vol. 44(5), pp. 885–99.

Farquhar, J. W. *et al.* (1981) 'The Role of Public Information and Education in Cigarette Smoking Controls', *Canadian Journal of Public Health*, vol. 72(6), pp. 412–20.

Fisher, J. V. *et al.* (1976) 'Physicians and Alcoholics: Modifying Behaviour and Attitudes of Family-Practice Residents', *Journal of Studies on Alcohol*, vol. 37(11), pp. 1686–93.

Grant, M. (1984) 'Alcohol Education Around the World', paper presented at the National Conference on Medical Education and Research on Alcohol and Drug Abuse, 7–9 November, Washington, DC.

Horverak, O. (1983) 'The 1978 Strike at the Norwegian Wine and Spirits Monopoly', *British Journal of Addiction*, vol. 78(1), pp. 51–66.

van Iwaarden, M. J. (1983) 'Advertising, Alcohol Consumption and Policy Alternatives', in Grant, M. *et al.* (eds), *Economics and Alcohol: Consumption and Controls* (London: Croom Helm).

Kendell, R. E. *et al.* (1983) 'Effect of Economic Changes on Scottish Drinking Habits 1978–82', *British Journal of Addiction*, vol. 78(4), pp. 365–79.

Mäkelä, K. *et al.* (1981) *Alcohol, Society, and the State: Volume 1: A Comparative Study of Alcohol Control* (Toronto: Addiction Research Foundation).

Medina-Mora, M. E. (1982) 'Comments on Smart, R. G., The Impact of Prevention Legislation: An Examination of Research Findings', in *Legislative Approaches to Prevention of Alcohol-related Problems: An inter-American Workshop, Proceedings* (Washington, DC: National Academy Press).

Moore, M. H. and Gerstein, D. R. (eds) (1981) *Alcohol and Public Policy: Beyond the Shadow of Prohibition*. Report of the Panel on Alternative Policies Affecting the Prevention of Alcohol Abuse and Alcoholism, National Research Council (Washington, DC: National Academy Press).

Moser, J. (ed.) (1985) *Alcohol Policies in National Health and Development Planning* (Geneva: World Health Organization) Offset Publication No. 89.

Reed, D. S. (1981) 'Reducing the costs of drinking and driving', in Moore, M. H. and Gerstein, D.R. (eds), *Alcohol and Public Policy: Beyond the Shadow of Prohibition*. Report of the Panel on Alternative Policies Affecting the Prevention of Alcohol Abuse and Alcoholism, National Research Council (Washington, DC: National Academy Press).

Reinhold, F. (1980) 'Overview of the Situation of Drug Dependence in Swaziland', in Anumonye, A. *et al.* (eds), *African Seminar on Problems of Drug Dependence, Lagos, Nigeria, November 1980* (Lausanne: International Council on Alcohol and Addictions)pp. 26–8.

Room, R. (1984) 'Alcohol Control and Public Health', *Annual Review of Public Health*, vol. 5, pp. 293–317.

Room, R. (unpublished draft) *Reducing alcohol problems by the year 2000*, paper prepared for the World Health Organization (Geneva: November 1982).

Ross, H. L. (1981) *Deterrence of the Drinking Driver: An International Survey* (Washington, DC; US Department of Transportation, National Highway Traffic Safety Administration).

Serpell, N. (1982) *The Alcohol Industry in Zambia* (unpublished WHO document).

Smart, R. G. (1982) 'The Impact of Prevention Legislation: An Examination of Research Findings', in *Legislative Approaches to Prevention of Alcohol-related Problems: An inter-American Workshop Proceedings* (Washington, DC: National Academy Press).

US Department of Health and Human Services (1982) *The Health Consequences of Smoking: Cancer*. A report of the Surgeon General, (Washington, DC: GPO) DHHS Publication No. (PHS)82-50179.

Wagenaar, A. C. (1983) *Alcohol, Young Drivers, and Traffic Accidents: Effects of Minimum Age Laws* (Lexington, Massachusetts: DC: Health).

Whitehead, P. C. (1983) 'Is Advertising Effective? Implications for Public Health Policy', in Rush, B. and Ogborne, A. (eds), *Evaluation Research in the Canadian Addictions Field*, proceedings of the record annual meeting of the Special Interest Group on Program Evaluation of the Canadian Addiction Foundation, 8–9 September 1982, Regina, Saskatchewan, Ottawa, Health and Welfare Canada.

WHO Expert Committee on Problems Related to Alcohol Consumption (1980) *Report* (Geneva: World Health Organization) Technical Report Series, No. 650.

World Health Organization (1984) *Mental Health Care in Developing Countries: A Critical Appraisal of Research Findings*. Report of a WHO Study Group (Geneva: Technical Report Series, Nop. 698).

Zimbabwe, Ministry of Health, Department of Mental Health (1984) Alcohol-related problems: Towards a National Plan of Action (draft).

5 The Costs of Addiction and the Costs of Control

Alan Maynard

INTRODUCTION

The policy debate about addiction and addiction control policies is permeated with inadequate data and the misuse of these limited data. The purpose of this chapter is to describe the UK consumption trends for alcohol and tobacco since 1960, to examine existing measures of harm associated with the use of these two substances, to indicate how these existing measures are of little policy relevance and to illuminate the nature and costs of some economic devices in the markets for legal addictive products.

CHANGES IN USE OF LEGAL ADDICTIVE PRODUCTS

Any analysis of the consumption trends of alcohol and tobacco must begin with caveats about the interpretation of the data. For each product, consumption trends can be presented in value and volume terms and these data, while indicating the general direction of changes in use give differing estimates of their magnitude. In Table 5.1 the value of expenditures on alcohol and tobacco is set out for selected years in the period 1960–87. These data are deflated to 1980 price levels to eliminate the effects of inflation over the 27-year period. It can be seen from this table that the real value of expenditure on alcoholic drink rose by over 120 per cent, peaking in 1979. However the fortunes of the individual products in the period 1963–87 were equal: the beer market expanded by 34 per cent, the spirits market by 127 per cent and the market for wines, cider and perry increased by 354 per cent. The real (1980 prices) value of the tobacco market in terms of expenditure peaked in 1973 and has declined steadily since then. Over the period 1960–87 real expenditure on tobacco fell by 36 per cent.

Table 5.1   Value measures of consumption expenditure on alcoholic
drinks and tobacco at constant 1980 prices (£ million)

Year	Alcoholic drink	Beer	Spirits	Wine, cider and perry	Tobacco
1960	4 750	3 409	1479		5 051
1961	5 103	3 601	1640		5 126
1962	5 210	3 672	1679		4 936
1963	5 388	3 705	1 192	632	5 095
1964	5 738	3 876	1 287	712	5 026
1965	5 686	3 907	1 236	695	4 842
1966	5 911	4 032	1 282	749	4 997
1967	6 154	4 165	1 304	841	5 023
1968	6 483	4 301	1 396	933	5 003
1969	6 609	4 558	1 330	913	4 943
1970	7 073	4 718	1 559	956	4 934
1971	7 544	4 941	1 654	1 105	4 759
1972	8 122	5 098	1 883	1 258	5 017
1973	9 211	5 394	2 334	1 522	5 309
1974	9 435	5 396	2 495	1 564	5 247
1975	9 350	5 567	2 378	1 459	4 995
1976	9 448	5 623	2 325	1 554	4 821
1977	9 487	5 467	2 428	1 618	4 602
1978	9 930	5 548	2 616	1 766	4 982
1979	10 382	5 588	2 890	1 904	4 960
1980	9 954	5 320	2 720	1 914	4 822
1981	9 612	5 000	2 561	2 051	4 470
1982	9 370	4 825	2 427	2 118	4 128
1983	9 730	4 914	2 494	2 322	4 083
1984	9 983	4 943	2 525	2 515	3 944
1985	10 224	4 934	2 658	2 632	3 837
1986	10 297	4 935	2 646	2 716	3 731
1987	10 574	4 987	2 716	2 871	3 704

Source: Central Statistical Office – National Income and Expenditure
Accounts.

Similar trends in the use of tobacco over time can be seen in the
volume data for the period 1960–87. In terms of numbers (thousands
of millions), it can be seen from Table 5.2 that use peaked in 1973
(137 400 million) and declined by 14 per cent over the period. In
terms of tobacco weight (millions of kilograms), use peaked in 1973
(103.8 m. kg) and declined by 26 per cent between 1960 and 1987.

The consumption of alcohol in volume, measured in terms of litres
per capita for the population aged 15 years and over, peaked in 1979
and rose by over 63 per cent during the 1960–87 period. (Further
details and discussion of these trends can be found in Hardman and
Maynard (forthcoming 1989).)

Table 5.2   Volume measures of consumption of alcoholic drink and
cigarettes, 1960 to 1987

Year	All alcoholic drink (litres of pure alcohol)	Cigarettes (by number 000s of million)	Cigarettes (by weight millions of kilo grams)
1960	6.0	110.9	108.4
1961	6.2	113.4	110.3
1962	6.2	109.9	104.7
1963	6.3	115.2	107.9
1964	6.7	114.4	104.7
1965	6.6	112.0	100.1
1966	6.6	117.6	101.3
1967	6.7	119.1	100.4
1968	7.0	121.8	99.9
1969	7.1	124.9	98.2
1970	7.5	127.9	97.7
1971	7.9	122.4	92.6
1972	8.3	130.5	98.1
1973	9.0	137.4	103.8
1974	9.4	137.0	102.3
1975	9.3	132.6	96.4
1976	9.6	130.6	93.2
1977	9.2	125.9	89.7
1978	9.9	125.2	98.9
1979	10.2	124.3	98.6
1980	9.7	121.5	97.2
1981	9.4	110.3	89.4
1982	9.3	102.0	82.6
1983	9.4	101.6	83.0
1984	9.6	99.0	81.6
1985	9.6	97.8	81.1
1986	9.6	95.5	79.8
1987	9.8	95.0	79.4

Source: Annual Abstract of Statistics, The Brewers Society: UK Statistical
Handbook; G. Hardman and A. Maynard, 'Consumption and Taxation
Trends', in A. Maynard and P. Tether (eds), *The Addiction Market.
Consumption, Production and Policy Development* (Aldershot: Avebury,
1989).

Thus for tobacco, using either expenditure or volume information, consumption peaked in 1973 and has declined significantly since 1960 by 36 per cent by value (1980 prices), 26 per cent by weight (millions of kilograms) and 14 per cent by numbers (thousands of millions).

The alcohol market on the other hand peaked in 1979 and has grown significantly over the period by over 120 per cent in value (1980 prices), and by 63 per cent in volume (litres of pure alcohol *per capita* aged 15 years and over). The size of the markets by alcoholic product (beer, spirits, and wine and cider) has grown unequally with modest growth for beer, significant gains for spirits and large gains for wines on volume and value measures.

WHAT IS KNOWN ABOUT THE CONSEQUENCES OF ALCOHOL AND TOBACCO USE?

The bases on which estimates of the harms, in terms of money and health, associated with the use of alcohol and tobacco are poor. First let us explore what estimates can be produced from the existing ignorance about the incidence and prevalence of harms and the health and resource consequences of them.

Social cost estimates

The work on the estimates of the social costs of alcohol and tobacco use originates in estimates produced by the Economic Advisers Office (EAO) of the UK Department of Health (e.g. Holterman and Burchell, 1981). The empirical basis for these estimates has improved little during the 1980s. Elaborating where possible and updating to 1987 prices gives the total social cost estimates shown in Table 5.3.

Including the unemployment and premature deaths associated with its use, the social cost of alcohol in 1987 was nearly £2 billion. However this estimate disguises some nice methodological issues such as why are sickness absence, unemployment induced by alcohol use and premature death regarded as a 'loss' if otherwise unemployed people can replace high alcohol users in the labour force with little consequent impact on National Income? Premature death and impaired quality of life for the user and their support groups at work and in the family are difficult to identify let alone quantify in monetary terms and do not enter the estimates in Table 5.3.

Table 5.3　The costs of alcohol misuse (in 1987 prices)

		£mn
1.	The social cost to industry	
	(a) Sickness absence	779.30
	(b) Housework services	52.35
	(c) Unemployment	179.58
	(d) Premature deaths	703.65
2.	Social costs to the National Health Service	
	(a) Psychiatric hospitals, inpatient costs (alcoholic psychosis, alcoholic dependence syndrome, non-dependent use of alcohol)	21.42
	(b) Non-psychiatric hospitals, inpatient costs (alcohol psychosis, alcohol dependence syndrome, alcoholic cirrhosis and liver disease)	8.66
	(c) Other alcohol-related inpatient costs	88.41
	(d) General practice costs	2.26
3.	Society's response to alcohol-related problems	
	(a) Expenditure by national alcohol bodies	0.35
	(b) Research	0.65
4.	Social cost of material damage	
	(a) Road traffic accidents (damage)	112.02
5.	Social costs of criminal activities	
	(a) Police involvement in traffic offences (excluding road traffic accidents)	5.28
	(b) Police involvement in road traffic offences (including judiciary and insurance administration)	15.65
	(c) Drink related court cases	19.54
Total	(excluding unemployment and premature death)	1105.90
Total	(including unemployment and premature death)	1989.14

Some of the social costs associated with the use of tobacco are set out in Table 5.4. These costs, perhaps as much as £535 million, are related only to the use of NHS resources. What are the losses to

Table 5.4   The social costs of smoking to the NHS in England (£m 1987)

		Low estimate	*High estimate*
(a)	Inpatient costs: Attribution category		
	Close (85–95%) association (e.g. lung cancer)	127.11	142.2
	Associated (10–25%) heart disease	18.2	45.5
	Other associated (30–50%) diseases (e.g. peptic ulcer and cancer of unspecified sites)	62.6	104.1
	Other associated (5–15%) respiratory disease	15.1	45.5
	Total inpatient costs	257.7	440.6
(b)	General practice, and outpatient costs	54.9	94.8
(c)	Inpatient, general practice, and outpatient costs	312.6	535.4

industry? What are the losses to length and quality of life? Again, these figures do not illuminate let alone answer these issues.

The estimates of the social cost consequences associated with the use of alcohol and tobacco are based on incomplete epidemiological data (McDonnell and Maynard, 1985c). These data have improved little over the last decade and, as a consequence, it is difficult to identify let alone cost the consequences of using these substances. Indeed the data in Tables 5.3 and 5.4 are little more than crude 'best guestimates'.

Mortality and life years lost

An alternative to social costs is the quantification of mortality and life years lost. Some data for 1985 are presented in Table 5.5. Using OPCS mortality data and the methodology set out in McDonnell and Maynard (1985a), the level of alcohol-related deaths was between 5163 (low) to 7964 (high) in 1985. The guestimate of the working days lost as a result of alcohol use is 63 000 (low) to 104 000 (high), with 116 000 (low) to 183 000 (high) life years being lost.

Table 5.5   Alcohol and tobacco-related deaths and life years lost, 1985

	Low estimate	High estimate
Alcohol-related deaths	5 163	7 964
Working years lost arising from alcohol-related premature death	63 854	104 397
Life years lost arising from alcohol-related premature death	116 225	183 472
Some tobacco-related deaths[a]	35 000	
Tobacco-related life years lost	526 000	

[a]Heart disease, neoplasms, chronic bronchitis and emphysema only.

The mortality and life years lost due to tobacco use are much higher. Using a conservative basis for tobacco-related mortality (heart disease, neoplasms, chronic bronchitis and emphysema only), there were 35 000 premature deaths and 526 000 life years lost associated with the use of tobacco.

However once again it has to be emphasised that these data are poor. Small sample, longitudinal research in Sweden (Malmo) suggests that alcohol-related mortality is under-reported by a factor of between 6 and 8 (Petersson *et al.*, 1980, 1982). Some relative orders of magnitude of mortality for alcohol, tobacco and illicit drugs are set out in Table 5.6. Alcohol-related mortality estimates range from 5 163 to 40 000 with the most recent estimate being 28 000 (Anderson, 1988). Tobacco related mortality in 1981 was estimated to be 100 000.

Thus alcohol and tobacco (especially the latter) do far more harm to health, as measured in terms of mortality, than do illicit drugs, and obviously merit relatively much more attention from policy makers.

WHAT IS THE RELEVANCE OF THESE ESTIMATES FOR POLICY FORMATION?

The social cost, mortality and life year guestimates of the consequences of alcohol and tobacco use are incomplete and of poor quality. It is unclear how much of the 'hidden iceberg' of resource and health consequences such estimates reveal. They must be used

Table 5.6   Mortality associated with legal addictive substances

		Mortality estimate	Year of data	Source
Illicit drugs	(i)	127	1982	DHSS (1985)
	(ii)	235	1984	BMJ (1986)
Alcohol	(i)	5 163–7 964	1985	Maynard (1988)
	(ii)	25 000	1984	BMJ (1986)
	(iii)	4 000	1983	Royal College of Psychiatrists (1986)
	(iv)	40 000	1984	Royal College of General Practitioners (1986)
	(v)	25 000	NK	Royal College of Physicians (1987)
	(vi)	28 000		Anderson (1988)
Tobacco	(i)	100 000	1981	Royal College of Physicians (1983)

Sources: Department of Health and Social Security (1985); *Cooperation at the Community Level on Health Related Problems*, Memorandum to the House of Lords Select Committee on the European Community, HMSO, London; *British Medical Journal*, 1986, 'Government hypocrisy on drugs', 292, 712–73, editorial, 16 March; Maynard, A. (1988), 'The mortality consequences of alcohol use', unpublished working paper, Addiction Research Centre, York; Royal College of Psychiatrists (1986) *Alcohol: Our Favourite Drug* (London: Tavistock,); Royal College of General Practitioners (1986), *Alcohol: a 'Balanced' View,* Report from General Practice 24, Royal College of General Practitioners, London; Royal College of Physicians (1987), *A Great and Growing Evil: the medical consequences of alcohol abuse* (London: Tavistock); Anderson, P. (1988) 'Excess mortality associated with alcohol consumption', *British Medical Journal*, 297, 824–6; Royal College of Physicians (1983) *Health or Smoking? A follow-up report* (London: Pitman).

with great caution as estimates of the total (resource and health) consequences, and their relevance in contributing to the process of informed policy making is limited. If the objective of the policy process in all markets, including those for legal addictive substances, is to achieve efficiency (i.e. a balance of costs and benefits – see Maynard and Powell, 1985), then two simple sets of rules have to be fulfilled:

- rules to decide whether to adopt a policy;
  if total costs (TC) exceeds total benefit (TB), cease the activity;
  if TC is less than TB, continue with the activity.
- rules to decide what level of activity to adopt.

If total benefits are greater than total costs, the activity or policy should be expanded until costs and benefits are equal at the margin (and TB = TC). The margin is one more or one less of the activity and the effects of such fluctuations are the marginal costs and marginal benefits.

The limited cost data presented in Table 5.3 and 5.6 are inadequate for the purposes of determining whether total costs exceed total benefits (TC > TB) and whether costs and benefits are equal at the margin (MC = MB). These data can be criticised in three ways:

- the cost and health estimates are poor because of the inadequate epidemiological and economic bases from which they are derived;
- the benefits of tobacco and alcohol use are ignored;
- the policy-relevant data are about the margin, not the average or the total.

The problems of the data are analysed elsewhere (McDonnell and Maynard, 1985b, 1985c) and as a consequence only the latter two items will be elaborated in this section.

The benefits of tobacco and alcohol consumption

The conventional argument in economic theory is that the price paid for a good or service is a minimum monetary measure of their benefit to the consumer. Thus, reverting to the data in Table 5.1, the value of the benefits to the consumer derived from the alcoholic drinks market in 1987 exceed £10.5 billion and the benefits of the tobacco market exceeded £3.7 billion (both in 1980 prices).

However these are minimum estimates due to the existence of consumer surplus. The price paid for a pint of beer may be less than its value to the drinker and the difference between the price and this value is the consumer surplus. To estimate this benefit it is necessary to be able to estimate the area under the demand curve and translate it into monetary values. This approach is used in Phelps (1988).

The approach to the estimation of the benefits derived by consumers from the use of alcohol and tobacco is based on the assumption of consumer rationality. However because of the addictive nature of these products, the validity of the rationality assumption can be disputed. Some of these complex issues are explored in the work of others involved in the work of the Hull–York Addiction Research Centre (e.g. see Posnett and Jones, 1988).

However even if such disputes are resolved, the use of these substances clearly gives benefits to consumers. To ignore these benefits is to approach the problem of controlling addictive substances with an eye to only half of the relevant cost–benefit equation. To reduce costs will reduce benefits: there is a trade-off between health and consumer satisfaction which cannot be ignored.

Formulating efficient policies: the importance of the margin

The importance of the margin in informing choices about the allocation of scarce resources amongst competing programmes of treatment is best demonstrated with a simple example. What is the efficient level of screening for high alcohol use in hospitals? Let us overcome the problem of measuring benefits by assuming that the 'benefit' of the screening programme is the identification of high alcohol users. Some illustrative data are presented in Table 5.7 and derived from a medical trial reported by Neuhauser and Lewicki (1976).

The policy choice that has to be made is how many screenings should be carried out to identify all the high alcohol users coming into the hospital system. The number of screens (1–6) is in column 1 and each screening process will generate false positives and false negatives. The screening of 10 000 people reveals 659 heavy drinkers. Carrying out another 10 000 screens of the same population increases the number of heavy drinkers found from 659 to 714, an addition of 55. After 6 screens 719 heavy drinkers have been identified. The total cost, as screening activity is expanded from 1 to 6, increases from £77 511 to £176 331. The final column shows the average cost per heavy drinker identified by these screens (*not* the average cost per screening) and this rises from £117 to £245.

Table 5.7   The importance of the margin: an illustrative case
study; yield and cost data

Number of screens	Number of heavy drinkers found	Total cost of programme	Average cost per drinker identified
1	659.46	77 511	117.57
2	714.42	107 690	150.737
3	719.00	130 199	181.083
4	719.38	148 116	205.898
5	719.4172	163 141	226.768
6	719.42	176 331	245.102

Source: Using numerical data derived from D. Neuhauser and
A. M. Lewicki, 'National Health Insurance and the Sixth
Stool Guaiac', *Policy Analysis*, vol. 24 (1976),Table 2. All
data per 10 000 screened.

What level of screening should be adopted? Some might argue that
the (average) cost rises little and 6 screens might be appropriate.
However simple rearrangement of these data to answer the question
what is the benefit (in terms of heavy drinkers identified) and what is
the cost arising from changed levels of screening gives different policy
implications. One screen generates 659 heavy drinkers at £77 511,
i.e. a marginal (equal to average) cost of £117. However Table 5.8
shows that as the level of screening activity increases it yields fewer
and fewer additional cases whilst the increase in total costs is not
inconsiderable. The consequence is that the marginal cost per case
found for successive screenings rises rapidly to marginal cost of £4.7
million per new case of heavy drinking identified by the sixth
screening.

Unfortunately the measure of benefit used here (additional cases
identified) is very limited. These data do not inform policy makers
about the benefit of diagnosis and treatment. As Phelps (1988) has
argued, what is needed when identifying an efficient policy is the
determination of the benefits gained (the value of lives saved) and the
costs imposed (the loss of benefits from consumption) on users by
changes in policy.

Table 5.8   The importance of the margin: an illustrative
case study; the margins

Number of screens	Increase in total costs	Increase in drinkers	Marginal cost per drinker found
1	77 511	659.5	117.523
2	30 179	54.956	549.148
3	22 509	4.5796	4 915.058
4	17 917	0.38159	46 953.536
5	15 025	0.0318	472 484.27
6	13 190	0.0028	4 710 714.200

Source: Using numerical data derived from D. Neuhauser and A. M. Lewicki, 'National Health Insurance and the Sixth Stool Guaiac', *Policy Analysis*, vol. 24 (1976), Table 2. All data per 10 000 screened.

Summary

All the cost and benefit data pertaining to alternative policies in the markets for alcohol and tobacco are very limited. However, despite these all too familiar limitations they are often used inappropriately. What is the relevance for policy formation of the guestimate that alcohol generates social costs of £2 billion? Such a result tells policy makers nothing about the costs and benefits at the margin of alternative policies aimed at reducing this problem. Without the use of the marginal approach in estimating the costs and benefits of alcohol and tobacco use, such total cost or damage data are of no use other than to illuminate how little is known about the epidemiology and costs of these product markets.

TOWARDS A MORE COMPREHENSIVE ANALYSIS OF POLICY CHOICES

The economist can contribute to the elucidation of policy choices in alcohol and tobacco in a variety of ways. One is to collaborate with the caring professions to evaluate the impact of interventions to reduce consumption. Another contribution is to determine the impacts of fiscal policy on substance use. All too often it can be seen that previous work has ignored the economic component of these policies and often dwelt on costs or benefits alone and ignored the importance of the margin.

Health care treatments

The use of clinical trials to evaluate the effects of treatment interventions for users of alcohol and tobacco is potentially very rewarding. However, there are a lot of compounding factors which may bias results. There appears to be a self cure rate amongst high users which may be as high as 20–25 per cent. Individual characteristics appear to be the best predictors of success, with those in stable jobs and marriages and in higher socio-economic classes achieving greater success in cutting consumption. Thus spurious 'successes' can be achieved if trials are not designed carefully with good controls.

The range of treatment options to be evaluated in such trials is wide. Some treatments might involve inpatient hospital episodes with varying lengths of stay. Outpatient treatments, with a wide range of activities inherent in individual treatment modes, are also used. Group therapy, for instance Alcoholics Anonymous, is available in many varieties as is the use of pharmaceuticals. There are 'half-way houses', other specialist units and even imprisonment which the judiciary appears to believe may influence the future use of alcohol of offenders.

Unfortunately, although there are hundreds of studies of such options in the literature, their design is often poor. Goodwin (1981) argues that this evaluative work has failed to demonstrate that one treatment is superior to another or superior to no treatment at all. It is apparent that few studies use controls who receive no treatment and often the population in the trials are self-selected volunteers. All too often in this literature, like the rest of the medical literature, there is no randomisation and few attempts to include the costs of competing treatment regimes.

Thus, as Russell (1987) argues, there is much ignorance about the costs and benefits of alcohol treatment policies. This does not prevent considerable investment in high cost treatments and ambitious programmes. Indeed there is great effort being made to increase service provision in the NHS at present. These efforts are not informed by good data about the costs and benefits of alternative treatments.

Hodgson is optimistic in Chapter 6 about the effectiveness of low cost responses. These require further validation, but are to be preferred to more expensive options whose effectiveness is unproven.

Using fiscal policy

For the majority of products (beer, spirits, wine and tobacco) both (tax) price and income (purchasing power) have significant influences on consumption. Other policies also have effects: advertising, health education and the number of outlets. The estimates of the magnitude of these effects are discussed in Chapter 7 by Christine Godfrey. However, as she points out, there is a range of estimates of the influence of these variables on use of alcohol and tobacco. This range is a product of researchers estimating different demand models with different data sets over the years.

The impact of control policies

As an example of forecasting the impact of a control policy let us analyse the impact of a tax-price hike on the tobacco markets. Godfrey has estimated a (tax) price elasticity for tobacco of −0.56 using a general model with rigorous statistical data and using data for the period 1956–84. Using this estimate it is possible to forecast the impact of a 10 per cent increase in the tax price of tobacco assuming a 3 per cent real annual increase in income and a continued trend in reduced use due to health education. Table 5.9 shows that consumption would fall by 3.65 per cent. This would increase the tax revenue to HM Treasury by 6.2 per cent and reduce employment by 3700 people between now and 1990 in the tobacco industry (Godfrey and Maynard, 1988, p.342).

Table 5.9   The costs of control: tobacco
(10 per cent real price rise)

Reduced consumption of	3.65%
Increased tax revenue of	6.2%
Reduced employment by 1990 of	3700

Source: C. Godfrey and A. Maynard, 'Economic Aspects of Tobacco Use and Taxation Policy', *British Medical Journal*, vol. 297 (1988).

This analysis is incomplete. There will be job losses, related to reduced consumption, arising in the distribution and sales of tobacco. However consumers will switch their consumption to other goods and services when they use less tobacco and this switch will create new (substitute) jobs, at home and abroad. Consequently the net (losses and gains) employment outcome is unclear, especially as part of it will be determined by whether the Government spends its increased tobacco tax revenues to create jobs or to reduce public borrowing.

The politics of control policies: an economic perspective

The politics of any control policy are complex, imposing costs and benefits on both the suppliers of regulations (politicians and civil servants) and demanders of regulation (the industry). These parties to the regulatory process trade to mutual advantage. For example, government regulation of the tobacco industry might be demanded by the producers if it keeps out foreign import competition, and politicians will supply such regulations in support for votes particularly in marginal constituencies, to maintain themselves in power.

Thus policy selection by politicians and civil servants will be a result of efficient decisions in the political market place which take into account the costs and benefits of alternative policies for politicians, a sub-set of society. Such decisions will be influenced by information about the costs and benefits of alternative policies for society but are likely to be at variance to efficient policy making which ignores the political market place.

Another way in which the pursuit of efficiency in the market for legal addictive substances is circumscribed is by the constraints imposed by international policy making. In Chapter 8, Melanie Powell explores the influence of EEC policy making on the alcohol and tobacco markets. The lesson to be learnt is that even if nationally efficient policies could be identified, they may be over-ridden by international treaties (e.g. because of 1992 or the Lomé Treaty).

For these and other reasons efficient policies which balance, at the margin, industrial wealth losses against health gains may not be adopted. The policy makers, particularly politicians, have goals other than efficient wealth-health trade-offs and to ignore the plurality of policy goals is to ignore the complexities involved in changing the use of alcohol and tobacco.

CONCLUSIONS

Much of the debate about the formulation of efficient alcohol and tobacco policies is ill defined and naive. The use of these legal addictive substances imposes resource costs on society and creates ill health for the UK population. However, the magnitude of these costs and the reduction in the length and quality of life of citizens who are users and third parties (e.g. affect by tobacco use as passive smokers) is poorly measured. The available measures indicate the aggregate costs and losses associated with the use of alcohol and tobacco. But these estimates ignore the benefits of using these products and available knowledge about the costs and benefits at the *margin* of alternative control devices is poor.

What is required is the formulation of policy option appraisals in the form of what additional benefits (economic and/or health) can be produced at what additional cost by small changes in policies, be they tax hikes or health education, or additional screening or treatment programmes. Alternatively it is necessary to investigate questions such as what tax-price hikes (or reductions) would equalise costs (e.g. the value of lives lost in road traffic accidents which are alcohol related) and benefits (in terms of consumer surplus) at the margin (Phelps, 1988).

At present the economic analysis of alcohol and tobacco price policies is limited and much of the policy debate, which all too often ignores this analysis, is ill-informed. It is essential to include benefits with costs in the evaluation of competing public policies and to concentrate on the margin in formulating policy.

References

Anderson, P. (1988) 'Excess Mortality Associated with Alcohol Consumption', *British Medical Journal*, vol. 297, pp. 824–6 (1 October).

Godfrey, C. and Maynard, A. (1988) 'Economic Aspects of Tobacco Use and Taxation Policy', *British Medical Journal*, vol. 297, pp. 339–43.

Goodwin, D. W. (1981) *Alcoholism: the Facts* (New York: Oxford University Press).

Hardman, G. and Maynard, A. (1989) 'Consumption and Taxation Trends', in A. Maynard, and P. Tether (eds), *The Addiction Market: Consumption, Production and Policy Development* (Aldershot: Avebury).

Holterman, S. and Burchell, A. (1981) *The Costs of Alcohol Misuse*, Government Economic Service Working Paper No. 37, Department of Health and Social Security, London.

Maynard, A. and Powell, M. (1985) 'Addiction Control Policies or there is no such Thing as a Free Lunch', *British Journal of Addiction*, vol. 80, pp. 265–7.

McDonnell, R. and Maynard, A. (1985a) 'Estimation of Life Years Lost from Alcohol Related Premature Death', *Alcohol and Alcoholism*, vol. 20, pp. 435–43.

McDonnell, R. and Maynard, A. (1985b) 'The Cost of Alcohol Misuse', *British Journal of Addiction*, vol. 80, pp. 27–35.

McDonnell, R. and Maynard, A. (1985c) 'Counting the Cost of Alcohol: Gaps in Epidemiological Knowledge', *Community Medicine*, vol. 7, pp. 4–17.

Neuhauser, D. and Lewicki, A. M. (1976) 'National Health Insurance and the Sixth Stool Guaiac', *Policy Analysis*, vol. 24, pp. 175–96.

Petersson, B., Kristenson, H., Sternby, N. H., Trell, E., Fox, G. and Hood, B. (1980) 'Alcohol Consumption and Premature Death in Middle Aged Men', *British Medical Journal*, vol. 280, pp. 1403–6.

Petersson, B., Kristenson, H., Krantz, P., Trell, E., Sternby, N. M. (1982) 'Alcohol Related Death: a Major Contributor to Mortality in Urban Middle Aged Men', *Lancet*, vol. 8307, pp. 1088–90.

Phelps, C. (1988) 'Death and Taxes', *Journal of Health Economics*, vol. 7, pp. 1–24.

Posnett, J. and Jones, A. (1988) 'Review of the Welfare Effects of Cigarette Taxes', *Applied Economics*, vol. 20(9), pp. 1223–32.

Russell, L. B. (1987) *Evaluating Preventive Care*, (Washington DC: Brookings Institution).

6 Low Cost Responses

Ray J. Hodgson

Behavioural change involves changes in two main types of expectations. The first, often referred to as *outcome expectancies*, relates to reasons why change should be encouraged. The second, usually called *efficacy expectations*, is to do with the level of confidence that change can be achieved. Whether we are deciding to replace a roof tile, enroll for tuba lessons or curb an addiction, we are influenced by both the expected consequences of the action and by an appraisal of our ability to carry it out. This chapter is concerned solely with the excessive use of alcohol and with low-cost methods of changing expectations.

One simple way of structuring an account of the available research literature is to consider three types of alcohol user. A number of excessive users will have encountered problems of such severity that they have already requested help. Another group will be experiencing some early problems. They might be contemplating reducing consumption but will not yet have made any commitment to change. Yet a third group will be regular heavy drinkers who are consuming alcohol in a hazardous way, but with no current problems relating to alcohol and no intention to change.

I will not be focusing upon total population interventions such as mass media campaigns or changes in fiscal policy since these approaches are covered in other chapters. My concern will be with relatively low-cost interventions which can be applied to each of the three worlds of alcohol use and for which there is some evidence of effectiveness.

LOW COST INTERVENTIONS FOR DRINKERS WHO ARE SEEKING HELP

One very *high-cost* approach to the treatment of alcohol dependence has been developed during the last thirty years even though there is no good evidence that the approach is at all effective. Throughout the world, hospital-based alcholism treatment units provide a relatively

101

costly service which involves weeks or months of in-patient treatment designed to detoxify and rehabilitate people with alcohol-related problems, usually the more severely dependent. It was not until 1977 that a good controlled trial was published which tested this traditional, treatment approach and reached some very salutary conclusions (Edwards *et al.*, 1977). Griffith Edwards, Jim Orford and their colleagues randomly assigned 100 married, male patients who were referred to the Maudsley Hospital Alcohol Service into two treatment groups. The relatively high cost treatment involved admission to hospital when appropriate as well as regular intensive treatment from a multidisciplinary team. Patients in this group received the 'best' treatments that were available at the time of the study. The relatively low-cost approach consisted of one 4-hour session of assessment and advice with monthly follow-up interviews carried out by a social worker. At both the one- and two- year follow-up interviews there were no significant differences between the two groups.

Orford and Edwards (1977) suggest that the most crucial events in the process of change are those which are involved in making a commitment to changed based upon outcome and efficacy expectancies. The act of requesting help, along with advice and the expectation of follow-up support, appears to be sufficient to influence a majority of patients. High-cost in-patient care does not appear to enhance the effectiveness of the relatively low-cost interventions, at least for the male, married alcoholics in this investigation.

The study described above was carried out in a psychiatric hospital. A high proportion of referrals were severely dependent drinkers and the advice given emphasised a total abstinence goal. In a rather different setting Miller and his colleagues looked at low-cost alternatives for those drinkers requesting help, for whom a controlled drinking goal was more appropriate (Miller *et al.*, 1980; 1981). This group of investigators focused mainly upon a relatively low-cost approach usually referred to as *behavioural self-control training*. Such an educational or counselling approach typically requires about ten sessions and includes:

- specific behavioural goal setting,
- self-monitoring,
- external cue training in blood-alcohol concentration discrimination,
- training in self-control of consumption rate,

- functional analysis of drinking behaviour,
- self-reinforcement training, and
- training in alternative behavioural competencies to substitute for previous functions of drinking.

Although ten sessions of therapist time constitutes a low-cost intervention when compared to a few weeks of in-patient treatment, Miller and his colleagues still wanted to check that all of these sessions are needed. In order to look at even lower cost alternatives they carried out one further piece of research which is very relevant to a discussion of low-cost interventions (Miller and Taylor, 1980). This study demonstrated that a self-help manual which teaches a self-control approach turns out to be as effective as ten sessions of training carried out by an experienced therapist. Furthermore, these findings have been consistent across populations varying widely in socio-economic and educational status. A more recent UK study has also confirmed the usefulness of a self-help manual (Heather *et al.*, 1986).

The results of these studies on relatively low-cost interventions directed towards both total abstinence and controlled drinking should change the way in which we view a comprehensive treatment service. Instead of using scarce resources to proliferate hospital treatment units, the first priority must be to ensure that each community has a widespread network of low-cost interventions. These could be based within a primary care setting, a community alcohol team, a community mental health centre or a District General Hospital out-patient department. Pamphlets and manuals should be easily available from health centres, social services, pharmacists and other centres involved in providing help. The main objective of an alcohol service should be to ensure that it is relatively easy to get some advice and support directed towards changing outcome and efficacy expectancies. Higher-cost alternatives would then be developed only for clients who require more intensive help and only when there is good evidence that such approaches are likely to be effective. For example, there is some evidence that group sessions which emphasise the repeated practice of coping skills can effectively prevent relapse (Chaney *et al.*, 1978). There is also evidence that more intensive help to develop social skills and social relationships can have beneficial effects (Azrin, 1976). In spite of these promising results it is clear that the treatment of alcohol dependence must involve a large number of busy people providing brief interventions rather than just a few specialists providing very intensive treatments. General practitioners, social workers, nurses and personnel officers, could all develop a low-cost but effective service.

INFLUENCING THE EARLY PROBLEM DRINKER

Responding to drinking problems involves more than the provision of a comprehensive service for those drinkers who request help. In addition, broad health promotion strategies should focus upon the diffusion of attitudes and beliefs, mass media communications, teaching self-help skills, ensuring a supply of alternative drinks so that healthier choices are made easier, influencing opinion leaders and policy makers as well as identifying and advising people with an early drinking problem. In this section only the latter strategy will be considered.

There is good evidence that low-cost early advice can prevent future problems and, furthermore, that such an early intervention programme can pay for itself. One important investigation carried out in Malmo by Kristenson *et al.* (1983) studied a group of middle-aged male heavy drinkers (age 46–49) who had been identified as a result of a general health screening project. The 585 men having a raised Gamma-GT on two occasions were randomly assigned to an intervention and a control group. The control group were simply informed by letter that the test indicated a liver problem and that they should reduce their consumption of alcohol. They were invited for further tests after two years. The intervention group were given a physical examination and a detailed assessment of alcohol consumption and alcohol-related problems. They were then offered an appointment with a doctor every three months as well as monthly appointments with a nurse for repeated assessments of Gamma-GT. The emphasis of the brief monthly intervention was upon simple advice and regular knowledge of results through Gamma-GT feedback. Progress was evaluated at two and four years after the original screening and the intervention was observed to lead to a very significant reduction in days sick and days in hospital.

This study clearly demonstrates that a relatively low-cost intervention, which focuses upon a biochemical marker of liver dysfunction, can have a very significant beneficial effect. The results indicate that a team set up by a Health Authority to carry out this type of intervention would quickly pay for itself by reducing hospital admissions.

A study carried out by Chick and his colleagues in a rather different setting has reached very similar conclusions (Chick *et al.*, 1985). This study involved men who were admitted for a medical condition to the Edinburgh Royal Infirmary. As a result of a ten-minute interview carried out by a nurse, heavy drinkers were identified on the basis of their alcohol consumption and dependence, current and past medical problems, as well as alcohol-related social problems. Of the 731 patients who were screened, 156 (or 21 per cent) were identified as heavy drinkers and randomly assigned to an intervention and a control condition. Patients assigned to the control group were given only the routine medical care for their particular condition. Those in the intervention group received between 30 and 60 minutes counselling from a nurse, as well as a booklet containing advice about techniques for reducing alcohol consumption. The results of this study are very encouraging. At one-year follow-up the intervention group were drinking less than the control group, had lower GGTs and obtained better scores on a global rating of improvement.

Putting together the results of the Malmo and the Edinburgh studies provides relatively strong evidence to support the view that early identification and intervention is a cost-effective way of preventing alcohol-related problems. One of the difficulties encountered in this approach to secondary prevention is to give the intervention at the right time. It is highly likely that admission to a medical ward, or the identification of a high GGT, concentrates the mind on health issues to such an extent that advice about behavioural change is likely to be more acceptable. As a result of our own work in Cardiff, carried out in both a district general hospital (DGH) and a general practice, we have concluded that the DGH is an ideal setting for early interventions. On a hospital ward patients ruminate about their health and have plenty of time to listen to advice. Furthermore, our change agents believe that great job satisfaction would be derived from being a member of a prevention or health promotion team covering alcohol, smoking, drug use, nutrition, exercise and stress. Such a team, composed of a nurse, a health education officer and a psychologist, could help to transform the way in which a DGH provides a comprehensive health promotion service. The research described above strongly suggests that such a health promotion team would pay for itself.

INFLUENCING THE HAZARDOUS DRINKER

Screening procedures designed to identify early drinking problems will not reach the large number of people within most societies who are drinking in a hazardous way but are not yet experiencing problems. For example, a recent study of life styles in Wales (Pulse of Wales, 1986) found that 41 per cent of the male population were consuming more than the recommended safe limit of 21 standard units per week. Current rough estimates of alcohol dependence and problem drinking suggests that, in a crowd of 50 000 men attending a Welsh rugby match, approximately 500 will be receiving help for a drinking problem and perhaps 3000 will be early problem drinkers.

In comparison, up to 18 000 men will be drinking in a hazardous way. Even though they are probably drinking less than the problem drinkers, it is likely that the harm that the hazardous drinkers are causing to themselves and others will be extensive simply because there are many of them.

Screening procedures would not be appropriate nor would they be cost-effective for this very large group of drinkers. Other approaches are required and there is now a need for some large-scale community studies which focus upon alcohol-related problems along the lines of those designed to prevent coronary heart disease, such as the North Karelia Project. A comprehensive health promotion approach involves many strands but one major component is to encourage a large number of people and groups to change their attitudes, policies and actions in order to make healthy choices easier and more probable (see Tether and Robinson, 1986; Robinson *et al.*, 1989). As examples, references will be made to two investigations which strongly suggest that excessive drinking is a behaviour which can be influenced in this way.

The first is based upon the hypothesis that the police can have a powerful preventive influence on drink-related problems simply by reminding both the publican and the drinker that excessive drinking can be illegal. Jeffs and Saunders (1983) were able to evaluate the effectiveness of a community policy strategy which was implemented in an English seaside resort during the summer of 1978 and then withdrawn the following year. Public houses in the harbourside area of the town were visited by two policemen and the first step was to remind licensees of their responsibilities under the licensing legislation. The licensees and the police agreed to co-operate fully in an attempt to ensure that the law was observed, particularly as it relates to under-age drinking and serving alcohol to those who are already intoxicated. During the summer months the selected premises were then visited regularly. Two or three uniformed officers amicably, but very conspicuously, checked for under-age drinking or the presence of persons who were the worse for drink. The checking was very thorough and was designed to bring home to both staff and patrons the seriousness of their intention to enforce the licensing laws.

In order to test the effectiveness of this preventive exercise the rates of recorded crime and public order offences for the summer of 1978 were compared with those for the year before as well as the year after. Such an analysis did indeed suggest that crime in 1978 was 20 per cent less than would be expected from an extrapolation of the figures for 1977 and 1979. The implication that this change resulted from the alteration in police practice is supported by two additional pieces of evidence. First, this result was not apparent in a control town within the same tourist region. Second, the reduction in 1978 was greater for alcohol-related crimes than for those, such as burglary and theft, which are not strongly related to alcohol consumption.

It would appear that a comparatively minor change in police practice, albeit a major change in policy, produced results which would be quite dramatic if they could be replicated throughout the world. There were 2000 fewer arrests in the experimental year than would be expected. This is not a trivial outcome. The study does suggest that a modern police force can do a great deal to prevent alcohol-related crime by altering the outcome and efficacy expectancies of publicans.

The second study also focuses upon ways of influencing alcohol consumption in the setting of a public bar (Geller *et al.*, 1987). This American investigation looked at the effectiveness of an intervention, usually called server training, designed to help servers to identify customers who are about to drink excessively. The training then covers a variety of tactics for dealing with such consumers; for example, offering food or alternative drinks, or discussing the catastrophic consequences that can result from drinking and driving. Seventeen servers of alcohol and 32 research assistants participated in the study, the latter visiting the server's place of work and posing as customers in order to provide double blind, before and after assessments. The pseudocustomers attempted to consume one drink every twenty minutes but they could be influenced by the server intervention strategies. All interactions between the servers and the pseudo-customers were recorded and independently analysed by other assistants. The results of the study were quite clear. Trained servers intervened more regularly and appropriately compared to the same servers prior to training, as well as a control group of untrained servers. The blood alcohol concentration of pseudocustomers was also assessed as they left the bar. Prior to the training 37.5 per cent of the pseudocustomers left the bars legally drunk. In contrast no pseudocustomers served by a trained server reached the legal limit of intoxication.

These studies of community policing and server training, when considered together, do strongly suggest that alcohol consumption can be influenced at the point of sale and that health promotion and crime prevention resources should be channelled into similar projects.

In summary, there is enough evidence to support the view that low-cost interventions are appropriate when providing help for those who request it and also when attempting to identify and advise the early problem drinker. Furthermore, it would appear that excessive drinking can be prevented in pubs and bars. Interventions by the police, publicans and servers might be expected to reach the very large numbers of hazardous drinkers who are not reached by screening strategies directed at the early problem drinker.

Low-cost strategies will only have a substantial effect on the drinking habits of a community if large numbers of individuals or groups accept the appropriateness of these approaches and have the skill to implement them. What is now needed are research studies or demonstration projects which focus upon the process of negotiating changes in the attitudes, policies and actions of a wide range of groups. There are good reasons why social workers would feel more effective if they could spot and help the early problem drinker. Similarly, the police constable would gain a great deal of credit if the crime rate on his patch could be reduced. What about publicans, servers, personnel officers, general practitioners, licensing magistrates, the Health and Safety Executive, Health Service Managers and many others. What will they gain from the implementation of low-cost responses? If they have a good reason to be interested in changing behaviour are they confident in their ability to implement changes? Again, the focus is upon outcome and efficacy expectancies. There is a need to research these expectancies, not only for the drinker but also for those groups who are in a position to implement low-cost strategies.

References

Azrin, N. H. (1976) 'Improvements in the Community Reinforcement Approach to Alcoholism', *Behaviour Research and Therapy*, vol. 13, pp. 339–48.

Chaney, E. F., O'Leary, M. R. and Marlatt, G. A. (1978). 'Skill Training with Alcoholics', *Journal of Consulting and Clinical Psychology*, vol. 46, pp. 1092–104.

Chick, J., Lloyd, F. and Crombie, E. (1985) 'Counselling Problem Drinkers in Medical Wards', *British Medical Journal*, vol. 290, pp. 965–7.

Edwards, G., Orford, J., Egert, S., Guthrie, S., Hawker, A., Hensman, C., Mitcheson, M., Oppenheimer, E., and Taylor, C. (1977) 'Alcoholism: a Controlled Trial of "Treatment" and "Advice" ', *Journal of Studies on Alcohol*, vol. 38, pp. 1004–031.

Geller, E. S., Russ, N. W. and Delphos, W. A. (1987) 'Does Server Intervention Training make a Difference? An Empirical Field Evaluation', *Alcohol Health and Research World*, vol. 2(4), pp. 64–9.

Heather, N., Whitton, B. and Robertson, I. (1986) 'Evaluation of a Self-help Manual for Media Recruited Problem Drinkers: Six-month Follow-up Results', *British Journal of Clinical Psychology*, vol. 25, pp. 19–34.

Jeffs, B. and Saunders, W. (1983) 'Minimizing Alcohol-related Offences by Enforcement of the Existing Licensing Legislation', *British Journal of Addiction*, vol. 78, pp. 67–77.

Kristenson, H., Ohlin, H., Hulten-Nosslin, M., Trell, E. and Hood, B. (1983) 'Identification and Intervention of Heavy Drinkers in Middle-aged Men: Results and Follow-up of 24–60 Months of Long-term Study with Randomized Controls', *Journal of Alcoholism, Clinical and Experimental Research*, pp. 203–9.

Miller, W. R. and Taylor, C. A. (1980) 'Relative Effectiveness of Bioliotherapy, Individual and Group Self-Control Training in the Treatment of Problem Drinkers', *Addictive Behaviours*, vol. 5, pp. 13–24.

Miller, W. R., Taylor, C. A. and West, J. C. (1980) 'Focused versus Broad-spectrum Behavior Therapy for Problem Drinkers', *Journal of Consulting and Clinical Psychology*, pp. 690–601.

Miller, W. R., Pechacek, R. F. and Hamburg, S. (1981) 'Group Behavior Therapy for Problem Drinkers', *International Journal of the Addictions*, vol. 16, pp. 827–37.

Orford, J. and Edwards, G. (1977) *Alcoholism: a Comparison of Treatment and Advice*. Maudsley Monograph No. 26 (London: Oxford University Press).

Pulse of Wales (1986) *Heartbreak Wales Report No. 4*. Cardiff.

Robinson, D., Tether, P. and Teller, J. (eds) (1989) *Local Action on Alcohol Problems* (London: Routledge).

Tether, P. and Robinson, D. (1986) *Preventing Alcohol Problems: A Guide to Local Action* (London: Tavistock).

7 Price Regulation

Christine Godfrey

INTRODUCTION

Many prevention policies are available to control legal addictions. These policies range from broad instruments which attempt to control consumption to more specific measures, designed to control some of the problems arising from consuming these commodities, e.g. drink driving legislation. The purpose of this chapter is to explore how price can be used to control legal addictions and to outline some of the barriers to the implementation of price control policies that exist in the UK. The discussion is illustrated by reference to alcohol and tobacco consumption and the harm they create.

The chapter has four main sections. The first section considers the effectiveness of price as a means of controlling alcohol and tobacco consumption. In the second section, current policy towards price regulation through tax changes is examined, and some factors which help determine these tax changes and the conflicts between the health and other objectives of governments are considered. Some alternative health-based tax policies are then outlined and their advantages and disadvantages discussed in the third section. In the final section, the strengths and weaknesses of the impediments to health-based policies are discussed and some concluding comments are made.

THE EFFECTIVENESS OF PRICE REGULATION

One of the major obstacles to the implementation of a policy of price increases (or any other prevention measure) is uncertainty about the policy's effectiveness. For both alcohol and tobacco, there has been some debate on whether price influences consumption and by how much. Price is clearly not the only factor that determines consumption. Other factors include income, advertising, health information and availability. Movements over time of these variables may not be the same as those of prices. Thus, in order to measure the effect of price on consumption accurately, it is necessary to use multivariate techniques (rather than simple correlations) to take account of the influence of these other factors. For example, suppose that consumption of tobacco would fall if its price increased, other things being constant, and would increase if consumers' incomes increased, other things being constant. Simultaneous increases in both price and incomes could lead to a higher, lower or constant level of consumption depending upon the relative magnitudes of the offsetting effects.

A number of studies have attempted to investigate the factors which influence tobacco and alcohol consumption. One means of comparing results from these studies is to calculate elasticities. An elasticity is a unit-free measure of responsiveness. A price elasticity, for example, will give the percentage change in consumption resulting from a 1 per cent change in prices, all other factors being held constant. Price elasticities for tobacco obtained in a number of different studies are given in Table 7.1.

As can be seen from Table 7.1, different studies have given different estimates of the effects of price and other variables on tobacco consumption. These variations seem to arise from the ways

Table 7.1   Tobacco price elasticity estimates

Study	*Elasticities*
Russell (1973)	−0.5 to −0.7
Atkinson and Skegg	0.0 (men)
(1973)	−0.45 (women)
Sumner (1971)	−0.8
Peto (1974)	−0.4 to −0.6 (men)
McGuinness and	
Cowling (1975)	−0.1
Witt and Pass (1981)	−0.3
Metra (1979)	−0.3 to −0.5
Radfar (1985)	−0.2 to −0.4
Treasury	−0.5
Godfrey and Maynard	
(1988)	−0.6

Source: C. Godfrey and A. Maynard, 'Economic Aspects of Tobacco Use and Taxation Policy', *British Medical Journal*, vol. 297 (1988), pp. 339–43.

in which models are specified and the type of data used. Few studies have used data covering the period after 1975. However, since 1975 there have been large decreases in consumption, and large variations in tobacco prices and in disposable income. In our own empirical work, data from 1956 to 1984 were used and a general model was adopted which included several earlier models as special cases (Godfrey and Maynard, 1988). Statistical tests were adopted to find the simplest model consistent with the data. A price elasticity of − 0.56 was obtained from one model which passed several statistical tests and was designed to explain variations in the weight of tobacco in cigarettes consumed per adult. This estimate is larger than many previous estimates, but close to the Treasury estimate of − 0.5. These estimates suggest a price increase of 20 per cent would be required in order to achieve a 10 to 12 per cent reduction in consumption, other things being equal.

Tobacco can be consumed in a number of ways, but cigarette smoking accounts for most of total consumption in the UK and estimated price elasticities have been similar whether consumption is measured in terms of total tobacco consumption, or just cigarette consumption. Like tobacco, alcohol is consumed in many different forms. In the UK, beer consumption was 53 per cent of the total in 1987, with spirits consumption being 24 per cent and wines, cider and perry 23 per cent. The shares of the alcohol market have changed considerably in the last 25 years. In 1963, for example, beer consumption was 58 per cent of the total, with spirits consumption 29 per cent and wines only 13 per cent (Hardman and Maynard, 1989). Studies have found that the responsiveness of consumption to prices varies between different beverages with, in general, the most popular form of beverage in any country being the least price responsive. It is therefore necessary to consider separately the price responsiveness of different alcohol beverages.

Some estimates of price elasticities from UK studies are presented in Table 7.2. Although there is a wide range of results for some beverages it can be seen that, in general, spirits and wine consumption are more responsive to price changes than beer consumption. As with tobacco, different data and model specifications have led to differences in the results. One of the major differences in the models used in Table 7.2 was the treatment of the number of licences and its effect on the consumption of alcohol. McGuinness (1983) and Walsh (1982) argued that the number of licences should be included as a determinant of consumption, and that increases in licences would

Table 7.2   Alcohol price elasticities

Study	Beer	Spirits	Wine
Walsh (1983)	−0.1 to −0.3	−0.5	−0.3 to −0.4
McGuinness (1983)	−0.3	−0.4	−0.2
Duffy (1983)	—	−0.8 to −1.0	−0.7 to −1.0
Treasury	−0.5	−1.3	−1.3
Godfrey (1988)	—	−0.6 to −3.0	−0.3 to −1.1

Source: C. Godfrey, 'Modelling Demand', in A. Maynard and P. Tether (eds), *The Addiction Market: Consumption, Production and Policy Development* (Aldershot: Avebury, 1989).

cause increases in consumption, other things being equal. In contrast, Duffy (1983) argued that increases in consumption would lead to increases in the number of licensed premises, but that licensing effects played no role in determining consumption. Duffy's argument implies that the models used by McGuinness and Walsh include an irrelevant variable and that their estimates may be affected by feedback bias. Given these differences in opinion about the specification and estimation of the models, it is not surprising that the corresponding estimated price elasticities in Table 7.2 are quite different.

The main purpose of the empirical work undertaken as part of the ESRC Addiction Research Centre's programme was to investigate the role of licensing on the demand for alcohol, but some new estimates of price elasticities were obtained. The empirical work compared the models of Duffy and McGuinness and tested for the inclusion of appropriate licensing variables (Godfrey, 1988). For wines and spirits, price was generally found to be an important determinant of consumption, but the sample data were consistent with a wide range of estimates. It is, therefore, difficult to choose a particular set of values, for example, for predicting the effects of price regulation. For beer, feedback effects between licensing and consumption were found. The existence of such feedback effects suggests that the statistical methods usually employed are invalid and, therefore, some doubt is cast on the results reported in previous research. Re-estimating the models using appropriate techniques resulted in poorly determined coefficients and no reliable new estimate of the effect of price on beer consumption could be obtained.

Thus there is evidence to suggest price increases are an effective means of controlling the consumption of tobacco, spirits and wine. For beer, the evidence is less conclusive. It is interesting to note that the Treasury has recently revised its estimate of beer price elasticity from -0.2 to -0.5. Our own empirical work used data ending in 1980, the last year licensing statistics were compiled on a UK basis. Since 1980, there have been large changes in beer prices and there may have been a corresponding change in price responsiveness.

The results presented above relate to aggregate *per capita* consumption. However, the price responses of groups of particular policy interest (for example, the young or heavy drinkers) may differ considerably from the aggregate figure. Further information is required to predict the effect of tax changes on the behaviour of groups of special interest. Research undertaken in the USA suggests that for young adults, consumption of alcohol and tobacco is more responsive to price changes than aggregate studies may suggest (Lewit *et al.*, 1981; Coate and Grossman, 1987). There have also been some studies of heavy drinkers which suggest that they do change their consumption of alcohol in response to price changes (Cook and Tauchen, 1982; Kendell *et al.*, 1983).

Additional information is also required to consider the effect of a change in the price of one good on the consumption of other alcoholic or tobacco goods. If alcoholic drinks are substitutes for one another, a rise in beer prices may induce a fall in beer consumption and an increase in the consumption of spirits and wine. Empirical work has not in general successfully identified interrelationships between prices and consumption of alcoholic beverages and tobacco goods. The estimated cross-price effects between alcholic beverages derived from many different types of model have been small and not precisely estimated (Godfrey, 1989). There has been less research into the possible relationship between alcohol and tobacco goods.

It will always be necessary to re-estimate and retest models of the relationships between consumption and the factors such as price. Models, even if adequately tested, can only be expected to accurately forecast changes in variables of a magnitude observed in data used for model selection and estimation. Mechanical predictions of the effects of unusually large price changes will be hazardous. Demand models and estimates of price elasticity are a useful input into the policy debate. While more research, for example, into the price responsiveness of different age and social class groups would be useful, existing research does indicate that price is potentially a useful instrument.

PRICE REGULATION AND CURRENT TAX POLICY

There are a number of ways governments might seek to regulate the price of alcohol and tobacco goods. In some countries where the production of goods is controlled by state monopolies, governments can directly control prices. State subsidies (such as for agricultural production) or retailing controls can also affect prices. In the UK, however, tax policy is the major potential means of regulating prices. In this section, trends in prices and taxes are considered. Current tax policy is described and the factors that have influenced current tax policy are identified. The impact of health arguments in determining tax changes is also assessed.

In Table 7.3 the prices of alcohol and tobacco goods relative to the prices of all goods for the period 1974 to 1988 are presented. The

Table 7.3   Indices of prices of alcoholic beverages and tobacco relative to the prices of all goods (1963 = 100)

Year	Beer	Spirits	Wine and Cider	Tobacco
1974	100	76	91	85
1975	101	77	92	88
1976	104	76	88	89
1977	105	74	83	95
1978	104	71	81	87
1979	105	69	82	84
1980	109	68	80	84
1981	117	71	80	93
1982	120	71	80	99
1983	124	72	79	100
1984	128	73	79	105
1985	134	74	79	110
1986	136	74	78	116
1987	135	74	78	116

Source: Central Statistical Office, *UK National Accounts* (various years) (London: HMSO)

figures suggest that there have been sizeable changes in prices of alcohol and tobacco goods relative to each other and also to all other prices. Only beer prices were at a similar level in 1974 relative to 1963. All the other alcohol and tobacco products were relatively cheaper in 1974 compared with general prices. For spirits and tobacco, the falls in relative prices were substantial. During the period 1974 to 1987, relative beer prices increased considerably particularly after 1981. In contrast, the relative prices of wines and cider decreased over the period. For spirits and tobacco, trends in prices were more varied, with tobacco prices in particular showing considerable changes from year to year.

However, tax is only one element of price. Prices will vary over time with production costs, profit margins, transport costs and retail margins. Increases in taxes are likely to increase prices, but the manufacturers or retailers can mitigate the effects of government policy by not fully passing on tax changes in final prices. While tax changes are one means of regulating price, it should be noted that a policy, for example, of maintaining the real value of tax cannot be guaranteed to ensure the stability of prices of alcohol and tobacco relative to other goods. The ability of manufacturers to absorb tax increases or substantially alter price is, of course, limited when tax is a large component of price.

It can be seen from Table 7.4 that tax is a large proportion of price for both cigarettes and spirits. The proportion of tax in price for a typical pint of beer or bottle of wine is much lower. Hence there is considerably more certainty that charges in taxes for spirits and tobacco will be passed directly on to consumers. For cigarettes, beer and wines, the changes in the proportion of tax in price show some correspondence to changes in prices. For spirits, however, the trends in price and tax in price are considerably different. This may reflect changes in the mix of spirits goods consumed. The figures shown in Table 7.3 are based on all spirits expenditure, whereas the figures in Table 7.4 are calculated for a typical 'low' price bottle of whisky. The reasons for changes in tax rates which help to determine the ratio of tax in price are now considered in more detail.

UK tax policy 1974 to 1988

Alcohol and tobacco taxation in the UK consist of an *ad valorem* component as a percentage of final price and a specific component as a fixed sum per quantity. Excise taxes are the specific element set in

Table 7.4 Duty and VAT as a percentage
of price, 1974 to 1988

Year	Cigarettes	Beer	Wine	Spirits
1974	70	32	32	90
1975	69	36	39	86
1976	70	34	37	82
1977	64	32	38	80
1978	70	31	35	78
1979	70	32	39	78
1980	71	34	42	78
1981	74	38	44	78
1982	75	38	46	77
1983	74	38	45	77
1984	75	39	39	75
1985	75	39	42	74
1986	75	36	45	72
1987	74	35	40	72
1988	74	35	40	70

Sources: Annual Reports of the Commissioners of HM Customs and Excise (London: HMSO). Prices for a typical bottle of wine for 1974 to 1977 kindly supplied by Marks and Spencer, PLC.

fixed monetary terms for a given characteristic. For example, excise is set per 1000 cigarettes and on alcohol content for spirits. The value added component, namely VAT, currently set at 15 per cent on all alcohol and tobacco goods with an additional *ad valorem* component for cigarettes of 21 per cent, will automatically rise with price increases.[1] The ratio of this tax component to final price, therefore remains constant. The specific elements are, however, set in monetary terms and will decline in real value in periods of inflation.

In the UK the excise and value added rates are set by means of budget decisions, usually annually in the spring. Changes in the structure of taxation are also generally announced in budget statements, although additional legislation may be required to enact the changes. In principle, therefore, the annual budget provides a mechanism to allow periodic adjustment of excise rates to at least maintain their value. (In many other countries without such mechanisms, there are more political impediments to changing the excise rates.) In practice, however, analyses of budget decisions reveal that tax changes are rarely closely linked to inflation, as can be seen from Table 7.5.

Although the chancellor receives representations and advice from both lobby groups and other government departments, he retains considerable autonomy in setting the levels of alcohol and tobacco taxes (Harrison and Tether, 1989). The discussions the chancellor may have on tax policy remain secret. However, by analysing statements and campaign material issued by lobbies, parliamentary and public opinion and the annual budget statements, it is possible to identify some of the different influences on chancellors' taxation decisions as set out in Table 7.5 (Leedham and Godfrey, 1989).

Table 7.5   Annual changes in retail price index and excise duties, 1974 to 1988

Year	Percentage change in RPI	Percentage change in Excise Duty			
		Cigarettes	*Beer*	*Wines*	*Spirits*
Denis Healey					
1974	14	35	29	57	10
1975	18	33	46	95	30
1976	21	1	16	11	12
1977	17	23	10	10	10
1978	9	0	0	0	0
Geoffrey Howe					
1979	10	2	0	0	0
1980	20	20	23	14	14
1981	13	31	38	17	15
1982	10	14	13	12	6
1983	5	5	6	6	5
Nigel Lawson					
1984	5	14	11	−20	2
1985	6	8	8	8	2
1986	4	13	0	0	0
1987	4	0	0	0	0
1988	4	4	5	5	0

Source: Annual Reports of the Commissioners of HM Customs and Excise, various years (London: HMSO).

Revenue

The principal concern of all three chancellors during the period 1974 to 1988 would seem to be revenue yield. Increases in excise taxes announced in the budget are generally introduced in terms of the extra revenue they will produce. For example, Geoffrey Howe in 1981 stated, 'I am proposing to increase the excise duties to produce in total about twice as much additional revenue as would be required to compensate for one year's inflation' (House of Commons, 1981). Alcohol and tobacco excise duties are an important source of revenue for governments. These duties (excluding VAT) at £11 781 m. accounted for 7.7 per cent of total current account government receipts in 1987 (Central Statistical Office, 1987).

During the period 1974 to 1988, for both Labour and Conservative administrations, economic policy has focused on the Public Sector Borrowing Requirement (PSBR), i.e. the balance between government receipts and expenditure, as a means of controlling the economy. Macroeconomic policies are, therefore, determinants of tax changes. It is not just as a source of general revenue that chancellors find excise taxes useful. An advantage of these taxes is that they can be adjusted with considerable flexibility to counter unexpected changes in the forecasted revenue flows which may be occasioned by sudden changes in economic variables prior to the budget, such as oil prices (Godfrey and Powell, 1985). Chancellors can also change duties by up to 10 per cent between budgets. Dennis Healey, for example, used this procedure in the autumn budget of 1976 in an effort to reduce the PSBR as necessitated by the agreement with the International Monetary Fund. The flexibility of tobacco duties was also shown in 1977 and 1981. In response to parliamentary pressure, plans announced in the previous Budget to increase petrol and derv duty were dropped and tobacco duties were increased to make up the expected shortfall in revenue.

Chancellors in their budget statements usually set the target for changes in revenue from excise duties as a whole before the changes in individual taxes are announced. There are some indications that tax decisions may also be taken in this order with an overall revenue target set and changes in individual duties varied with political and other representations. So, for example, in 1986 there was a considerable increase in cigarette taxes and some rise in petrol duties, but alcohol taxes remained unchanged (and hence fell in real value). The Chancellor noted that the overall effects of excise changes on petrol and tobacco were expected to raise the same amount of revenue as would have resulted from increasing all the excise duties in line with inflation (House of Commons, 1986).

Thus revenue considerations may not always conflict with health concerns. When governments require revenue, tax rates are likely to be increased at least in line with inflation. Within these tax targets, it may also be possible for health lobbies to persuade chancellors to increase taxation and possibly alcohol duties in preference to other excise duties. In the last two years, however, revenue has been buoyant and, as can be seen from Table 7.5, tax rate changes were considerably lower than previous years. It is apparent that governments value the flexibility of revenue these duties afford and they also wish to maintain the revenue generating capabilities of alcohol and tobacco duties. There may, therefore, be considerable opposition within the Treasury to health-based tax policies which require consistent and possibly large increases in tax rates (Harrison and Tether, 1989).

Inflation

Another feature of the period 1974 to 1988 was the concern with inflation. Prices at the beginning of the period rose at a rapid rate and the real value of excise duties set in monetary terms could also fall considerably between budgets. One consequence of these rapidly changing prices was a gradual public acceptance that excise rates would be annually uprated. However, as was indicated in Table 7.5, the actual tax changes rarely correspond to the change in prices in the previous year. The need to annually increase duty levels in line with inflation was stressed by successive chancellors during this period. Such changes had become so accepted that there was considerable surprise expressed by both the health and trade lobbies when the Chancellor changed neither alcohol or tobacco duties in the 1987 Budget. In periods of high inflation, or when the level of inflation is an important policy objective, there are, however, considerable constraints on a chancellor's ability to increase alcohol or tobacco duties for fear of fuelling the inflationary process.

Political cycles

A feature of the figures presented in Table 7.5 is that tax changes are either small or zero in pre-election budgets. Clearly chancellors will be under some pressure to avoid unpopular tax changes in such circumstances. There is, however, some evidence to suggest that governments have not lost support from tax hikes on tobacco. During the period 1974 to 1988 there has been a growing understanding of the health consequences of smoking and a fall in the number of people who smoke. So, for example, in 1986 a National Opinion Poll commissioned by DHSS suggested 48 per cent of the respondents approved of increased taxation with only 30 per cent disapproving of such increases. There seems to be far less support for increases in alcohol taxation (Leedham and Godfrey, 1989). For example, Wood (1987) reports a survey where 73 per cent of respondents thought that it was a bad idea to increase tax on beer in order to cut down the amount people drank. Unless information and other prevention policies change these attitudes and drinking behaviour, politicians may continue to be concerned about the public attitudes to alcohol taxation, especially in pre-election budgets.

Trade and health lobbies

The period 1974 to 1988 has seen a growth in activity of both health and trade lobbies. Lobbies not only submit proposals to chancellors but they also lobby MPs and attempt to influence public opinion. The tobacco industry, for example, has in the past spent considerable sums in mass advertising campaigns prior to budgets (Leedham and Godfrey, 1989).

As part of its lobbying, the tobacco industry has made several claims about the adverse economic consequences of tax increases. In particular, they have emphasised the effect on employment, trade and the poor. Employment in the alcohol and tobacco industries has declined dramatically in the last 20 years. Many other industries have also lost jobs and the role of prevention policies such as tax in causing job losses, or other adverse effects for industry, is unclear (see Chapter 10 in this volume). The industry's claims concerning job losses in associated industries can also be questioned (Godfrey and Hartley, 1988). The Chancellor has not made any concessions to the tobacco industry, despite a large rise in imports in the 1980s. By contrast, the Scotch Whisky industry has seemed to have received favourable tax concessions.

Health considerations have been linked to tobacco tax changes in several budget statements. For example, in 1986 the increase in cigarette tax was justified 'in the light of the representations that I have received on health grounds' (House of Commons, 1986, column 180). Cigarette taxes have not, however, increased consistently as would be required by health based policy. In 1987 following the tax hike, the Chancellor failed to revalorise duties and hence their value fell in real terms. There has been no recognition of the health effects of alcohol.

To conclude, it is interesting to note that most health and trade lobbies take the view that, despite chancellors' statements concerning the effects of representations, their influence is small relative to other factors.

Effects on the poor

Political pressure, inflation and revenue as determinants of tax policy were common to all three chancellors. An additional factor mentioned only by Denis Healey was the effect of raising duties on particular groups of the population. For example, in announcing cigarette duty changes in 1976 he stated ' . . . I had to pay some regard to the level of prices and to the burden of those, particularly the poor, who found it difficult to cut back on their smoking' (House of Commons, 1976, column 260).

Taxes on cigarettes and beer do fall more heavily on the poor. Heavy smokers and drinkers with low incomes can pay a very large proportion of their income in tax. For example, in 1985 taxes on alcohol and tobacco made up 13 per cent of income of the retired and 12 per cent of the income of the non-retired for those smokers and drinkers with the lowest 20 per cent of income. For single non-retired male households who smoke and drink in the lowest income group, £5 per week went in alcohol and tobacco taxes out of a net disposable income of £32 (Godfrey and Posnett, 1988). Whether the distributive burden of these taxes would worsen when tax increases depends on the responsiveness of different groups to price increases. There is some evidence for cigarette consumption to suggest that lower social classes may be more responsive to price changes than higher social classes and, therefore, the distributive effects of increased taxation on the poor may be less than is sometimes feared (Godfrey and Maynard, 1988).

Some of the variations in tax changes in Table 7.5 are explained by the factors discussed in this section. A number of impediments to a health-based policy have been identified from this analysis. The central position of chancellors in the current tax policy-making process may also be significant. Individual preferences of chancellors may remain an important determinant of tax changes.

ALTERNATIVE TAX POLICIES

The examination of the present system suggests that there are difficulties in introducing a health-based price regulation policy to increase tax rates and that duty rates can fall in real value by a considerable amount. For example, spirits duties have fallen in real terms by 15 per cent since they were last uprated in 1985. A number of alternative policies have been suggested by lobby groups (Godfrey and Harrison, 1989). The purpose of this section is to examine some of the advantages and disadvantages of these health-based alternative policies and discuss difficulties in implementing them.

The alternative tax policies set out in Table 7.6 have been divided into two groups: those that can be implemented within the present system of current tax bands and budgetary adjustments; and those that require special legislation or a major restructuring of duties. There are obvious advantages to proposing tax reforms that fit within the present system as new regulation is both costly and difficult to implement (see Chapter 12 in this volume). The different policies are now examined in turn.

Table 7.6   Alternative tax policies

Changes within the present system
- Revalorisation
- Increase the real levels of taxation
- Benchmark policies

Alternative taxation structures
- Changes to the budget system
- Value added versus specific taxation
- Differential taxation

Revalorisation

Some degree of revalorisation can be seen as a common component of all health-based policies. Most health groups have advocated that taxes should be maintained in real terms. Such a policy would not necessarily maintain prices of alcohol and tobacco relative to other goods or hold the ratio of tax in price constant, as was discussed in an earlier part of the chapter.

Revaluing tax rates in line with inflation is the usual, but not the only, form of revalorisation. Policies could be designed to maintain relative prices, prices adjusted for income changes, or be linked to manufacturers' costs and profits. These various revalorisation schemes would have different effects on economic variables such as consumption and revenue. A policy designed to maximise revenue yields may lead to a different choice of scheme than one designed to control consumption.

The major barrier to the adoption of any indexation policy would, however, seem to be that those taking part in the present budget policy-making process have considerable incentives to maintain the flexibility and secrecy of annual budget changes. Rules for alcohol and tobacco could, however, be devised so that indexation was automatic unless the Chancellor made explicit proposals for other tax changes. It is also clear that indexing rules would give more certainty for the trade and, therefore, they might not be strong opponents of such a scheme.

Increasing the real levels of taxation

Indexation of the tax level to general prices to maintain the real tax rate will not automatically fulfil either health or revenue policy objectives. Many bodies concerned with health have advocated a gradual increase in the real rate of taxation. Implementing a policy of steadily rising real tax rates would require a commitment to a health perspective and the consistent application of the policy throughout political cycles.

Opponents of such tax increases have suggested that punitive taxation might lead to a fall in revenue. The values of price elasticities discussed earlier, combined with the ratio of tax in price, suggest, however, that revenue yield for beer and tobacco would be likely to increase at least in the short run if such a policy were adopted. For example, using the cigarette price elasticity estimate of -0.56 and other parameters from the demand model, Godfrey and Maynard (1988) projected a 27 per cent increase in real revenue yields (and a similar size fall in consumption) if a policy of 10 per cent yearly price increases had resulted from Government tax policy between 1985 and 1990.

Benchmark policies

Most health policy recommendations have been presented in the form of benchmark targets. These targets have either concerned some historic level of tax rates, or some consumption target as set out by the World Health Organisation (described by Robinson in this volume). Restoring tax rates to historic levels could imply large changes in price. For example, adjusting spirits tax in the 1986 Budget to account for income changes since 1965 would have added over £11 to a bottle of spirits (Godfrey *et al.*, 1986). It is difficult to predict the revenue and consumption consequences of such changes because of the limitations of using price elasticity estimates discussed above. Also the large once and for all effects of the Retail Price Index (RPI) may act as a deterrent to Government action.

Alcohol and tobacco goods could be removed from the RPI so that concern about the effects of tax changes on the level of inflation would no longer be an impediment to a public health policy. The weights of tobacco and alcohol in the index are, however, small, for example at 36 and 78 respectively out of a total of 1000 in 1988. Only very large changes in the price of these goods add significantly to inflation. Using the 1988 weights, for example, a 10 per cent rise in all alcohol and tobacco duties would only add just over 1 per centage point to the RPI. With the numbers of smokers declining, however, there is some question as to the appropriateness of a general price index that includes an item only a small declining section of the population consume. For smokers, the percentage of tobacco expenditure in their total budget will generally be much larger than the 3.6 per cent implied by the RPI weights (Godfrey and Posnett, 1988).

Benchmark consumption levels may be difficult to achieve with tax policy alone. Taxes would have to be manipulated to take account of the other factors influencing consumption. To achieve consumption goals, it may be necessary to increase duties on different goods at unequal rates. The changes in relative prices which could occur if such a policy was implemented may have considerable effects on the structure of industries (see Chapter 10 by Keith Hartley).

A major problem with any benchmark policy is, however, deciding on the appropriate benchmark. Should consumption be reduced by 25 per cent at any cost? Would it be more efficient to have some other target level? As Maynard observes in Chapter 5, to consider appropriate policy objectives we require considerably more knowledge about the exact relationship between the social costs and benefits from the consumption, and the policies that can influence these consumption levels.

To avoid some of the adverse consequences of the present system, a number of changes to the structure of the present system of taxing alcohol and tobacco goods have been proposed.

Changes in the budgetary process

At present there is generally a minimum gap of a year between budgets and the possible revalorisation of excise duties. An alternative system is the gradual adjustment of tax rates throughout the year. This would result in less conspicuous increases, but could involve increased administrative costs, and costs to industry because of frequent price changes. Such a change in the system may, however, make increases in the real level of taxation more difficult to achieve.

Ad valorem *versus specific taxation*

Another alternative which would ensure a maintenance of a constant proportion of tax in price is to change the system so that all taxes are set in *ad valorem* terms. *Ad valorem* taxes will maintain the tax to price ratio, but do not necessarily ensure constant real prices or constant levels of tax per item. A decline in manufacturers' costs passed on in prices, for example, would also mean a fall in the amount of duty. Specific taxes also have the advantage that they can be directed at specific characteristics, e.g. alcohol content, rather than just value. Within a specific tax system, it is therefore possible to construct rates that are set according to the harm of the consumption of the goods. Also, research suggests that tax structures have effects on the industries. *Ad valorem* taxes tend to encourage the production of lower quality (low cost) products and lead to decreases in product variety (Kay and Keen, 1985). In evaluating tax policy change, it is important to consider such hidden costs.

Differential taxation

One prevention strategy is to tax commodities by the harm they create (Godfrey and Powell, 1987). So, for example, one proposal would be to equalise tax or price per unit of alcohol. At the moment, spirits are taxed at a higher rate per unit of alcohol than either beer or wine. Further, tax rates per unit of alcohol vary within beverage type. For example, wine of 14 per cent alcohol content is taxed at £7.3 per litre of pure alcohol, whereas wines of 15 per cent which fall in the higher tax band are taxed at a rate of £11.7 per litre of pure alcohol. The abolition of the minimum duty charge for beer, announced in the March 1988 Budget, was designed to encourage both the production and consumption of low alcohol beers. There is no indication that the Government is concerned with equalising taxes across different beverages although the spirits industry has advocated such a change.

IMPEDIMENTS TO A HEALTH-BASED TAX POLICY AND CONCLUDING REMARKS

A number of impediments, political, administrative and economic, to the implementation of a preventative health-based tax policy can be identified from the analyses of current and alternative tax policies. These impediments are summarised in Table 7.7. The strengths and weaknesses of these barriers will vary over time. For example, the boom in consumer spending in 1987 and 1988 and a general increase in prosperity has led to increases in revenue from sources other than alcohol and tobacco. Increases in alcohol and tobacco duties may, therefore, only be considered in response to major economic crises. Problems with rising levels of inflation may also act as a barrier to excise rate charges. On the other hand, there has been recent concern expressed both by the government and commentators on the level of alcohol-related problems, particularly amongst the young. Public opinion and attitudes to health may strengthen the arguments of the health lobby for increases in alcohol duties.

The most obvious impediment to major tax changes is, however, the EC tax harmonisation proposals described by Melanie Powell in Chapter 8.[2] The Government's objections to these proposals are similar to many of the alternative tax policies described above in that

Table 7.7   Impediments to a price regulation policy

- Government economic objectives
- Economic consequences of raising taxation levels
  - e.g.   Employment
          Inflation
          Trade and industry
          Effects on the poor
- Administrative costs
- Lobby pressure
- Public opinion
- EC tax harmonisation

---

they will lose fiscal sovereignty and flexibility. Whether tax rates will be harmonised across Europe is still uncertain. Whatever the final outcome of the EC negotiations, there will be considerable inertia effects. The process involves a moratorium on changes in tax structures until 1992 and, therefore, no radical changes in tax policy can be considered. Also, given the present levels of taxes in the UK are on average higher than other EC countries and any compromise will involve a fall in rates, chancellors may decide not to annually uprate taxes in order to avoid the possibility of excessive adjustments if agreement is reached.

To conclude, price regulation is one means of controlling consumption. Other factors, however, such as income and the effects of other policies (such as information and regulation) are also important. Offsetting effects may occur if there is no co-ordination of prevention policies. It must also be recognised that tax while important is not the only determinant of price. There may also be some short-run adverse economic consequences, for instance on inflation, trade and employment, arising from particularly large tax changes. A consistent health-based tax policy may help minimise these adverse effects and ease adjustment costs for industries. The usefulness and flexibility of excise duties as one of the tools used by governments in managing the economy is a major barrier to the adoption of a more consistent tax policy. EC tax harmonisation may help to remove this particular impediment at a European level, but at a considerable health cost within the UK. Finally, whether the forum for debate is in the UK or the EC, health lobbies have to be prepared to continue to present arguments for price regulation.

Notes

1. The VAT rate was changed twice during the period 1974 to 1988. In the autumn of 1976, the rate was reduced from 10 to 8 per cent, thereby effectively lowering the prices of alcohol and tobacco and all goods subject to VAT. In Geoffrey Howe's first budget in 1979, VAT was raised from 8 to 15 per cent. The rise in VAT was cited as a reason for not changing excise duties in the same budget. As a result of this lack of revalorisation however, alcohol and tobacco goods became cheaper compared to other goods that attracted VAT.
2. British tax rates and the tax system have already been influenced by EC regulations and harmonisation. The structure of wine and tobacco duties was changed at the beginning of the period. The EC negotiations on the harmonisation of tobacco tax structures forced the withdrawal of the tax on higher tar cigarettes introduced in the 1978 Budget. Further, a

European Court relief in 1983 implied that the UK overtaxed wine relative to beer, and wine duties were reduced by 18p a bottle in the 1984 Budget.

References

Atkinson, A. B. and Skegg, J. L. (1973) 'Anti-smoking Publicity and the Demand for Tobacco in the UK', *The Manchester School*, vol. 41, pp. 265–82.

Central Statistical Office (1987) *UK National Accounts, 1987* (London: HMSO).

Coate, D. and Grossman, M. (1987) 'Change in Alcoholic Beverage Prices and Legal Drinking Ages', *Alcohol, Health and Research World*, Fall, pp. 22–5.

Cook, P. J. and Tauchen, G. (1982) 'The Effect of Liquor Taxes on Heavy Drinking', *Bell Journal of Economics*, vol. 13, pp. 370–90.

Duffy, M. (1983) 'The Demand for Alcoholic Drink in the United Kingdom, 1963–78', *Applied Economics*, vol. 15, pp. 125–40.

Godfrey, C. (1988) 'Licensing and the Demand for Alcohol', *Applied Economics*, vol. 20, pp. 1541–8.

Godfrey, C. (1989) 'Modelling Demand', in A. Maynard and P. Tether (eds), *The Addiction Market: Consumption, Production and Policy Development* (Aldershot: Avebury).

Godfrey, C., Hardman, G. and Powell, M. (1986) 'Data Note, Alcohol and Tobacco Taxation', *British Journal of Addiction*, vol. 81, pp. 143–9.

Godfrey, C. and Harrison, L. (1989) 'Preventive Health Objectives and Tax Policy Options', in A. Maynard and P. Tether (eds), The Addiction Market: Consumption Production and Policy Development (Aldershot: Avebury).

Godfrey, C. and Hartley, K. (1988) 'Employment and Prevention Policies',*British Journal of Addiction*, forthcoming.

Godfrey, C. and Maynard, A. (1988) 'Economic Aspects of Tobacco Use and Taxation Policy', *British Medical Journal*, vol. 297, pp. 339–43.

Godfrey, C. and Posnett, J. (1988) *An Analysis of the Distributional Impact of Taxes on Alcohol and Tobacco*. ESRC Addiction Research Centre, University of York, Working Paper.

Godfrey, C. and Powell, M. (1985) 'Alcohol and Tobacco Taxation, Barriers to a Public Health Perspective', *The Quarterly Journal of Social Affairs*, vol. 1(4), pp. 329–53.

Godfrey, C. and Powell, M. (1987) *Budget Strategies for Alcohol and Tobacco in 1987 and Beyond*. Discussion Paper 22, Centre for Health Economics, University of York.

Hardman, G. and Maynard, A. (1989) 'Consumption and Taxation Trends', in A. Maynard and P. Tether (eds) *The Addiction Market: Consumption, Production and Policy Development* (Aldershot: Avebury).

Harrison, L. and Tether, P. (1989) 'Tax Policy: Structure and Process', in A. Maynard and P. Tether (eds) *The Addiction Market: Consumption,*

Production and Policy Development (Aldershot: Avebury).

House of Commons (1976) Budget Statement, *Parliamentary Debates, 1975–1976*, 909, col. 232–82.

House of Commons (1981) Budget Statement, *Parliamentary Debates, 1981–1982*, 1000, col. 773.

House of Commons (1986) Budget Statement, *Parliamentary Debates, 1985–1986*, 94, col. 286–305.

Kay, J. A. and Keen, M. J. (1985) 'Alcohol and Tobacco Taxes in the European Community: Criteria for Harmonisation', in S. Cnossen (ed.) *Tax Coordination in the European Community*, (Netherlands: Kluwer Academic).

Kendell, R. E., de Roumanie, H. and Ritson, E. B. (1983) 'Effects of Economic Changes on Scottish Drinking Habits 1978–82', *British Journal of Addiction*, vol. 78, pp. 365–79.

Leedham, W. and Godfrey, C. (1989) 'Tax Policy and Budget Decisions, 1974 to 1988', in A. Maynard and P. Tether (eds) *The Addiction Market: Consumption, Production and Policy Development* (Aldershot: Avebury).

Lewit, E. M., Coate, D. and Grossman, M. (1981) 'The Effects of Government Regulation on Teenage Smoking', *Journal of Law and Economics*, vol. 14, pp. 545–69.

McGuinness, T. (1983) 'The Demand for Beer, Spirits and Wine in the UK, 1956–1979', in M. Grant, M. Plant and A. Williams (eds) *Economics and Alcohol* (London: Croom Helm).

McGuinness, T. and Cowling, K. (1975) 'Advertising and the Aggregate Demand for Cigarettes', *European Economic Review*, vol. 6, pp. 311–28.

Metra Consulting Group Limited (1979) *The Relationship between Total Cigarette Advertising and Total Cigarette Consumption in the UK* (London: Metra).

Peto, J. (1974) 'Price and Consumption of Cigarettes: a Case for Intervention', *British Journal of Social and Preventive Medicine*, vol. 28, pp. 241–5.

Radfar, M. (1985) 'The Effect of Advertising on Total Consumption of Cigarettes in the UK', *European Economic Review*, vol. 29, pp. 225–31.

Russell, M. A. (1973) 'Changes in Cigarette Price and Consumption by Men in Britain 1946–1974', *British Journal of Preventive and Social Medicine*, vol. 27, pp. 1–7.

Sumner, M. T. (1971) 'Demand for Tobacco in the UK', *The Manchester School*, vol. 39, pp. 23–36.

Walsh, B. M. (1982) 'The Demand for Alcohol in the UK: a Comment', *Journal of Industrial Economics*, vol. 30, pp. 439–46.

Witt, S. F. and Pass, C. L. (1981) 'The Effects of Health Warnings and Advertising on the Demand for Cigarettes', *Scottish Journal of Political Economy*, vol. 28, pp. 86–91.

Wood, D. (1987) *Beliefs about Alcohol* (London: Health Education Council).

8 Tax Harmonisation in the European Community

Melanie Powell

INTRODUCTION

The European Commission White Paper on completing the internal market for trade between member states was published in June 1985. Six months later, the Single European Act (1986) specified the target of unification to be the creation of 'an area without internal frontiers in which the free movement of goods, persons, services and capital is ensured'. This is to be achieved by removing remaining physical, technical, fiscal and administrative barriers to trade between countries. The deadline is December 1992, and the harmonisation of tax structures and approximation of indirect tax rates on alcohol and tobacco form a central part of the internal market strategy. If the tax proposals currently under consideration are adopted, tax differentials between member states on alcohol and tobacco will be removed. Any increase in trade and consumption which results could impede the progress of internationally agreed goals for health policy (WHO, 1980).

When the UK entered the European Community (EC) in 1973, it became legally committed with other member states to the trade policy of the Treaty of Rome. Economic progress under the Treaty was to be achieved through the formation of a large integrated market, and through the use of intervention agencies to regulate essential trade and production. The benefits of increased trade would be gained by furthering specialisation and efficiency in production, and ensuring stability of inputs, self sufficiency in outputs, and a balance-of-trade surplus with external trade partners. To date, the combined impact of the initial removal of tariff barriers under the Treaty, together with the support of wine and tobacco leaf output under the Common Agricultural Policy, the stabilisation of less developed markets in alcohol and tobacco and the progress of competition policy, has been to increase trade, production and consumption of alcohol and tobacco. The costs of past and future trade progress, however, may be measured in terms of the health consequences for European consumers amongst other factors. There is no provision under the Treaty of Rome for a co-ordinated health strategy which involves restricting trade.

The conflict between the goals of EC, trade policy in alcohol and tobacco and the embryonic European preventive health policy is examined in this chapter with reference to the proposals for tax harmonisation. A brief outline of the role of alcohol and tobacco production in EC trade is given in the first sections, together with a discussion of consumption trends, and the nature of current health policy action. Three-quarters of the White Paper proposals of the internal market have been tabled by the European Commission (EC, 1985), including those required to achieve fiscal goals. It is argued in the final sections of this chapter that the tax proposals are likely to lead to substantial price changes for alcohol and tobacco products in some member states, which may result in higher rates of consumption and rising levels of associated harm. In addition, given the current trends in trade and consumption, the proposals will restrict the use of tax policy by Member States as an instrument of health policy. To achieve and maintain the targets adopted under international health agreements, the EC must adopt a co-ordinated approach to trade and health policy.

PRODUCTION AND TRADE IN ALCOHOL AND TOBACCO IN THE EEC

Both internal and external trade in alcohol and tobacco products have expanded with the accession of new countries to the EEC (Powell, 1987). The UK, Ireland and Denmark joined in 1973, followed by Greece in 1981 and Spain and Portugal in 1986. However, even between periods of accession, the trade policies of the EC have encouraged specialisation in production, and supported external trade and agricultural output in the alcohol and tobacco markets.

Figures in Table 8.1 highlight the importance of trade in alcohol and tobacco products to the EEC in 1986. Manufactured alcohol and tobacco provide a continuous balance-of-trade surplus valued at 4 916.9 million ecu in 1986 (ecu: currency uit derived from a weighted basket of all currencies of EEC member states). Because the EC is only 48 per cent self-sufficient in raw tobacco leaf, a balance-of-trade

Table 8.1 Balance of external trade in alcohol and tobacco in the EC (12) 1986

	Volume (1 000 000 kg)	Value (1 000 000 e.c.u.)
Beer	+797.4	+663.8
Wine	+1 198.6	+1 766.9
Spirits	+518.9	+1 959.8
Unmanufactured tobacco	−276.7	−1 643.8
Manufactured tobacco	+38.4	+526.4
		+3 273.1

Source: Eurostat, Foreign Trade Statistics.

deficit is shown on unmanufactured tobacco. The EC is a major world exporter of wine and spirits, and beer exports are expanding in the new internationalised beer market. Exports of cigarettes to less developed countries have increased steadily over the last decade. The value of internal trade between member states in alcohol and tobacco products constituted approximately 2 per cent of the total value of all internal trade in 1986.

Alcohol and tobacco products are manufactured in most EC countries as shown in Table 8.2. Beers are produced in every member state, the majority of which originates in West Germany, the UK, France and Spain. Output increased by 33 per cent between 1965 and 1985 and EC production of beer comprised 28 per cent of world

Table 8.2 Production of alcohol and tobacco in the EC (12) 1986

Product	Main producers	Percentage of world output
Beers	All member states	28
Wine	France, West Germany, Italy	57
Spirits	UK, France, West Germany and Spain	25
Tobacco leaf	Italy, Greece and France	6
Tobacco products	All member states	15

Source: Eurostat.

output in 1986. The main wine producers are France, West Germany, Italy and Spain. The EC is the world's largest wine producer and Community wine output increased by 30 per cent betwen 1965 and 1985 under the Common Agricultural Policy wine programme. Spirit production, mainly from the UK, France, West Germany and Spain, increased by more than 25 per cent between 1970 and 1985, and accounts for a quarter of world output. Comparable figures are not available prior to 1970. Tobacco leaf production is an important agricultural product in Italy, Greece and France. Production increased by 45 per cent between 1965 and 1985, but forms only 6 per cent of world output. Whereas, tobacco products (80 per cent of which are cigarettes) are manufactured in all member states and account for 15 per cent of world production.

TRENDS IN ALCOHOL AND TOBACCO CONSUMPTION

Data on alcohol and tobacco consumption have been used to support arguments for control policies across Europe. Particular attention has been paid to *per capita* consumption of alcohol on the basis of an observed positive relationship between *per capita* consumption and indicators of harm (Davies and Walsh, 1983).

Absolute volumes of different alcoholic drinks can be converted to units of pure alcohol using an average value of alcohol content per litre. Between 1965 and 1975, consumption of pure alcohol increased in all member states except France.Figures in Table 8.3 show that the trends since 1975 have varied between countries, ranked by consumption in 1975. Consumption has declined mainly in countries which recorded high levels of wine consumption and high levels of *per capita* consumption overall. The exception is the relatively large reduction in recorded alcohol consumption in Ireland, where tax policy has resulted in a substantial rise in the real price of alcoholic drinks. *Per capita* consumption of pure alcohol has continued to increase in most countries with high rates of beer and spirit consumption.

An example of the changing trends in consumption of different drinks and the trend towards more homogeneous drinking patterns in the EC, is given in Table 8.4. Several features can be identified from the figures. Both countries with high levels of wine consumption also record high levels of *per capita* consumption of pure alcohol. Although wine consumption decreased, consumption of beer and spirits increased between 1960 and 1985. The UK and Denmark have

Table 8.3 Consumption of alcohol in the EC (litres of pure alcohol *per capita*)

	1975	1985	Percentage change
France	16.1	13.3	−17.4
Italy	12.8	11.6	−9.4
W. Germany	11.3	10.8	−4.4
Luxembourg	11.1	11.6	+4.5
Belgium	10.1	10.5	+4.0
Denmark	9.1	9.9	+8.8
Netherlands	8.7	8.5	−2.3
Ireland	7.7	6.2	−19.5
UK	6.6	7.1	+7.6
Greece	5.3	6.8	+2.8
EC 10 average	9.9	9.8	−0.1
Spain	14.1	11.8	−16.3
Portugal	13.3	13.1	−1.5

Source: Dutch Distillers, *How Many Alcoholic Beverages are being Consumed throughout the World?* Produktschap voor Gestilleerde Dranken; Schiedam, Holland, 1986.

high levels of beer consumption, but lower levels of *per capita* consumption of pure alcohol. However, consumption of beer continues to increase with that of wines and spirits. Most countries have shown a relative decline in alcohol consumption since 1980.

Approximately 85 per cent of all tobacco products consumed in the EC are cigarettes. *Per capita* consumption of cigarettes increased in most member states up to 1978, but subsequently declined. The decline may be explained by increasing taxation and prices, the extent of health promotion campaigns, and also a fall in real incomes. The latter effect would also explain part of the parallel decline in alcohol consumption after that date. Figures in Table 8.5 show *per capita* rates, ranked in 1981. Unlike trends in alcohol consumption, cigarette consumption has not fallen in all countries recording the highest rates. Consumption rose 20 per cent over the period in Greece, continuing a long-run increasing trend. By comparison, consumption fell by 27 per cent in the Netherlands.

Table 8.4   Disaggregated trends in alcohol
consumption (litres of pure alcohol *per capila*)

Countries with high levels of wine consumption		1960	1980	1985
France	Beer	35.3	44.3	40.1
	Wine	126.9	91.1	80.0
	Spirits	2.0	2.5	2.3
Italy	Beer	5.1	16.7	21.6
	Wine	108.3	92.9	84.8
	Spirits	1.0	1.9	1.2

Countries with high levels of beer consumption		1960	1980	1985
UK	Beer	85.1	117.1	108.9
	Wine	1.6	7.2	10.0
	Spirits	0.7	1.8	1.7
Denmark	Beer	71.4	121.6	121.2
	Wine	3.1	14.0	20.7
	Spirits	0.6	1.5	1.6

Source: Dutch Distillers, *How Many Alcoholic
Beverages are being Consumed throughout the
World?* Produktschap voor Gestilleerde Dranken;
Schiedam, Holland, 1986.

Per capita cigarette consumption figures, however, disguise
changes in consumption by weight of tobacco, which may be important for analysing associated health problems. For example, as part of
the move towards harmonising tax structures, the EC has enforced
indirect taxation on cigarettes by number rather than by weight.
King-size cigarettes are therefore taxed at a relatively lower rate for
tobacco content. A switch to king-size cigarettes has tended to
increase the weight of tobacco consumed in cigarettes in the UK. By
contrast, a shift towards filter-tipped standard size cigarettes in other

Table 8.5 Consumption of cigarettes in the EC (number *per capita*)

	1981	1985	Percentage change
Greece	2 415.5	2 902.2	+20.2
W. Germany	2 107.8	1 951.7	−7.4
Ireland	2 091.2	1 737.3	−16.9
UK	1 968.9	1 743.3	−11.5
Belgium/ Luxem- bourg	1 937.9	1 916.8	−1.0
Italy	1 764.1	1 842.8	+4.5
France	1 582.5	1 716.5	+8.4
Netherlands	1 495.1	1 083.4	−27.5
Denmark	1 386.2	1 506.0	+8.6
EC 10 average	1 860.3	1 538.0	−17.3
Spain	1 705.0	2 051.7	+20.3
Portugal	1 347.8	1 368.5	+1.5

Source: Tobacco World.

regions of the EC has tended to reduce the average weight of tobacco per cigarette. Overall, the weight of tobacco per 1000 cigarettes fell from 1.24 kg in the early 1970s to 0.8 kg in 1985. The dramatic reduction in cigarette consumption in the Netherlands must be balanced against a distinct rise in the use of tobacco for roll-your-own and make-your-own cigarettes. Between 1981 and 1985, roll-your-own tobacco sales by volume increased by 18.8 per cent, although the increase did not outweigh the volume reduction from cigarettes.

ALCOHOL AND TOBACCO RELATED HEALTH POLICY IN THE EC

The goals of EC policy were originally centred on economic growth, with minimal reference to social policy under the Treaty of Rome to ensure a free and mobile workforce. However, health and social policy are linked directly to economic growth through public expenditure. Accelerating expenditure on welfare led to the acceptance of social policy as an equal goal to economic policy at the EC summit of

1972. Health policy, however, was not seriously considered until a meeting of Health Ministers in 1978. No further action was taken until 1982.

Concern over rising health care expenditure and potential inflationary pressure has generated interest in the development of a Community health policy (Abel-Smith and Maynard, 1978; Abel-Smith, 1983). Four documents have been presented to the Council for consideration; a Directive on dialysis, a Recommendation on European health care, a Resolution on identification of poisons and a Communication from the Commission on co-operation in health related problems. The latter proposed joint action on drug addiction, smoking and infectious diseases. No action was recommended on alcohol-related health problems, and there is still no policy to co-ordinate preventive action under the Treaty of Rome. However, documents from the Commission in relation to smoking and health have been forthcoming. The Commission set out proposals for preventive health action on smoking-related disease in a report to Parliament in 1982 (EC, 1982) and finalised the action programme 'Europe Against Cancer' in 1986 (EC, 1986). These programmes are intended to alter individual patterns of consumption, but have also been used to support harmonisation proposals in relation to tar content and tax rates. The legal competence of the Commission has yet to be tested.

In addition to action by the Commission on smoking and health, member states have agreed on prevention policies aimed at reducing consumption of alcohol and tobacco. In 1984, member states individually agreed to the targets of the World Health Organisation (WHO) programme, Health for All in the Year 2000 (WHO, 1984). Consumption of alcohol and tobacco products is to be reduced by 25 per cent by the year 2000 in the European Region. A progress report on the strategy was produced in 1985 which revealed poor results for alcohol consumption, and negative European scores on heart disease (WHO, 1985). Countries are now required to monitor their performance every two years.

The Europe Against Cancer campaign was launched in October 1987, with the publication of a public opinion survey on knowledge of preventive action (EC, 1987). The survey showed that more than 70 per cent of Europeans were aware of the effect of tobacco on health, but only 30 per cent were informed about alcohol consumption. Of those surveyed, 88 per cent were aware of the prevention potential of not smoking, but less than 50 per cent were aware of the need for moderate alcohol consumption. The figure for alcohol awareness varied widely between countries, being as low as 11 per cent in the UK and as high as 68 per cent in France. In February 1988 the Council of Health Ministers announced proposals in a directive to harmonise health warnings on cigarettes and to set 'tar' limits by 1992. However, the survey indicated that only 36 per cent of smokers take notice of tar content in cigarettes.

The early stages of an EC health policy are firmly focused on tobacco use. There is evidence, however, that tobacco producers will attempt to fight the programme on the basis of restrictions to free trade and on the grounds that the Council of Health Ministers have overstepped their authority. The industry intends to fight the label harmonisation and tar directives on the basis that there is no legal competence for restrictive public health action under the Treaty of Rome (Tobacco Reporter, March and April 1988). Proposals for tax harmonisation on tobacco may also be challenged where changes increase prices on the grounds of public health considerations, but the overall impact on alcohol is likely to promote trade and consumption.

HARMONISATION OF INDIRECT TAX ON ALCOHOL AND TOBACCO PRODUCTS

It is argued that differences in the structures and rates of indirect tax adopted by member states result in a distortion of competition and the continuation of frontier controls, restricting free trade. The internal frontier arises because member states must ensure that duties imposed under domestic laws are paid on all imported goods. To create a complete internal market, the internal frontiers must be removed. There are two elements in the EC proposals; the harmonisation of tax structures, establishing a unified set of tax methods; and the approximation of tax rates, reducing differential tax rates between states. The proposals are intended to eliminate the existing distinction between suppliers in different states and thereby the need to continue relieving goods from tax at export and import.

There are two components of indirect tax affecting alcohol and tobacco products in the EC. All member states have now implemented the same system of VAT, although differences exist in the number of rates and the level of rates charged. VAT is an *ad valorem* tax, or a tax as a percentage of the final price of goods purchased.

Member states also raise excise tax on alcohol and tobacco products, which may take the form of an *ad valorem* tax, but is more usually levied as a specific tax. Specific duties are specified as a value per physical unit.

Harmonisation of the system of indirect tax has been partly achieved. All member states raise specific duties on alcoholic drinks and a combination of specific and *ad valorem* excise on tobacco products, in addition to VAT. As a result of previous Commission action, member states must tax cigarettes and must use a combination of both specific and *ad valorem* tax within given limits. The UK, Denmark and Ireland raise the maximum specific element, whereas France, Greece, Belgium, Luxembourg and Italy apply the lowest specific rates allowed. A high *ad valorem* content favours producers of low-cost cigarettes, and the system can therefore be used to protect domestic producers where applicable. The proposals represent the minimum required change to achieve a sufficient degree of approximation in order to remove internal frontiers.

Proposals for harmonising VAT

More than one rate of VAT is applied in all member states except the UK and Denmark, and rates vary from 1 per cent in Belgium to 38 per cent in Italy (Powell, 1988). In addition, the UK and Ireland make extensive use of zero rates. Rates on tobacco products vary widely because tobacco carries an additional *ad valorem* component.

Two rates of VAT are proposed: a standard rate to be applied to most goods including alcohol and tobacco, and a reduced rate for special goods, including foods, energy, water, pharmaceuticals, books, newspapers and transport. The standard rate is to fall between 14 and 20 per cent of final price and the reduced rate between 4 and 9 per cent. Figures in Table 8.6 give details of rates applying in April 1987. The proposals will lead to reductions in the rate of VAT in Belgium, Denmark and Ireland, and increased rates in Greece, Luxembourg and Spain. Italy and Portugal will have to agree unique rates.

Member states would be allowed to change the number and levels of existing rates of VAT only where they complied with proposed limits. A clearing mechanism has also been outlined to redistribute revenues.

Table 8.6   Rates of VAT on alcohol and tobacco products in the EC (% of final price, 1 April 1987)

Member state	B	DK	D	F	GR	IRE	I	L	NL	UK	E	P
Alcohol												
Spirits	25	22	14	18.6	6[1]	25	18	12	20	15	12	16–30[2]
Still wine	25	22	14	18.6	6	25	9–18[3]	6–12[4]	20	15	12	8–16[5]
Sparkling wine	25	22	14	18.6	6	25	18–36[6]	12	20	15	12	16
Beer/cider	19–25[7]	22	14	18.6	—	25	9	12	20	15	12	16

	B	DK	D	F	GR	IRL	I	L	NL	UK	E	P
Tobacco												
Cigarettes	5.66	18.03	12.28	25.60[8]	26.47	20.00	15.25	6.00	15.50	13.04	11.94	13.79
Other tobacco products	5.66	18.03	12.28	25.60[8]	26.47	20.00	15.25	6.00	16.67	13.04	10.70	13.79

Notes:
[1] With the exception of ouzo, brandy and liqueurs, subject to VAT at 18 per cent.
[2] Lower rate applies to non-aged wine brandy and grappa brandy.
[3] Lower rate applies to wine less than 12 per cent alcohol by volume.
[4] Lower rate applies to still wine less than 13 per cent alcohol by volume.
[5] Lower rate applies to table wine.
[6] Higher rate applies to champagne only.
[7] Higher rate applies to cider.
[8] Includes BAPSA (Budget Annexe des Prestations Social et Agricoles)
Source: European Commission DGXXI Customs Union and Indirect Taxation Excise Duty Tables, XXI/C/2, 1987.

Proposals for excise rates

The Commission has proposed precise rates of specific duties on
alcohol and cigarettes to minimise the potential for tax-induced price
differentials. Proposed rates are shown in Table 8.7. Fixed specific
rates have been proposed on alcoholic drinks and cigarettes. In
addition, limits have been set on the *ad valorem* components of
cigarettes including VAT, and *ad valorem* rates have been chosen for
all other tobacco products. Lower rates will apply on cigars and
cigarillos than on smoking tobacco.

The approximation proposals on cigarette taxation are based on
the arithmetic average of current rates, with a large proportion in the
form of *ad valorem* tax. This will tend to reduce the ability of
countries producing high-cost cigarettes to protect domestic markets,
while supporting use of lower quality Community produced tobaccos.
However, the Commission has specifically set tobacco rates with a
view to increasing overall revenue from tobacco across the Commun-

Table 8.7   Proposed rates of excise on alcohol and tobacco in the EC (in
e.c.u.)

Alcohol

	e.c.u.
Potable spirit per hectolitre pure alcohol	1271
Intermediate products per hl pure alcohol	85
Still wine per hl volume	17
Sparkling wines per hl volume	30
Beers per degree Plato per hl at 15°C	(1.32)
At average strength of 12.5 degrees Plato	17
Tobacco	
Cigarettes per 1000	19.5
Ad valorem plus VAT (% of final price)	52–54%
Cigars and cigarillos	
Ad valorem plus VAT (% of final price)	34–36%
Smoking tobacco	
Ad valorem plus VAT (% of final price)	54–56%
Other *ad valorem* plus VAT (% of final price)	41–43%

Source: EC (1987b) *Proposals for Council Directives on VAT and Excise
Tax and Responses by UK Customs and Excise*, Com (87) 324/2/final and
Com (87) 325/2/final and Com (87) 326/2/final and Com (87) 327/2/final
and Com (87) 328/2/final of 21.8.87.

ity, in line with health proposals. The combined impact of *ad valorem* and specific changes will probably lead to increased tax rates in most member states, and subsequent price increases, but the rates of tax are expected to fall in Denmark.

Approximation of alcohol excise rates has been proposed in two forms, based on existing rates. Spirits and beers are to be taxed on alcohol content, but at different rates, and wines at a specific rate per volume without reference to alcohol content. An arithmetic average of existing rates has been used to set the rate on spirits. However, the Commission argues that a rate equal to the arithmetic average on beers and wines would lead to major disruptions in Community markets because of existing differentials. The rates on wine and beer have therefore been set to be equal per litre volume at the average strength, so that the overall tax effect is neutral. It is likely that Denmark, Ireland and the UK will reduce tax rates on all alcoholic

Table 8.8   The likely impact of EC proposals on tax harmonisation on alcohol

VAT reductions in	
Belgium	
Ireland	
Denmark	
Excise reductions (percentage change from 1987 rates on average products)	
Beer	
UK	72%
Ireland	84%
Denmark	78%
Netherlands	30%
Spirits	
UK	42%
Ireland	49%
Denmark	64%
Wines	
UK	88%
Ireland	93%
Denmark	89%
Netherlands	52%
Belgium	50%

drinks. A net reduction in tax rates on wines and beers is also likely in the Netherlands and on wine in Belgium. By comparison, tax rates will tend to increase on alcoholic drinks in Greece, Luxembourg and Spain, with higher rates on beers and wines in France and West Germany. These effects are summarised in Table 8.8 (Powell, 1988). The net effect on revenue will depend upon the responsiveness of demand to changes in price in each country, on the degree of substitution between drinks and on changes in cross-border trade which result.

THE IMPLICATION OF TAX PROPOSALS FOR EC HEALTH POLICY

The immediate implications for health from proposed changes in tax rates and structures, will depend on the impact on consumption and subsequent changes in associated mortality and morbidity. There may also be consequences associated with changes in the joint consumption of alcohol with tobacco products. However, reductions in tax, when other factors influencing consumption are constant, are likely to result in lower prices and increased consumption rates.

Tax rates and prices could rise on tobacco products in most member states as a result of the proposals. However, increased consumption of tobacco may result in Denmark, where tax is expected to fall, and where consumption rates on cigarettes have been increasing. If increasing trends in consumption in countries like Greece are not related to price, but to rising incomes, increased tax rates may not reduce consumption.

Reductions in the tax incidence on alcohol are expected in Denmark, Ireland, Belgium, the UK and the Netherlands. If prices fall as a result, consumption of individual drink types will probably increase. *Per capita* consumption of pure alcohol may also increase, given the weight of tax reductions on wines and spirits in these countries, and the relatively low *per capita* rates obtaining at current tax levels. Increased rates of *per capita* consumption of pure alcohol have been associated with rising levels of harm.

In the longer run, the purpose of tax harmonisation is to remove internal barriers and extend free trade. If successful, tax harmonisation should lead to increased trade in alcohol and tobacco products, given other factors, and increased consumption within the Community. These goals run in direct opposition to the existing targets of

European health policy, particularly in relation to alcohol consumption. If increased trade results in higher consumption levels and increased levels of harm, the costs to the European Community should be balanced against the gains in terms of trade wealth. Costs may take the form of tangible increased expenditure on health care and in lost productivity, but also in the form of intangible costs to individuals through ill health and death (Maynard and Powell, 1985). The benefits of increased trade in alcohol and tobacco to EC wealth and growth may be reduced or even be outweighed by the costs of adverse consequences.

In addition to the counteracting effects of health consequences there is limited evidence to suggest that the tax harmonisation proposals will improve competition and trade within the internal markets (Lee *et al.*, 1988). A unified system of tax is required in order to remove the barriers to border controls, but differential tax rates need not distort competition. VAT and excise rates are applied in the countries where goods are sold. Only a tax on inputs into the production process would be likely to give an unfair cost advantage to inefficient producers in low tax states. However, tax differentials may lead to increased cross-border shopping, but the extent of this problem is limited. Individuals must bear the cost of travel and high tax rate states must bear the cost of lost sales. One factor might be the potential downward pressure on tax rates as countries attempt to undercut tax rates to attract cross-border shopping in an internal market. There is therefore a purpose in setting minimum tax rates rather than precise rates.

An important consequence of the proposals for tax harmonisation is the resulting restriction on fiscal sovereignty in individual member states. Because both the method of tax on wines and beers, for example, and the rates of tax have been specified, little scope is left for the use of indirect tax as an instrument of health and fiscal policy. Changes in *ad valorem* components, including VAT would allow little flexibility in tax policy. West Germany has already supported the proposals, but excise rates there are low and VAT is charged at the proposed rate. The UK and Denmark have been the strongest opponents to date. Both countries rely heavily on indirect taxation for revenue and stand to lose flexibility and fiscal choice. Recent proposals put forward by the UK in response to the EC proposals argue that market forces will tend to lead to tax harmonisation if restrictions on cross-border shopping are reduced and simpler frontier checks introduced. However, the UK now states that excise rates on alcohol and tobacco should not be left to market forces, but to individual member states because of health considerations. These proposals would tend to lead VAT rates downward towards the UK rates but leave high excise rates unaffected.

CONCLUSIONS

The current proposals put forward by the EC on tax harmonisation are intended to increase trade and consumption in all goods, but are likely to support current trends in trade in alcohol and tobacco products. The purpose of expanding trade is to increase the benefits derived from economic growth. However, trade policy should not proceed in isolation from health policy. The direct and indirect consequences of increased trade in alcohol and tobacco products on health and social welfare may counteract the increased benefits from trade. Current tax proposals are likely to result in changes in consumption which conflict with the goals of agreed international health policy. In addition, member states will be restricted in their ability to choose tax as an implement to achieve agreed targets, and future health policy will be constrained. Tax proposals should be assessed in the light of prevention health policy requirements and also in relation to the impact of past and future trade policy. The EC must accept the inherent conflict between the goals of health and trade policy and seek to establish a co-ordinated approach under the Treaty of Rome. However, this cannot be achieved without further investigation of the substitution effects in consumption and production of alcohol and tobacco, both within and between different states as a result of tax changes, and an amendment to the bias on economic goals within the Treaty of Rome.

References

Abel-Smith, B. (1983) *Cost Constraints in Health Care*. Occasional Papers on Social Administration, No. 7, NCVO, London.
Abel-Smith, B. and Maynard, A. (1978) *The Organisation, Financing and Cost of Health Care in the EC*, Commission of the EC, Social Policy Series No. 36, Brussels.
Davies, P. and Walsh, D. (1983) *Alcohol Policies and Alcohol Control in Europe* (London: Croom Helm).
Dutch Distillers (1986) *How Many Alcoholic Beverages are being Consumed throughout the World?*, Produktschap voor Gestilleerde Dranken: Schiedam, Holland.

EC (1982) *Communication (82) 61 final* (Brussels: European Commission).

EC (1985) *Completing the Internal Market*. White Paper from the Commission to the European Council, June (Brussels: European Commission).

EC (1986) *Europe Against Cancer*. Communication (86) 717 final (Brussels: European Commission).

EC (1987) *Europeans and the Prevention of Cancer: A Public Opinion Survey*, Working Document of the Services of the EC, 30 September 1987 (Brussels: European Commission).

Lee, C., Pearson, M. and Smith, S. (1988) *Fiscal Harmonisation: An Analysis of the European Commission's Proposals*, Institute for Fiscal Studies, Report Series No. 28, London.

Maynard, A. and Powell, M. (1985) 'Addiction Policies, There's No Such Thing as a Free Lunch', *British Journal of Addiction*, vol. 80.

Powell, M. (1987) 'Data Note – Alcohol Data in the European Community', *British Journal of Addiction*, vol. 82, pp. 559–66.

Powell, M. (1988) 'Alcohol and Tobacco Tax in the European Community, Data Note 15', *British Journal of Addiction*, vol. 83, pp. 971–8.

Tobacco World, Various issues containing figures from the International Maxwell Reports.

WHO (1980) *European Strategy for Health for All*, Agreed 30th Session of the Regional Committee (Eur/RC30/8).

WHO (1984) *Regional Targets in support of the Regional Strategy for Health for All*, 34th Session of the Regional Committee, (EUR/RC34/7) Rev. 1 and (EUR/RC34/13).

9 The Politics of the Market

Rob Baggott

In most countries today alcoholic drink and tobacco can be classified as legal addictions. In such cases the manufacture, consumption and sale of these products are not prohibited outright. Instead, the state seeks to regulate and restrict production, sale and use, while at the same time attempting to discourage, monitor and treat misuse. This approach gives rise to a complex business and political environment, in which legitimate market forces interact with the political system. In order to clarify and explain some of the implications of 'the politics of the market' for the prevention of alcohol and tobacco-related problems, this chapter outlines the main characteristics of the alcohol and tobacco markets and examines the four main groups of actors in the political environment: the alcohol and tobacco industries; the consumers and the general public; the anti-alcohol misuse and the anti-smoking lobbies; and the government and other political institutions.

THE ALCOHOL AND TOBACCO MARKETS

The main features of the alcohol and tobacco markets are; private production for profit; diversification and concentration of production; macroeconomic importance; large and mature product markets; and externalities of consumption.

Private ownership and profit

In the UK both alcoholic drinks and tobacco are produced for profit by privately owned companies. This has been the case since 1971 when state management of the drinks industry in a small number of areas (Carlisle, Gretna and Cromarty Firth) ended. Full scale nationalisation of the drinks industry was on the agenda during the First World War, but never materialised. Even so in a number of other

148

countries today, including capitalist countries, alcohol and tobacco industries are in state ownership. Examples include Norway's wines and spirits industry, and Italy's tobacco industry.

It would be impossible here to go into the highly ideological debate about the comparative performance of state and private enterprises. Suffice it to say that there is little evidence to suggest that ownership makes a big difference to the level of alcohol misuse and smoking in the country in question. This is largely because, particularly in capitalist states, most public enterprises are generally market oriented anyway. As a result the objectives of most state-owned alcohol and tobacco firms are broadly in line with their private sector counterparts.

Even so public ownership does appear to give more scope for the introduction of social objectives alongside commercial targets. For example 20 per cent of the profits made by Norway's nationally owned wines and spirits monopoly are channelled into prevention and treatment programmes (Davies and Walsh, 1983). However, the actual extent to which this kind of potential is exploited is in most cases limited.

Although public ownership does have this potential, it would not be true to say that private ownership precludes the achievement of social objectives. It is possible within the framework of the private market to give incentives and disincentives, through subsidies and taxation for example, in an attempt to encourage and discourage certain forms of business activity which are socially harmful. Also, it should be remembered that private companies have public images, which if tarnished could have implications for long-term profitability.

Diversification and concentration of producers

Alcohol and tobacco companies have diversified in recent years. In the UK alcoholic drinks market there has been a considerable amount of internal diversification. The most marked trend has been the movement of brewers into wines and spirits, largely due to the relative decline of their own sector. Drinks companies have also expanded their alcohol related retail operations, and this has led more recently to a movement into leisure services. Diversification is greatest among the larger drinks companies (Company Reports 1987). In 1986 the top five British drinks companies derived 71 per cent of their profits from alcohol. For the smaller companies alcohol contributes anywhere between 80 per cent and 100 per cent of total profits.

Tobacco companies have diversified to a much greater extent. Less than half of the profits (42 per cent) made by the top four British tobacco companies in 1986 was derived from tobacco. Diversification by tobacco companies has often involved a movement into areas with little obvious relation to tobacco. British American Tobacco for example is involved in financial services and non-food retailing; Gallaher in engineering, office products and optical services.

As well as being increasingly diversified, the largest alcohol and tobacco companies dominate their domestic markets (Booth *et al.*, 1986). This is particularly the case in tobacco, where the market for cigarettes is dominated by three companies holding over 90 per cent of the market. Large producers also capture the market in beer, where the top seven companies are responsible for around 85 per cent of the market (*The Economist*, 4 May 1985, pp. 78–9). The wines and spirits markets are more competitive, though even here the diversification of the larger brewers into these sectors has increased concentration.

One reason for the concentration of production in beer and cigarettes has been the low level of imports. Beer imports have stayed below 6 per cent of domestic sales, and until the 1980s cigarette imports did not achieve a 1 per cent market share. Increasingly, though, alcohol and tobacco markets are becoming international in scope (*The Economist*, 16 April 1988, pp. 75–6). '1992' may give further impetus to this trend.

In contrast the retail trade in alcohol and tobacco appears to be much more fragmented than the production side. Alcohol is sold in on-licensed premises, like public houses, restaurants and hotels (99 600 in Britain in 1980); off-licensed premises like supermarkets, grocery stores and specialist off-licences (42 200 in 1980); and registered clubs (29 600) (Brewers Society, 1983a). But the retail trade in alcohol is not as atomistic as it could be, for two reasons. First the licensing system regulates the ability to retail alcohol and presumably limits to some extent the overall number of outlets. Secondly, the brewers' ownership of licensed premises leads to a considerable degree of concentration. Brewers own over 60 per cent of on-licensed premises and just under 10 per cent of off-licensed establishments (Brewers Society, 1983b).

Compared with alcohol the retail tobacco trade is highly diffuse. This is because there is no longer a licensing system restricting permission to sell tobacco. Moreover there is less ownership of the retail trade by the tobacco manufacturers (though there is some integration – for example Gallaher owns a newagent chain and a number of tobacco kiosks).

Macroeconomic importance

A further feature of the alcohol and tobacco industries is their importance to the economy. This is summarised in Table 9.1. In addition to these statistics one has to be aware of the importance of the alcohol and tobacco industries to other sectors like engineering, agriculture, packaging, and advertising. A few examples illustrate this. Around a fifth of UK barley production and around two thirds of domestic hop production is used by British brewers and distillers. On average this represents around 6 per cent of the value of British crop production, and 2 per cent of the agricultural output. Another industry whose fortunes are closely related to both alcohol and tobacco is advertising. Approximately 5.4 per cent of press and television advertising expenditure is attributable to alcohol and tobacco.

Table 9.1   The economic significance of the alcohol and tobacco industries in the UK (1986)

	Alcohol	Tobacco	Comb
Number of companies in top 50	4	3	7
Profits from production (£m)	1300	814	2114
Employment (000)	512	16.9	529
Indirect taxation as percentage of exchequer revenue	4.5	4.1	8.6
Percentage of visible exports (£m)	1.8	0.5	2.3
Percentage of consumer spending	7.4	8.3	10.7

Sources: Company Reports 1987; *The Times* Top 1000 Companies; Central Statistical Office, *UK National Accounts;* Department of Employment, *Employment Gazette*; Department of Trade and Industry, *Overseas Trade Statistics.*

Large, mature markets

The alcohol and tobacco markets are both well differentiated. Alcohol is divided into a number of sectors; beer, wine, spirits, cider. Beer is still the largest single sector, accounting for 54 per cent of spending, while the market share of spirits is currently around 24 per cent. The share of beer and spirits has fallen over the last twenty or so years as a result of the growth in the consumption of wine and cider, which now account for around a quarter of expenditure (Godfrey *et al.*, 1986).

Within each sector drinks can be further subdivided, (for example red and white wine, beer and lager) and are differentiated even more by branding. Branding is the main form of differentiation in the tobacco market, in view of the dominance of manufactured cigarettes. Though in recent years cigars have increased their share of the tobacco market by weight (Godfrey *et al.*, 1986).

Both alcohol and tobacco are large markets. But where the market for alcoholic drinks in the UK has grown dramatically over the last thirty or so years, the tobacco market has declined. Expenditure on alcohol doubled between 1960 and 1984, while the expenditure on tobacco fell by 22 per cent over the same period (Godfrey *et al.*, 1986). Alcohol is consumed by 90 per cent of the adult population, while tobacco is now smoked by a minority, around a third of the adult population (OPCS, 1984; 1985).

Externalities

The final and perhaps the most important characteristic of the alcohol and tobacco markets is externalities. The consumption of both products gives rise to social problems, such as ill-health, which can be seen as external costs imposed by the industry (and also the consumer) on society. Alcohol and tobacco-related problems can be costed. The most comprehensive estimates available put the annual cost of alcohol misuse at around £1900m and the costs of smoking at as much as £500m (Maynard *et al.*, 1987; Hardman, personal correspondence).

There are also significant differences in the chain of causation between alcohol consumption and social problems on the one hand and tobacco consumption and its problems on the other. The relationship between smoking and health is relatively straightforward. We can identify smokers and we can measure their health. As a result scientific opinion with a few exceptions overwhelmingly supports a positive relationship between smoking and ill-health (Collingridge and Reeve, 1986). But not all the adverse consequences produce such a consensus. The effect of smoking on non-smokers for example is more difficult to establish accurately, as is the role of cigarettes in fire accidents.

Alcohol problems generally tend to have a more complex aetiology, because alcohol tends to interact with a greater number of other factors. Road accidents for example may involve alcohol, but they also involve roads, cars, and other people. Yet this is perhaps the most straightforward chain of causation in the family of alcohol-related problems. The precise role of alcohol in violent crime, for example, is even more complex.

THE ALCOHOL AND TOBACCO INDUSTRY

The focus of this section is the main implications of the nature of the alcohol and tobacco markets for first, the political stance and second, the political organisation of the alcohol and tobacco industries.

Political stance

The differences in the nature of the externalities help shape the stance taken by each industry when they defend their markets against intervention. The close statistical relationship between smoking and ill-health has almost paradoxically prevented an admission by the tobacco industry that its products are harmful. Such an admission could further encourage legal action by those suffering from smoking-related diseases. Instead the tobacco industry continues to publicly deny any link between smoking and ill-health.

The drinks industry on the other hand does accept that alcohol is a factor behind a number of social problems. But it can do this because the evidence linking the level of alcohol consumption and harm is much more circumstantial. The drinks industry is also able to emphasise other factors, for example human nature, in the causation of such problems, while the overall level of alcohol consumption in society is played down almost as a secondary factor. The industry then goes on to argue that a vast majority of drinkers benefit from alcohol consumption without coming to any obvious harm.

These public stances feed through into collective aims and action, though not always in a straightforward way. For example, while the tobacco industry's public stance would appear to make it opposed to virtually all types of government intervention, it is in practice willing to negotiate with government on issues such as the restriction of tobacco advertising for example.

The alcohol industry's main aim has been to project an image of public responsibility. Its public opposition to intervention has therefore been much more selective, focusing upon measures aimed at reducing or restricting overall alcohol consumption. At the same time the drinks industry tries to protect its public image by supporting health education about alcohol, policies to deal with alcoholism in the workplace, and measures aimed at preventing drinking and driving (see Brewers Society, 1982; 1983b).

Each industry demonstrates a fairly high degree of cohesion in the face of pressure to regulate their products and markets. In both industries retailers and producers combine to resist policies which they feel will undermine their economic welfare. There are some exceptions however. The public house landlords' associations have in recent years called for restrictions on the growth of off-licence outlets. In this they agree with some parts of the alcohol misuse lobby, although the main concern of the landlords is the threat which off-licences pose to their livelihood. Their view, however is opposed by the rest of the industry which basically sees the expansion of outlets as leading to increased sales. Another source of conflict can be found in the tobacco industry where the increase in imports in recent years appears to have strained the relationship between tobacco importers and domestic manufacturers, thus undermining to an extent the basis for cooperation between them.

For the most part then the alcohol and tobacco industries have a clear incentive to oppose policy ideas put forward by others. Diversification into other markets ensures that not all the eggs are in one basket, but this does not appear to have lessened the vigour with which these industries defend themselves. Profits (or economic surpluses in the context of state-owned enterprises), livelihoods and jobs provide a firm basis for mobilisation. Such economic fruits will not be easily given up by those who currently benefit from them.

Political organisation and leverage

The concentration of market power facilitates strong political organisation. In the tobacco industry the manufacturers, through their association the Tobacco Advisory Council, have taken a lead role in defending the industry (Baggott, 1987a). This is largely because of the fragmentation of the retail trade, which makes it difficult to organise.

In the case of alcohol it is also the producer associations such as the Wines and Spirits Association, the Scotch Whisky Association and the Brewers Society which have taken on similar responsibilities for defending the industry as a whole. In particular the brewers appear to have a major co-ordinating role. There are four possible reasons for this. First, beer is the largest single sector in the market. Second, the brewers are more heavily dependent on domestic markets than on export markets, compared with the distillers. Third, they have considerable influence over the retail trade through the tied house system. Finally the diversification of brewery firms into wines and spirits has given them some influence over the policies of the trade association which represents these other sectors.

The producers of alcohol and tobacco also represent the wealthiest part of the two industries and this further explains their lead role. They have a lot to lose. Furthermore their wealth ensures that they dominate the industry's political campaigns. In addition the economic leverage of these industries ensures contact with government and politicians. As already demonstrated, alcohol and tobacco make important contributions to shareholders' wealth, jobs, exports, national revenue, and the wider economy. The producers are at the apex of a sizeable economic and political interest that cannot be ignored by politicians and senior government officials.

THE CONSUMERS

In many ways the consumers are at the centre of a number of political and economic forces. It is consumer behaviour which ultimately has to be changed if alcohol and tobacco-related problems are to be diminished. Yet without consumers there would be no market for alcohol and tobacco. Both these points illustrate the potential power of consumers in relation to the government on the one hand and the producers on the other.

Consumers and government

Consumers are often in conflict with both government and the industry. Consumers may oppose government policies and could refuse to co-operate with the spirit of legislation. Perhaps the most extreme example of non-cooperation in practice was the prohibition period in the United States (Coffey, 1975). But consumer consent is also crucial to the success of a range of less draconian measures. Banning smoking in public places, is one example where only mild sanctions can be realistically imposed on those who disobey the rules.

Other policies can still be effective in spite of consumer hostility. Taxation on alcohol and tobacco, as a means of discouraging consumption, may be unpopular with consumers, but there is little they can do but grumble. However even in this case, if the tax increases are significant, practices such as smuggling and illicit production may appear to thwart the original policy aims. Furthermore if policies are unpopular, this may ultimately rebound on the government through the ballot box.

Consumers, and the public generally, have to be convinced of the need for alcohol and tobacco policies. Their support and consent will be more forthcoming if two conditions hold. First, they must perceive alcohol and tobacco-related problems as social problems requiring a government-backed solution. Secondly, they must believe that the measures proposed will be effective in reducing these problems.

Consumers and industry

Consumers interests conflict with industry, on the other hand, in many ways. The market power of the large manufacturers suggests the possibility of consumer exploitation, particularly higher prices. Though ironically higher prices, by discouraging consumption may reduce alcohol and tobacco-related problems, and this may in the long run be to the benefit of consumers and industry.

Consumer organisations in the alcohol field are publicly critical of the large breweries in particular. The Campaign for Real Ale (CAMRA) for example has in recent years challenged brewery policies on price, the quality of beer, and the closure of 'traditional pubs'. But consumer organisations are not the only source of public pressure. Another is that mass, unorganised consumer tastes cannot always be shaped and predicted to order. For example the 'health and fitness' vogue, which has become fashionable in Britain in the last few years, has no doubt caused some headaches for alcohol and tobacco producers, who are well aware of the health implications of their products. Nevertheless the clever marketing of 'light beers' and 'slim cigarettes', illustrates the extent to which these industries can accommodate changes in consumer tastes articulated through the market.

Consumer weakness

As the previous point suggests, consumers are not always able to fully exploit their potential economic and political power. Consumer sovereignty in the marketplace can be undermined by advertising and other promotional techniques (Packard, 1957). Moreover, both alcohol and tobacco products are addictive, and addiction often begins at a relatively early age. This further undermines the conventional assumptions of rational consumer choice.

Similarly, from a political perspective there can detected a number of factors which undermine the power of the consumer. First, consumers are fragmented and difficult to organise. There is a clear incentive for consumers to 'free ride' – that is allow others to represent their interests while personally not contributing to the costs of collective action (Olson, 1965). Secondly, the alcohol and tobacco consumer groups which do emerge are as a result small (CAMRA for example has around 20 000 members, a small proportion of the millions of beer drinkers), possibly unrepresentative of mass consumer opinion, and of limited financial strength. In this context it is interesting to note that FOREST, the smokers group which campaigns against smoking restrictions, is sponsored by the tobacco industry itself.

THE ANTI-SMOKING AND ALCOHOL MISUSE LOBBIES

Although strictly speaking not part of the market, being neither buyer nor seller, the anti-smoking and the alcohol misuse lobbies nevertheless affect the market for alcohol and tobacco in two main ways. First of all their campaigns can have a direct impact on consumer attitudes and behaviour. For example it is widely believed that the periodic reports by the Royal College of Physicians (1962; 1971; 1977; 1983) on smoking and health, and the publicity given to these reports, may have discouraged smoking. The same may also apply to the medical professions' reports on alcohol misuse (Royal College of Psychiatrists, 1979; 1986; Royal College of General Practitioners, 1986; Royal College of Physicians, 1987). The publicity given to anti-smoking and alcohol misuse campaigns can therefore be seen as negative advertising, reducing demand in the market. But it may also have the effect of educating the consumer and the public to accept new policy initiatives to tackle alcohol and tobacco-related problems.

The second way in which the activities of these lobbies can affect the market is through the political system. Pressure on government and Parliament, if it is strong enough, can ultimately lead to state intervention in the alcohol and tobacco markets.

Motivation and organisation

What motivates these lobbies? The anti-smoking lobby seeks to restrict smoking in view of the relationship between smoking and ill-health. Indeed, the lobby consists wholly of health pressure groups; the British Medical Association (BMA), the Royal College of Physicians (RCP), and Action on Smoking and Health (ASH) (Baggott, 1987a). The motiviation of the alcohol misuse lobby is more complex (Baggott, 1987b). Public health appears to be a primary concern, given the relationship between alcohol and ill-health and injury. But the preservation of public order is also a major motivation. A third area of concern is the protection of public morality. Though in today's more liberal society this latter considera-tion has not yet acquired the importance it held when Victorian values reigned supreme.

In view of the above the alcohol misuse lobby is more diverse and fragmented than the anti-smoking lobby. It includes the representat-ives of the caring professions and law enforcement professions, as well as the temperance movement and voluntary organisations. There is also less direction within this lobby. The groups within it frequently push in different directions and have rarely in the past co-ordinated their activities. One reason for this lack of co-ordination lies in differences of opinion. There has been considerable division for example on the question of policies aimed at limiting overall alcohol consumption, although in recent years opinion on this issue has hardened, and most within the lobby now support this approach.

The fragmentation of the alcohol misuse lobby has been its major weakness in the past (Baggott, 1986), but it has also suffered from other problems. Politically the lobby has not had a good public image. In particular its association with the temperance movement has given it something of a 'killjoy persona'. Moreover, alcohol abuse has not been a popular cause and it has proved difficult to motivate public support for both preventive and treatment policies.

On the credit side, the lobby contains a number of well connected high status professional groups like the police, magistrates', and doctors' associations. There has also been a growth in contacts between the lobby and Parliament, resulting in a growing interest by the latter. But the economic and political leverage of the lobby in no way matches that of the drinks industry. As a result the achievements of the alcohol misuse lobby have been fairly limited.

The anti-smoking lobby on the other hand has been a more effective lobby, in spite of facing a similarly powerful adversary. The lobby is integrated and has been well co-ordinated, particularly in recent years. It has good contacts with central government, largely through the Department of Health and Social Security (DHSS), and with Parliament. On the whole the anti-smoking lobby has been highly successful in getting policies on to the political agenda (Baggott, 1987a). Even so it has been less successful in promoting specific policies (such as an advertising ban on tobacco products) than similar lobbies abroad which have faced a weaker tobacco industry, as in Norway for example (Baggott, 1988a).

Relationship with industry

The relationship between the tobacco industry and the smoking and health lobby is extremely hostile. This is largely because the policies proposed by the latter directly harm the economic interest of the former.

In the case of alcohol the situation is different. As I have already pointed out the drinks industry supports policies such as alcohol education, medical research into the causes of individual alcohol problems, and programmes aimed at identifying problem drinkers. The drinks industry is willing to fund this kind of activity and has a good relationship with those within the alcohol misuse lobby who are engaged in this area. On the other hand the industry is hostile to those that stand in the way of its commercial objectives and this includes those groups which support policies aimed at restricting the total level of alcohol consumption in an attempt to limit overall misuse.

THE GOVERNMENT

It is the task of government when formulating public policy to balance the interests of the industries, the consumers, and the anti-smoking and alcohol misuse lobbies. Its ability to do this however is frustrated by four factors: departmental divisions, party divisions, lack of Parliamentary consensus, and a lack of public consensus.

Departmental divisions

Government departments take different views on the question of regulating alcohol and tobacco (see Baggott, 1986; 1987a; Taylor, 1984). The health departments generally desire greater control, while the economic departments (Employment, Trade and Industry, Agriculture and the Treasury) generally oppose policies which restrict alcohol and tobacco consumption.

These conflicts of interest within central government prevent the emergence of a coherent stance. They also help to explain a number of contradictions in government policy. For example the government gives financial support to tobacco companies at the same time as backing anti-smoking campaigns. A more recent contradiction was the decision to relax the licensing laws prior to a review of alcohol policy.

Party divisions

Divisions within government are compounded by divisions within governing parties. Alcohol misuse and smoking are cross-party issues. Within the same party, one will find some politicians who will oppose policies aimed at restricting the alcohol and tobacco markets, and some who support such intervention. Even the Conservative Party, which receives around 5 per cent of its company contributions from alcohol companies (Baggott, 1987b), contains such prominent anti-alcohol campaigners as Sir Bernard Braine and Sir George Young.

Division within a governing party creates great uncertainty. The main problem facing governments is that party discipline with Parliament – which normally ensures that backbench MPs support the Party leadership's policies – cannot be relied upon. This raises the prospect of an embarrassing defeat for the leadership. As a result alcohol and tobacco issues are rarely the subject of government legislation, except where there is a clear Parliamentary consensus on a specific matter.

Lack of Parliamentary consensus

A Parliamentary consensus rarely forms around alcohol and tobacco policies. One exception was the drinking and driving legislation of the 1960s where a visible majority of MPs of all parties supported the introduction of the breathalyser (Baggot, 1988b). More recently the government perceived similar support for a relaxation of the licensing laws. But such a consensus is exceptional. MPs are generally divided on alcohol and tobacco issues. Some MPs feel more sympathy for the industries, as a result of constituency, personal economic interests, and political contacts. Around 47 MPs have some obvious connection with the drinks industry (Triple A, 1987), while some claim that the tobacco industry may be able to rely on the support of as many as 100 MPs (*The Times*, 17 November, 1981, p. 2). Other MPs are linked with the anti-smoking and alcohol misuse; 48 MPs are members of the all-party group on alcohol misuse (Triple A., 1987); while the number of MPs supporting the anti-smoking cause has been put at around 100 (Baggott, 1987a). A further factor which inhibits the formation of a Parliamentary consensus, is the absence of public consensus on most of these issues.

Lack of public consensus

The lack of public consensus on alcohol and tobacco issues creates a number of difficulties for government. Not only does public opinion reflect in the public stance of many MPs, it also raises the problems of unpopularity and non-compliance mentioned earlier. Occasionally a consensus does emerge, again, for example, the overwhelming public support for restrictions on drinking and driving, but this is comparatively rare. In recent years, however, there have been sign of increasing public support for anti-smoking policies. If this trend continues a more courageous response from government may be expected (Leedham, 1987).

The four factors mentioned tend to push alcohol and tobacco policy down the political agenda. Government sees that it has a lot to lose and little to gain politically by pursuing policies which provoke a hostile response from the industries or from consumers. Yet at the same time government cannot evade its responsibilities. Indeed, it has a key role to play in shaping opinions and improving public understanding about the nature of alcohol and tobacco problems and the policies needed to deal with these problems.

One suggestion, which has been made on a number of occasions in the past, is that the government should establish special agencies to co-ordinate and formulate policy on alcohol and tobacco. Similar bodies exist in a number of other countries. Norway for example has special agencies to formulate, co-ordinate and review both alcohol and tobacco policies.

In the British context co-ordination of alcohol and tobacco policy is performed by interdepartmental committees of officials and by cabinet subcommittees. More recently a special ministerial committee has been established to co-ordinate policy on alcohol (Home Office, 1987). Another idea, however, would be to create entirely new agencies independent of existing government departments. The members of this agency could be directly appointed by the Prime Minister, or by a number of departmental ministers, but should not be seen as representative of any particular vested interest. The membership should be multidisciplinary and would also include civil servants seconded from all government departments. The task of the agencies would be to formulate strategies aimed at preventing alcohol and tobacco problems. In compiling these studies, the agencies would consult and involve all interests, and would make the findings public knowledge. The agencies could also be given the responsibility for health education campaigns and executive powers to regulate advertising and promotion of alcohol and tobacco.

The establishment of a new non-departmental agency goes against the grain of current government policy (Cabinet Office, 1985). However, the deregulation of British Gas and British Telecom has led to the creation of new non-Ministerial departments charged with protecting the public's welfare. An Office of Alcohol and Tobacco Regulation (or Office of Legal Addictions perhaps?) may therefore fit more easily into the current administrative vogue than a new non-departmental body.

CONCLUSION

This analysis has shown that there is no simple solution to the political problems of dealing with legal addictions. However, by examining the complexity of the business and political environment it is possible to be aware of some of the pitfalls of simplistic prescriptions. The central argument is that economic and political realities have to be faced by those seeking to reduce alcohol and tobacco-related problems. If they are to formulate an effective strategy, the following points should be borne in mind.

First policy makers have to be aware of the commercial environment. In particular they cannot ignore market forces. Wherever possible a strategy should attempt to work with the market rather than against it. This could involve reducing the profitability of alcohol and tobacco production through the tax system and encouraging diversification into less harmful products. Commercial advertising could be more extensively used to positively promote healthy activities. Alcohol advertisements for example could be positively used to discourage certain harmful drinking habits.

Second, to admit the power of market forces does not necessarily mean compliance with the demands of the industrial lobbies, influential though these may be. Especially in the case of alcohol, it is important that a degree of co-operation be sought wherever possible. The drinks industry is highly conscious of its public image, and could be persuaded to compromise on a range of policies which might be in its long-term interest. There is less scope for compromising with the tobacco industry, though the threat of draconian measures may provoke a more co-operative response. The present system of voluntary restriction of cigarette advertising illustrates that the industry is prepared to negotiate.

Third, each industry may be economically and politically powerful, but they are not monolithic. Power is concentrated amongst producers and there is a degree of conflict within the industry. This raises the possibility of fragmentation where interests diverge, and could undermine the power of the industry lobbies. Any strategy should therefore avoid uniting the industry in question, and ideally should have strong appeal for some sectors.

Fourth, no strategy can succeed without public support. Hence it is important that public pressure be mobilised and that policies be made popular. It is the anti-smoking and alcohol misuse lobbies who must play the largest role in educating public opinion, though government too must be involved. In so doing they must be careful not to alienate the consumer and the general public. Instead they must continue to build public support by creating consumer awareness about the range of problems associated with alcohol and tobacco consumption. The lobbies must moreover show themselves to be public interest groups, not merely 'killjoys' or 'moralisers'. Such images could stick and be very damaging to their credibility.

Fifth, the organisation of the lobbies is also a key factor. The alcohol misuse and anti-smoking lobbies must build a broad coalition of support for their aims. They should key into other more emotive issues like child health, hard drugs, violent crime, and fire accidents, stressing the relationship with alcohol or tobacco. This may bring in other groups who may not at first see the relevance of alcohol and tobacco problems for their particular cause or interest. Yet at the same time a coherent organisation is needed to present a united platform to the public and to politicians.

Also, structural reform is needed to deal with the problems in hand. Present political structures are not conducive to the formation of coherent policies on alcohol and tobacco. The division of governmental functions and responsibilities on alcohol and tobacco appears to be particularly damaging, and there is a need to reorganise these functions, perhaps under an Office of Alcohol and Tobacco. Furthermore, there is a strong case for more intergovernmental co-operation, particularly in view of the international nature of alcohol and tobacco markets.

Ultimately political will is the main key to action on public health generally and legal addictions in particular (Baggott, 1986, 1987b). Politicians have to be persuaded to take risks and to think long term if anything is to be achieved. There are signs that this is now beginning to happen. A number of ministers are now making noises about alcohol and tobacco, and the government is reviewing its policy on alcohol. There is however at present little sign of a comprehensive strategy on legal addictions emerging. This analysis has shown that such an approach is urgently needed not only to deal with the problems of alcohol and tobacco but to tackle the political complexities of the addiction market.

References

Baggott, R. (1986) 'Alcohol, Politics and Social Policy', *Journal of Social Policy*, vol. 15, pp. 467–88.
Baggott, R. (1987a) 'Government-Industry Relations in Britain: The Regulation of the Tobacco Industry', *Policy and Politics*, vol. 15, pp. 137–46.
Baggott, R. (1987b) *The Politics of Public Health: Alcohol, Politics and Social Policy*, University of Hull Phd Thesis (unpublished).

Baggott, R. (1988a) *Health v Wealth: The Politics of Smoking in Norway and the UK*, Strathclyde Papers on Government and Politics No. 57, University of Strathclyde.

Baggott, R. (1988b) 'Drinking and Driving: the Politics of Social Regulation', *Teaching Politics*, vol. 17, pp. 66–85.

Booth, M., Hardman, G. and Hartley, K. (1986) 'Data Note 6: The UK Alcohol and Tobacco Industries', *British Journal of Addiction*, vol. 81, pp. 825–30.

Brewers Society (1982) *Action on Alcohol Abuse: A Guide to Projects Funded by the Brewing Industry* (London: Brewers Society).

Brewers Society (1983a) *UK Statistical Review* (London: Brewing Publications).

Brewers Society (1983b) *A Strategy for the Prevention of Problem Drinking* (London: Brewers Society).

Cabinet Office and HM Treasury (1985) *Non-Departmental Bodies: A Guide for Departments* (London: HMSO).

Coffey, J. M. (1975) *The Long Thirst* (New York: Norton).

Collingridge, D. and Reeve, C. (1986) *Science Speaks to Power* (London: Pinter).

Davies, P. and Walsh, D. (1983) *Alcohol Problems and Alcohol Control in Europe* (London: Croom Helm).

Godfrey, C., Hardman, G. and Maynard, A. (1986) 'Data Note 2: Measuring UK Alcohol and Tobacco Consumption', *British Journal of Addiction*, vol. 81, pp. 287–93.

Home Office (1987) *Press Release*, 18 September.

Leedham, W. (1987) 'Data note 10: Alcohol, Tobacco and Public Opinion', *British Journal of Addiction*, vol. 82, pp. 935–40.

Maynard, A., Hardman, G. and Whelan, A. (1987) 'Data note 9: measuring the Social Costs of Addictive Substances', *British Journal of Addiction*, vol. 82, pp. 701–6.

Office of Population Censuses and Surveys (1984) *General Household Survey* (London: HMSO).

Office of Population Censuses and Surveys (1985) *General Household Survey*. OPCS Monitor GHS 85.2 (London: HMSO).

Olson, M. (1965) *The Logic of Collective Action* (Cambridge (Mass.): Havard University Press).

Packard, V. (1957) *The Hidden Persuaders* (London: Longman).

Royal College of General Practitioners (1986) *Alcohol: A Balanced View* Reports from General Practice No. 24.

Royal College of Physicians (1962) *Smoking and Health* (London: Pitman).

Royal College of Physicians (1971) *Smoking and Health Now* (London: Pitman).

Royal College of Physicians (1977) *Smoking or Health?* (London: Pitman).

Royal College of Physicians (1983) *Health or Smoking?* (London: Pitman).

Royal College of Physicians (1987) *The Medical Consequences of Alcohol Abuse: A Great and Growing Evil* (London: Tavistock).

Royal College of Psychiatrists (1979) *Alcohol and Alcoholism* (London: Tavistock).

Royal College of Psychiatrists (1986) *Alcohol: Our Favourite Drug* (London: Tavistock).
Taylor, P. (1984) *Smoke Ring* (London: Bodley Head).
Triple, A. (Action on Alcohol Abuse) (1987) *Personal Correspondence*.

10 Industry, Employment and Control Policy

Keith Hartley

INTRODUCTION: WHY FOCUS ON THE INDUSTRY?

If society and governments are to make informed choices about prevention policy, they need information on the gains and losses (benefits and costs) from different policies. Who gains, who loses and by how much? In principle, governments can be viewed as collectors and assemblers of all relevant information on the size of benefits and costs, on the basis of which public choices are made about the social desirability of various prevention policies. However, some of the information for public choices will be supplied by those groups most likely to be affected (favourably or unfavourably) by policies aimed at reducing drinking and smoking. Interest groups in the political market-place will try to influence and modify government policy in their favour. Those groups likely to lose from, say, higher taxes or advertising controls, will obviously oppose such policies and will form barriers to change.

Supporters of measures to reduce drinking and smoking cannot ignore the implications of such policies for the firms supplying these products in the UK alcohol and tobacco industries. Amongst the suppliers, the groups likely to lose from prevention measures comprise the managers, workers and shareholders in the UK alcohol and tobacco industries, their suppliers of equipment, materials and services both at home and overseas, together with the advertising agencies and retail outlets such as pubs, shops and supermarkets. Questions arise as to how these supplying groups are likely to respond and adjust to policies aimed at reducing their domestic sales.

Immediately new prevention policies are expected or are introduced, various interest groups representing the industry will lobby the government to modify its policies. Trade associations and unions will threaten plant closures and job losses, especially in high unemployment areas and in marginal constituencies. References will be made to the adverse effects on the balance of payments and to

167

reduced profitability resulting in lower investment leading to a further decline in the UK's manufacturing base. While opposing prevention policies, firms will also respond and adjust so as to minimise the adverse effects on themselves. For example, firms might shift the burden of higher taxes to part-time and unorganised workers or to foreign suppliers rather than to UK consumers and the firms' shareholders. In response to advertising controls, firms can substitute more salesmen or sponsorship campaigns. Over time, firms will respond to actual or expected government prevention measures designed to reduce their domestic sales by seeking new markets. They can introduce new products such as low alcohol drinks or safer cigarettes, they can merge with and take-over rivals, and they can diversify into other markets in the UK and overseas.

Governments need to know how firms are likely to respond to different prevention policies. It needs to be recognised that responses and adjustments by firms can be complex, they might occur over a number of years and some responses might be both unexpected and socially undesirable. Also, it has to be recognised that the opponents of prevention policies whose future income depends on the continued sales of alcohol and tobacco have every incentive to exaggerate their adverse effects, particularly the likely job losses. Clearly, in making informed public choices, there is scope for independent analysis, critical scrutiny and empirical testing of the various claims, myths and special pleading which often dominate the debates about prevention policy. This chapter focuses on the UK alcohol and tobacco industries, showing that the supply side is an important component of the market which has been relatively neglected in the prevention debate. Three policy issues are considered:

- Are mergers and diversification a possible response to actual and expected prevention policies?
- Have mergers created large producer groups able to influence government prevention policies and are large firms in the public interest?
- Have prevention policies affected industry profitability and caused job losses?

THE UK ALCOHOL AND TOBACCO INDUSTRIES

In recent years, the UK brewing and tobacco industries have experienced a declining output and substantial job losses. By 1986, the output of the UK brewing industry was 70 per cent of its 1979 peak and employment was some 40 per cent of its 1963 level. Moreover, between 1963 and 1986, the brewing sector's share of the total output of the UK alcohol industry declined substantially, while spirits together with British wines, cider and perry increased their share of the UK industry's output (Table 10.1). Some of these changes reflect varying consumer tastes and substitution effects, further influenced by the impact of fiscal policy on relative prices in the alcohol market (Booth *et al.*, 1989).

Not surprisingly, the output of the UK tobacco industry has declined substantially. By 1986 it was slightly more than 50 per cent of its 1973 peak, with employment at 47 per cent of its 1963 level. Various explanations have been offered for this reduction in output, including the recession and unemployment in the UK, higher taxation, advertising controls, health education campaigns and competition from foreign suppliers. Clearly, the UK tobacco industry has every inducement to attribute all its problems to the British Government's taxation policy. At the same time, faced with an actual as well as possible future declining trend in cigarette sales, profit-conscious firms will search for alternative market opportunities both at home and overseas. In response to declining domestic sales, the UK tobacco industry has increased the proportion of its output for export: such a response favourably affects the economy's current performance and its balance of payments (contrary to the claims of industry). Also, as a result of mergers and take-overs, the UK tobacco companies have become large diversified groups with an extensive and varied range of other products, all of which offers some protection from the immediate impact of anti-smoking campaigns. A study of individual companies can provide insights into the size and other features of firms which are often regarded as powerful producer groups which will oppose prevention policies.

The companies

The major brewing and tobacco companies are amongst the largest enterprises in the UK. The large national brewers have their tied outlets (except for Guinness), an international business and diversification into related markets, particularly wines, spirits and hotels. The tobacco companies are all large diversified enterprises with a wide range of other activities such as engineering, financial services, luxury consumer products, optics, retailing, paper manufacturing and printing (Table 10.2).

Table 10.1 The UK alcohol and tobacco industries

Year	Brewing and malting		Spirit distilling		British wines cider and perry		Tobacco	
	Output (£m)	Employment (000s)	Output (£m)	Employment (000s)	Output (£m)	Employment (000s)	Output (£m)	Employment (000s)
1963	2993	86.8	986	16.8	67	4.2	4550	43.3
1968	3373	80.4	1279	19.9	89	4.4	4284	40.8
1970	3403	74.5	1662	22.2	124	5.2	4487	39.7
1975	3660	66.2	1678	26.0	176	5.1	4672	39.8
1980	3524	53.5	1924	26.2	208	5.0	4159	35.7
1985	2723	35.6	1486	16.4	304	4.3	3055	23.9
1986	2728	35.3	1523	16.1	305	4.1	2724	20.5

Notes: (i) Output data are in constant 1980 prices. (ii) Selected years only are shown.

Source: Census of Production, Business Statistics Office (annually).

Table 10.2   UK brewing and tobacco companies

Company	UK ranking by sales	Tur-nover (£m)	Employment (000s)	Profit rate (%)	Main activity
BAT Industries	3	13623	176.4	22.3	Tobacco, financial services, retailing, paper, packaging
Grand Metropolitan	13	5291	131.5	14.6	Hotels, consumer services, brewers, wines and spirits
Hanson Trust (Imperial)	17	4312	92.0	13.9	Industrial services, building products, tobacco, food
Allied-Lyons	23	3615	77.6	16.8	Brewers, wines, spirits, food, hotels
Gallaher	26	3405	30.3	27.0	Tobacco, optical, pumps and valves, houseware
Bass	37	2710	76.9	19.7	Brewers, soft drinks, wines and spirits merchants, hotels, holidays
Guinness	39	2602	32.1	14.6	Brewers, distillers, retailing, publishing
Whitbread	73	1554	47.7	12.4	Brewers, wines, spirits, restaurants
Rothmans	76	1467	21.8	15.9	Tobacco, luxury consumer products
Scottish and Newcastle	137	774	20.4	16.6	Brewers, wines, spirits, hotels

Note: Profit are net profits before interest and tax as a return on capital
Sources: Times 1000, 1987–88, London: Times Books. Company reports.

The current size of firms and the structure of the UK alcohol and tobacco industries are the results of firms growing through either internal expansion or mergers and takeovers. Both the alcohol and tobacco industries have been extensively involved in the acquisition of other companies, including some of the largest UK mergers. Examples are BAT–Farmers (insurance USA) in 1988, Hanson–Imperial and Guinness–Distillers in 1986, BAT–Eagle Star in 1983, together with Grand Metropolitan–Watney Mann and Imperial–Courage in the early 1970s. Interestingly, numerous studies in both the UK and the USA have found post-merger declines in performance as reflected in productivity, market share and profitability (Schmalensee, 1988).

The tobacco industry is one of the most highly concentrated industries in the UK (a 5-firm concentration ratio for output of 99 per cent). Four firms which are also large multinational corporations dominate the industry (Table 10.2). With such a high level of concentration, the acquisitions by the tobacco companies have involved diversification into completely different markets creating large conglomerates. Diversification can be explained by two factors. First, the relative profitability of tobacco has provided funds for acquisition. Second, diversification enables a firm to spread its risks and reflects the UK industry's response to the actual and expected decline in cigarette smoking, starting with the home market and the first Royal College of Physicians report in 1962 (Booth *et al.*, 1988). In contrast to tobacco, mergers in the UK brewing sector have had a major impact on industry structure.

Most of the mergers and take-overs in brewing during the 1960s were between firms in the same industry. Industrial concentration increased substantially between 1958 and 1968 (5-firm concentration ratio for output of 62 per cent in 1968), and there emerged a small number of large national breweries with a network of tied houses. Inevitably, the merger boom of the 1960s, the trend to increased concentration and its association with tied houses raised major policy questions about monopoly and competition in the UK brewing industry (Cmnd 659, 1989).

Acting against the public interest?

Even without using health arguments, critics of the industry can find much to support their case. Both the UK alcohol and tobacco industries are oligopolies, dominated by a small number of firms which are large both in relation to the market and in terms of absolute size (giant enterprises). Where there are small numbers of firms, there is the possibility of collusion either implicitly or explicitly through cartels and restrictive practices aimed at creating a monopoly position. Or, with oligopoly, competition usually takes non-price forms such as advertising, marketing, sponsorship and brand proliferation. Critics point to the 'excesses and wastes' of such competition (e.g. too many brands; too much wasteful advertising) and to the possibility of large-scale advertising forming a barrier to entry. An alternative view regards advertising as part of the process by which firms search the market and provide consumers with information in a world of ignorance and uncertainty. On this alternative view, markets are dynamic, competition is a continuous process and, in the absence of government support, monopoly is a temporary phenomenon which will attract profit seeking rivals (Kirzner, 1973).

The brewers are involved in a further aspect of non-price competition through their tied houses. This arrangement has been criticised as a restriction on both competition and consumer choice and as a barrier to new entry into the industry. The 1969 Monopolies Commission Report concluded that in England and Wales the tied house system operated against the public interest and it recommended a 'substantial relaxation' in the licensing system (Cmnd 216, 1969). This is an interesting recommendation in the context of current debates (1988) about the licensing laws and competition in the brewing industry. However, recent developments in economic theory stress contestability claiming that the *threat* of entry will force existing firms (even small numbers) to behave competitively. In alcohol, new entry has occurred and competition for the tied house system has emerged through the expansion of alternative outlets (e.g. supermarkets, clubs). There are, though, potential conflicts between competition policy (lower prices, greater output) and health and prevention policies. Supporters of reduced drinking and smoking might welcome the higher prices, output restriction and lack of dynamism often associated with monopoly power!

While critics of the alcohol and tobacco industries can condemn many aspects of structure, conduct and performance, they have to work within the framework of current UK monopoly and competition policy. A two-stage approach is used, concerned with identifying a monopoly situation and then determining whether it is acting against the 'public interest'. UK policy defines a monopoly as a situation where 25 per cent of the market is supplied by one firm or by a group of firms acting together or is likely to result from a proposed merger. Mergers can also be referred to the Monopolies and Mergers Commission if the assets involved exceed £30m. On this basis, the high concentration ratios in the tobacco industry suggest a monopoly situation requiring investigation (for example, Imperial and Gallaher each with over 25 per cent of the UK market: Booth *et al.*, 1986). Moreover, the tobacco industry's profitability has usually exceeded the national average which could indicate monopoly profits (Table 10.3). There are at least two possible explanations for the lack of monopoly reference to the Monopolies Commission. First, the belief that tobacco is a declining industry operating in a contestable market (for example, competition from foreign firms and Rothmans). Second, the tobacco lobby might have been successful in persuading the Government not to refer the industry to the Monopolies Commission.

Table 10.3   Profitability in selected industries

| Year | *Rate of return on capital (%)* | | |
	Brewers and distillers	*Tobacco*	*All industrial groups*
1970	14	17	14
1973	15	18	18
1976	15	18	18
1980	13	18	14
1983	15	22	15

Note: Profits before interest and tax on capital on an historic cost basis.
Source: Bank of England Quarterly Bulletin, September 1984.

The UK brewing industry is not as highly concentrated as tobacco. Indeed, none of the leading brewers had 25 per cent or more of the market which is the UK policy definition of a monopoly (Booth *et al.*, 1986). Nor does there appear to be any evidence of monopoly profits: the industry's profit rates have usually been below the national average (Table 10.3). However, the tied house system remains controversial. Also, it has to be recognised that even if a firm has monopoly power, it might choose not to exercise it so as to deter new entrants or because it is concerned with objectives other than maximum profits (such as a quiet life). There is also one distinctive feature of both the major brewers and the tobacco companies, namely, their large absolute size (Table 10.2). If absolute size is necessary for creating producer groups able to influence government policy in their favour, then the leading brewing and tobacco companies must be amongst the major interest groups in the UK.

Producer groups

Public choice models predict that the policies of democratic governments will favour producers more than consumers. Producers can combine to form an interest group to influence government policy in their favour. They will lobby against tax increases on their products and advertising restrictions, referring to the jobs and export benefits of their industry. They will try to capture any regulatory agency for the industry and will seek to ensure that regulation benefits producers rather than consumers. While producer groups have a major role in public choice models, few efforts have been made to operationalise the concept.

The brewing and tobacco companies are often presented as powerful and influential producer groups forming a major barrier to prevention policies. Insights into the characteristics of such pressure groups can be obtained by analysing the major companies and their market environment. The UK brewing and tobacco industries are dominated by a small number of firms and small numbers facilitates agreement on key issues. The major firms are also large both in relative and absolute size and have an international business. In the case of tobacco, the industry is highly concentrated and characterised by large conglomerates. Both brewers and cigarette companies have specialised trade associations (Brewers Society and Tobacco Advisory Council), each of which is involved in lobbying, advertising and public relations on behalf of their industry. For a producer group, the ultimate indicator of successful performance will be its ability to protect the industry's profitability.

What is the evidence on profitability?

Profitability is an indicator of industry performance. Continuously high profits (excessive) could reflect the presence and exercise of monopoly power whereas successive losses would signal the need for some adjustment in either efficiency or in the size of the industry. The profitability records of UK brewing, distilling and tobacco for selected years between 1970 and 1983 are shown in Table 10.3. The industrial group provides a national average benchmark for comparative purposes. For brewing and distilling, profitability was below that for tobacco and usually less than the industrial average. This does not suggest above average (excessive) profits which are likely to be associated with monopoly power. In fact, since 1968 concentration in brewing has declined (from a five firm concentration ratio for output of 62 per cent in 1968 to 50 per cent in 1985).

Tobacco's profitability has generally exceeded the national average. Indeed, since 1978, tobacco showed increases in profitability to a peak of 22 per cent in 1983 at a time when the industrial group's profits moved in the opposite direction. Throughout the period, the level of concentration in the tobacco industry has remained unchanged and so cannot explain the rise in profitability after 1978. However, the high concentration ratio for tobacco might partly explain why its profitability levels exceeded the national average between 1970 and 1983. There are, though, at least two other possible explanations for tobacco's profitability record. First, declining home sales might have shocked the industry into improved efficiency. Second, the industry has responded to reduced cigarette sales by diversifying into other profitable markets at home and overseas. All of which raises questions about the effects of prevention policies on the industry's profitability.

Have prevention policies harmed profits?

Industry representatives and pressure groups often claim that increased taxation and other prevention policies such as advertising regulations have adversely affected profitability. And if profits are reduced, this might eventually persuade capitalists to re-allocate resources to other uses, with implications for plant closure, job losses and exports in the 'penalised' sectors. Here, the tobacco industry is especially interesting. Given the continuous protestations about the effects of penal taxation, it might be expected that the UK tobacco industry would have a relatively poor profit record and would be characterised by exits from the industry. Yet the industry's profitability record which has continuously exceeded the national average does not support this view of a relatively poor profit performance. Obviously profitability is determined by a variety of factors, with prevention policies forming only one element in a complex model.

A statistical model was tested to estimate the possible effects of prevention policies on the profitability of the UK brewing and tobacco industries for the period 1960–83. In the model, industry profitability was determined by the concentration ratio, output, exports, advertising and labour productivity. Public policy variables were included in which the impact of prevention policy was measured by taxation (the real tax yield), Health Education Council expenditures and variables for health shocks, the 1964 changes in the licensing laws and whether there was a Conservative or Labour administration. It was expected that industry profitability would be reduced by increased taxation, Health Education Council spending and by health shocks (for example, Royal College of Physicians reports on the dangers of smoking). The results were tentative and suggestive rather than conclusive.

For brewing, it was found that taxation had the expected negative effect on industry profitability (higher taxes reduced profitability). However, for the tobacco industry, the statistical results were much less satisfactory, with many of the variables showing no significant relationship with profitability. Interestingly for prevention policy, the results were particularly important for the variables which were *not* statistically significant. Health Education Council spending and health warning shocks appeared to have no impact on profitability. Also, changes in taxation seemed to have no effect on the tobacco industry's profit rates. In other words, there was no support for the industry's claims that taxation has adversely affected its profitability. Of course, it could be that the costs of prevention policies are shifted to other groups, such as workers. Opponents of prevention policies will stress their adverse effects on employment, both directly in the industries affected and indirectly amongst suppliers and distributors. Indeed, unions, professional and trade associations whose members' future incomes depend on the continued sales of alcohol and tobacco products have every incentive to exaggerate likely job losses and their impact on local communities. This is an area which is long on emotion and short on independent economic analysis and supporting evidence.

EMPLOYMENT ISSUES

In evaluating the employment effects of prevention measures, policy makers need to know the number of jobs likely to be lost, their type (e.g. skilled or unskilled), their location and the likely effects on local unemployment rates. Of course, reliable data might not be available for a fully-informed public choice, which is where producer groups have every incentive and opportunity to attribute all job losses to prevention policies. However, employment depends upon a variety of factors such as output, technical progress, the price of machinery and wage rates. On this basis, factors other than prevention policy can cause job losses. Nor does it follow that job losses will result in higher unemployment. Much depends upon the availability of alternative employment together with how well and how quickly local labour markets are working (for example via labour mobility or wage adjustments).

The number of jobs lost

Total employment in the UK alcohol and tobacco industries has declined from some 151 000 in 1963 to 76 000 in 1986, resulting in a loss of 75 000 jobs over the period of which some 23 000 were in tobacco (Table 10.1). These figures might be regarded as the *maximum* possible direct employment effects of prevention policies, on the unrealistic assumption that there were no other factors causing job losses (cf. the downward trend in manufacturing employment). Even if these are the maximum job losses from prevention measures, they are obviously small in absolute numbers. For tobacco, where there have been health warnings, education campaigns, advertising restrictions and tax increases, the figures are equivalent to an average loss of 1000 jobs per annum. Such small numbers raise doubts about the reliability of industry claims about the likely employment effects of prevention measures. However, the industry's representatives respond by claiming that the true numbers affected are much greater than shown by the losses in direct employment. There are reputed to be large numbers of other jobs indirectly dependent on the alcohol and tobacco industries. There are jobs in the industries supplying materials and equipment for alcohol and cigarette production and further jobs in distribution and retailing. Industry estimates have claimed employment multipliers of 7.5 for tobacco and 8.5 for brewing (that is, the total number of direct and indirect jobs to direct jobs: Mackay and Edwards, 1982). But estimation in this area is not without its problems.

Accurate data are not always available, especially on employment in the retailing of alcohol and tobacco. How much of a newsagents' employment should be attributed to tobacco sales and how many jobs in a supermarket depend on the sales of beer, spirits, wine and cigarettes? Difficulties also arise if the numbers of full-time and part-time jobs are simply aggregated into an unadjusted total without converting into full-time equivalents. It is also the case that alternatives estimation methods can give widely different results. Our own estimates are shown in Table 10.4, which presents upper and lower bound figures of the total number of jobs directly and indirectly attributable to the UK alcohol and tobacco industries (Godfrey and Hartley, 1988). The estimates in Table 10.4 have two implications for policy. First, the upper bound multipliers are usually less than the industry's estimates. Second, the employment multipliers have not remained constant throughout the period 1974–84: hence constant employment multipliers cannot be used to make reliable predictions about the effects of prevention policy. On the basis of the estimates in Table 10.4, the loss of every 1000 direct jobs in the tobacco industry in 1984 meant a total annual employment reduction of 3000 to some 6000 full-time equivalent jobs (say, 4500 jobs). In addition to the numbers involved, the location of job losses might also be an important element in lobbying, with threats to close plants in high unemployment areas and in marginal constituencies.

Table 10.4 Employment multipliers in the alcohol and tobacco industries, 1974 and 1984

Year	Alcohol	Tobacco
1974	3.2–3.7	2.7–4.3
1984	5.9–7.3	3.0–6.2

Note: Employment multiplier shows total jobs (direct and indirect) as a multiple of the number of direct jobs in full-time equivalents.
Source: C. Godfrey and K. Hartley, 'Employment and Prevention Policy. Data Note', *British Journal of Addiction*, vol. 83 (1988), pp. 1335–42.

Where are the jobs?

The regional distribution of jobs in alcohol and tobacco identifies which areas might lose from prevention policy. Past job losses have already been incurred and, in assessing the future impact of policy governments need to know the current location of jobs. Unfortunately, published data are only available on the location of direct employment and not of indirect jobs. Also, figures are available only at the regional level and do not show employment in plants in villages, towns and cities (Godfrey and Hartley, 1989).

Brewing is concentrated in the South-East, the Midlands and Northern England (including the North-West and Yorkshire), these regions accounting for about 75 per cent of the industry's direct employment. Spirit distilling is concentrated in Scotland, where there are over 85 per cent of the industry's jobs. Tobacco is concentrated in the South, the East Midlands and the North-West which provided 60 per cent of the industry's employment. For tobacco, the main locations include Bristol, Nottingham, Manchester and Liverpool (Godfrey and Hartley, 1989). A similar geographical mapping showing the locations of major plants is needed for the alcohol industry. The locations then need to be related to local unemployment rates and to the political map, including marginal constituencies and as Baggott makes clear in Chapter 9 the desire of governments to be re-elected.

A cause for concern?

Direct job losses in the UK alcohol and tobacco industries are not disputed. There are, though, genuine differences of opinion on the 'knock-on' effects and the size of the indirect employment losses. Questions also arise about the extent to which job losses have been due to prevention policies or reflect other factors such as labour-saving technical progress and changing competitiveness in the UK and overseas markets. For the future, it has to be recognised that employment in the UK tobacco industry totalled some 20 000 in 1986, which is an indication of the *maximum* direct job losses if the industry ceased to exist. The virtual elimination of an industry is not a new and unique experience. Historically, the UK economy has survived and adjusted to changing economic circumstances (for example, the decline of the UK motor-cycle, civil shipbuilding and textile industries). This does not mean to say that there will not be adjustment costs imposed on particular regions and groups of workers which might require compensatory public policies (such as, retraining). However, job losses in, say, tobacco production do not necessarily mean higher local unemployment. Other jobs might be available. Also, effective prevention policies will release spending power for other purposes which will create new jobs. Consumers who no longer smoke and drink will spend their incomes on other goods and services so creating new jobs in industry and retailing.

CONCLUSION

The industry and the supply side is an important component of the overall market for alcohol and tobacco products which cannot be ignored in debates about prevention policy. In formulating prevention measures, it cannot be assumed that firms are passive organisations. Firms are active and adaptable agents which will respond to new prevention policies by seeking alternative ways of making money in a world of ignorance and uncertainty about market opportunities. Higher taxes on a firm's product might not be passed on to consumers through higher prices. Instead, they might be shifted to workers, shareholders or suppliers in the UK or overseas. Firms will also respond to an actual or expected reduction in their home market sales by greater advertising or sponsorship, by acquiring rivals or by diversifying into completely new markets in the UK and abroad.

For governments, the variety of reactions by firms and the years over which adjustments occur means that the analysis of the supply side and market effects of prevention measures can be extremely complex. Nor can economists confidently offer universally accepted and tested models of firm behaviour and market structure which explain the facts of the UK alcohol and tobacco industries. Indeed, recent research in industrial economics ' . . . has cast doubt on many positive and normative relations that were once widely believed to be generally valid' (Schmalensee, 1988, p.677). In the circumstances, public choices about prevention measures are even more likely to be determined by various interest groups.

References

Booth, M., Hartley, K. and Powell, M. (1989) 'The Industry: Structure, Performance and Policy', in A. Maynard and P. Tether (eds) *The Addiction Market: Consumption, Production and Policy Development* (Aldershot: Avebury).
Booth, M., Boakes, R., Hardman, G. and Hartley, K. (1988) 'Data Note 14, Mergers in the UK Alcohol and Tobacco Industries', *British Journal of Addiction*, vol. 81, pp. 825–30.

Booth, M., Hardman, G. and Hartley, K. (1986) 'Data Note 6, The UK Alcohol and Tobacco Industries', *British Journal of Addiction*, vol. 81, pp. 825–30.

Cmnd 216 (1969) *Report on the Supply of Beer* (London: Monopolies Commission, HMSO).

Cmnd 659 (1989) *The Supply of Beer* (London: Monopolies and Mergers Commission, HMSO).

Godfrey, C. and Hartley, K. (1988) 'Employment and Prevention Policy, Data Note', *British Journal of Addiction*, vol. 83, pp. 1335–42.

Godfrey, C. and Hartley, K. (1989) 'Employment', in A. Maynard and P. Tether (eds) *The Addiction Market: Consumption, Production and Policy Development* (Aldershot: Avebury).

Kirzner, I. (1973) *Competition and Entrepreneurship* (Chicago: University of Chicago Press).

Mackay, D. and Edwards, R. (1982) *The UK Tobacco Industry: its Economic Significance* (Edinburgh: Peida).

Schmalensee, R. (1988) 'Industrial Economics: an Overview', *Economic Journal*, vol. 98, pp. 643–81, September.

11 The Information Component

Larry Harrison

Two recommendations recur, almost with monotonous regularity, in virtually every report on the prevention of alcohol and tobacco-related problems produced over the past 25 years. These are the need to spend more on health education and the need for greater controls over advertising. Both of these measures involve intervention in the market for information. Together, the measures adopted in these two areas constitute the government's information policy; that is, how government attempts to communicate health information to the public and how it responds to activities that could prejudice or undermine that communication. Of course, health education involves far more than the communication of information, but providing information is a basic and an integral part of the educational process. The dissemination of health information is not all there is to health education, but it is an essential component. Indeed, it is an essential component of all prevention policy options. As Christine Godfrey notes in Chapter 7, controls over the price of alcohol or tobacco are unlikely to be introduced, or to survive for long, without the support of a well-informed public. The provision of information is not an alternative to the use of other policy instruments like legislation or fiscal controls, but an indispensible accompaniment.

Much of our work on the ESRC Addiction Research Centre programme has been concerned with identifying the impediments to the adoption of a coherent information policy. By a coherent policy I mean, quite simply, one in which government intervention is geared towards the objective of minimising alcohol- and tobacco-related harm. Anything that stands in the way of such a policy impedes the development of a national prevention strategy and is – or should be – a key matter of concern for everyone concerned with health problems.

In order to understand the obstacles that stand in the way of more effective information policies we have to look at policies in related areas; we have to consider how the dissemination of health information is affected by more general policies adopted towards broadcasting and the maintenance of advertising standards. Indeed it is hard to understand the rationale for the current voluntary agreements governing alcohol and tobacco advertising unless we remember that they are essential to what the Department of Trade and Industry calls the 'British System' of self-regulatory control, and that one of the original ideas behind the agreements, in the early 1970s, was to make advertising into the 'ally of health education', by engineering a shift towards the consumption of low tar cigarettes (Department of Trade, 1980; *The Times*, 17 March 1971, pp.1–2).

Broadening the focus to information policy involves going beyond such well-rehearsed debates as whether we should permit any alcohol or tobacco advertising. Indeed, I shall argue that those who still believe that individual European governments can take unilateral action over such matters, except within very narrow limits, have failed to take account of changing realities. We are moving into a new age, the age of information technology, yet our thinking on policy belongs to the age of the printing press and the megaphone. Like a group of ageing generals, we are busy preparing to fight the next war with the weapons of the last. Satellite broadcasting, and other new technologies, have made national controls over advertising largely irrelevant. In future, the key decisions are going to be made at the supra-national level.

Technological innovation is only part of the problem. Three things stand in the way of a coherent information policy. These are the nature of information technology and the impact it will have on policy; the division of policy responsibilities within government and the way this prevents many opportunities for health promotion being utilised; and the consequences of policy decisions taken by the European Communities.

THE POLICY ENVIRONMENT

Information policies have to be understood in the context of the major technological, political and economic developments that will undoubtedly affect the mass media over the next few years. These developments include the introduction of satellite broadcasting; the growing power of multi-media conglomerates like News International, which link satellite television companies with international news agencies like Reuters and with video, press and cinema interests across several continents; and, finally, European plans to create a single market for broadcasting by 1992. By the early 1990s there will be ten European television channels broadcast directly by satellite, with an additional 90 channels available for satellite programmes to be re-broadcast by local television transmitters or cable networks (European Commission, 1986). This expansion of broadcasting is being matched by rapid developments in communication networks and in computer technology, providing access to massive central databanks and computer processing power. The resulting changes will be far-reaching and irreversible. Already, the introduction of new technology into the newspaper industry has reduced costs and increased competition in what used to be known as Fleet Street. Within a few years, it will be impossible to imagine how business was conducted without word processors and electronic mail, viewdata information services, Fax machines and cordless telephones, while the erosion of national boundaries in broadcasting will generate new advertising markets and methods.

The immediate beneficiaries of the single European Market will be the large transnational corporations referred to by David Robinson in Chapter 1. These corporations already market products in every European country and are expecting to achieve substantial reductions in costs when they no longer have to manufacture six or seven versions of each product to conform to different regulations in each member state. Transnational corporations are moving into industries like telecommunications, data transmission and broadcasting, which are seen as growth areas. As broadcasting becomes more competitive, British television companies are attempting to gain economies of scale and access to overseas markets by taking over foreign television companies, particularly in America.

British advertising agencies are also preparing to exploit new markets. The advertising agencies have experienced a remarkable rise in wealth and status over the past thirty years. It seems strange to recall that advertising was regarded as rather disreputable when commercial television was introduced in 1955, even by many members of the Conservative Party. In the 1980s, advertising is engaged in by banks, building societies, solicitors, State-owned industries and even comprehensive schools. Advertising agencies are regarded as a safe investment by pension funds and are rich enough to attempt to take over one of the Big Four clearing banks, the Midland. Eleven advertising agencies feature in the *Times 1000*, as being amongst the largest UK companies (*The Times*, 1987). The foremost British agency, Saatchi and Saatchi, is ranked 47th, which makes it bigger than most of its clients (*The Times*, 1987).

Saatchi and Saatchi were one of two advertising agencies involved in planning the Conservative Party's campaign at the 1987 election. Even if we ignore the advertising industry's economic importance – and total advertising expenditure was estimated at £5117 million in 1986 – and leave out the industry's lobbying activities, which are considerable, there is no doubt that the industry is extremely influential (Waterson, 1987; Harrison and Tether, 1989). Advertising executives get to know ministers and senior civil servants extremely well through the work their agencies undertake for government departments and political parties. Indeed there is almost a symbiotic relationship between politicians and the advertising industry. Both need each other. The industry benefits from expenditure on government and party advertising, while political parties are increasingly dependent on advertising agencies to sell their policies to the electorate. Over the past thirty years there has been a growing awareness, by all political parties, of the role of professional advertising and marketing skills in shaping public perceptions of party policy. The 1987 election campaign was characterised by a greater emphasis

Table 11.1   Government advertising expenditure through the Central Office of Information, 1978 to 1987

Year	Expenditure in current prices (£ million)
1978–79	18.8
1979–80	20.6
1980–81	20.0
1981–82	18.5
1982–83	18.8
1983–84	21.3
1984–85	21.9
1985–86	25.1
1986–87	98.5
1987–88	88.0

Source: House of Commons, *Parliamentary Debates, 1987–88*, Weekly Hansard, 3 May 1988, vol. 1448, col. 398 (London: HMSO).

on media presentation than in any previous election, with the Labour Party mounting what was universally acknowledged to be a very sophisticated media-oriented campaign.

Since re-election, the present Government has placed a much greater emphasis on the management of information than in their previous terms of office. The Prime Minister's Press Office has assumed greater importance than under any previous administration, and every major department of state possesses an information division with a press office, which liaises with Downing Street and handles all departmental news for the press, radio and television. Table 11.1 shows that government expenditure on advertising has risen from £18 million in 1978, at current prices, to £88 million in 1987.

These figures are an underestimate, as the data only refer to expenditure by the Central Office of Information (COI). Many departments fund advertising campaigns directly, but there is no central record of their expenditure. If departmental advertising budgets were added to that of the COI the total would probably exceed £100 million. As it is Table 11.2 shows that the size of the

Table 11.2 The top ten holding companies' advertising expenditure, 1987–8

Rank	Holding company	Total press and TV expenditures (£000)
1	Unilever	104 126
2	HM Government	88 102
3	Procter and Gamble	57 682
4	Mars	52 740
5	Nestle	40 882
6	Woolworth	38 035
7	Kelloggs	37 810
8	Electricity Council	37 551
9	Allied Lyons	36 549
10	Dixons Group	32 076

Source: Campaign, *The Top Ten Holding Companies' Advertising Expenditure, 18 April 1988.*

COI's advertising budget makes HM Government the second largest advertiser in the United Kingdom, just behind Unilever.

Ten years ago it would have seemed unbelievable if someone had predicted that the government would become a larger advertiser than Procter and Gamble, a manufacturer of soap powder. It is as if the presentation of policy has become as important, a cynic might say more important, than its implementation. Yet this is the changing world that health policy makers are faced with. It is a world in which the growing economic and political importance of the advertising industry influences government information policy, and in which there is so much competition for the public's attention that health messages are in danger of being overwhelmed. Clearly, if governments are to achieve the health objectives outlined by David Robinson in Chapter 1, policy makers must ensure that these concerns are addressed and that future policies on broadcasting and advertising are consistent with the overall objective of developing 'healthy public policy'. Is there any evidence that this is taking place? Have health considerations been to the forefront in the Government's response?

THE POLICY RESPONSE

The commercial opportunities presented by satellite broadcasting and the European pressures to remove barriers to the free movement of goods and services across national frontiers have provided a tremendous challenge, and government has responded with a number of changes in broadcasting policy. These are designed to permit greater commercial freedom by introducing some measure of deregulation, while at the same time introducing selective controls in controversial areas, such as the depiction of sex and violence on television. This dual approach is partly a reflection of ideological strains within the Conservative Party, but even the socialist government in France is dismantling controls over broadcasting. European nations are hurrying to reform their own broadcasting systems before the introduction of the single audio-visual market in 1992.

The first aspect of this policy, the de-regulation of broadcasting, has manifested itself in government concern over restrictive labour practices and higher programme costs in independent television, and proposals to change the existing structure of broadcasting or expose the broadcasting authorities to market pressures. The Independent Broadcasting Authority (IBA) will be replaced by a body that will exercise a lighter regulatory touch, and independent radio is to be removed from the jurisdiction of the IBA and controls over radio advertising relaxed. The British Broadcasting Corporation (BBC) has been forced to reduce costs since its licence fee was pegged to the Retail Price Index, and BBC radio will face greater competition from independent companies in the future. By 1992, when the European Common Market in broadcasting is due to be established, there will be three new national commercial radio stations in Britain, and about 500 new local stations, and all broadcasting companies will face competition from new electronic media, like cable television and videotex.

Videotex is the generic term for computerised information services like Prestel. In France, videotex has become an important advertising medium and it is already possible for those with access to a computer terminal to order a crate of wine, pay for it, and have it delivered to the door without leaving the house. Videotex illustrates how technology is changing the rules of the game: it would be virtually impossible to enforce statutory controls over videotex services, as information is supplied and updated from so many sources at once. There may be no permanent record of advertising messages that have been deleted from the database, so it could be difficult to investigate complaints from consumers. The new technology makes industrial self-restraint essential, but at the same time the greater competition for advertising revenues which will follow deregulation and the introduction of new media like videotex could lead to a relentless downward pressure on advertising standards, ending in the destruction of the self-regulatory system.

The Government's response to these and similar regulatory issues has been to adopt a strategy of selective control. At the same time that government has favoured liberalising the controls over broadcasting to create greater diversity and competition, it has sought stronger and more specific controls over all media. These are being sought on grounds of individual privacy, national security, public morality and the public health. The threat to individual privacy posed by the amount of confidential information held on computer data banks led to the introduction of the Data Protection Act (1984), while backbench MPs have been encouraged to introduce private member's bills aimed at strengthening the law on libel. National security was given as the reason for attempting to prevent the appearance of books, articles and television programmes about the intelligence services in 1988 and for government proposals to strengthen parts of the Official Secrets Act in the same year. Concern over public morality, pornography and violence on television led to the censorship of video tapes under the Video Recordings Act (1984) and to the Broadcasting Standards Council being established in 1988.

The present Government's apparent commitment to deregulation has not been accompanied by a retreat from the paternalistic approach to broadcasting controls favoured by their predecessors; rather, there has been a change in emphasis, with the elimination of such things as violence on television becoming relatively more important, and the maintenance of cultural standards – in the way that Lord Reith would have understood them – relatively less. There has certainly not been a retreat from controls over advertising standards, as Philip Tether shows in Chapter 12. Governments have negotiated progressively tighter voluntary controls over tobacco and alcohol advertising, the most recent example being the initiatives from the Inter-Ministerial Group on Alcohol Misuse to restrict both alcohol advertising and the media portrayal of drinking.

POLICY RESPONSIBILITY IN GOVERNMENT

Government pursues its information policy in two ways. It intervenes in the information market by providing information, largely through mass advertising campaigns, but also through a range of government information services, the National Health Service and organisations which are wholly or partly funded by government, like Alcohol Concern and Action on Smoking and Health; and it restricts information, through the use of laws, covert pressure and voluntary agreements. But the picture is actually much more complicated than this. It is complicated because governments are not monolithic entities having something recognisable as a policy on every issue. When we were conducting research into current prevention policy we found that each government department appeared to pursue its own objectives largely in isolation (Harrison and Tether, 1987). Government consists of a diverse collection of competing bureaucracies, regulatory boards and law enforcement agencies, with little in common apart from their source of funding. With issues like prevention and health, which cut across the administrative responsibilities of many government departments, the policy process is fragmented. Different departments have responsibility for different aspects of a problem. Table 11.3 shows the eleven departments involved in some

Table 11.3   British government departments with an interest in some aspect of information policy

---

1   Health
2   Education and Science
3   Defence
4   Transport
5   Agriculture, Fisheries and Food
6   Environment
7   Home Office
8   Trade and Industry
9   Welsh Office
10   Scottish Office
11   Northern Ireland Office

Source: L. Harrison and P. Tether, 'The Coordination of the UK's Policy on Alcohol and Tobacco: the Significance of Organisational Networks', *Policy and Politics*, vol. 15, pp. 77–90.

aspect of information policy. Not all of them recognise the relevance of their activities for alcohol and tobacco policy nor fully exploit the opportunities for health promotion.

Seven of these departments have a direct interest in alcohol or tobacco education. The Department of Health has lead responsibility for health education in England, with the Welsh, Scottish and Northern Ireland Offices having responsibilities for their respective countries. At the Department of Health, policy on health education is dealt with by CPM1, a branch of the Children, Maternity and Prevention Division, which has overall responsibility for the government response to alcohol and tobacco related problems. CPM1 liaises with the Health Education Authority (HEA), which is funded by the Department and constituted as a special Health Authority.

In Scotland, health education is provided by the Scottish Health Education Group (SHEG), oversight of which is vested in Division 5b of the Scottish Home and Health Department (SHHD), part of the Scottish Office. Wales has its own Health Promotion Authority, which has taken over the work of the former Health Education Council and is linked with one of three Health and Social Services divisions in the Welsh Office. In Northern Ireland, health education is the responsibility of the Northern Ireland Office. Unfortunately, the Northern Ireland Office have not released details of their alcohol and tobacco policy-making responsibilities, administrative structures and interdepartmental relationships, despite repeated requests (Tether and Harrison, 1988).

In all four countries – England, Wales, Scotland and Northern Ireland – a distinction is made between public education and health education in schools and other educational institutions, which is seen as a matter for the education authorities. In Scotland, health education in schools comes under Division 2 of the Scottish Education Department (SED). In England, it comes under Division B of Schools Branch 3 at the Department of Education and Science (DES). Division B is responsible for the national curriculum working groups and is concerned to develop policy on health and social education within the context of the Government's plans for the curriculum as a whole. DES officials work in close liaison with Her Majesty's Inspectorate, who report directly to the Secretary of State for Education on the quality of education, and provide health education training courses for teachers. In Wales, health education for young people involves the Schools Division, Further Education Division and Educational Services Division of the Welsh Office's Education Department.

Given these complicated administrative arrangements, it is not surprising that the priority accorded to the development of alcohol and tobacco education varies in each country. While the White Paper *Better Schools* (DES, 1985) made it clear that the Government regards health education as an essential part of the schools curricula, policy interest in alcohol and tobacco education has, in England, come some way behind concern to develop drugs and sex education. In Scotland, these issues have always had a higher profile, largely as a result of the activities of the Scottish Health Education Coordinating Committee, which brings together representatives of the SHHD, SED, local authorities, health boards and others concerned with health education (Scottish Health Education Coordinating Committee, 1983; 1985). Alcohol and drugs education is integrated into the Standard Grade Science Course in Scottish schools.

Yet another division of responsibility exists in relation to health education directed at the civilian population and that designed for the armed forces. The Ministry of Defence has its own health and welfare policies for all men and women serving in the armed forces, at home and abroad, and the services mount their own health education campaigns. The army, navy and airforce develop their own programmes, responsibility for which is shared between their personnel and medical officers. Inter-service co-ordination on health education is achieved through a number of committees at the Ministry of Defence, the most important of which is the Principal Personnel Officers Committee, with its sub-committee on alcohol and drug abuse. A separate structure, the tri-service Defence Medical Services Directorate, co-ordinates the medical officers' contribution.

A further division of responsibility for health education can be seen in relation to public education on drinking and driving, which is considered a matter for the Department of Transport. The Department's Road Safety Division, part of the Road and Vehicle Safety Directorate, contains one branch that has specific responsibility for these safety campaigns and for the Highway Code. They are assisted in planning and evaluating these campaigns by the Transport and Road Research Laboratory (TRRL), which undertakes specific programmes of research for the UK Transport Departments. The TRRL also collates the drink driving statistics for Great Britain which are published, together with an analysis of current trends, in the Department of Transport's annual *Road Accidents GB*. The dissemination of information on drinking and driving is as much a part of alcohol education as advice on 'safe drinking levels' but the division of administrative responsibility has led to the drink driving programme developing largely in isolation from other initiatives on alcohol education. Despite the fact that the Department of Transport has spent between £0.5 million and £2.5 million on publicity campaigns since 1976, making them the largest funder of alcohol education, their contribution is often ignored or undervalued in policy debates.

The Ministry of Agriculture, Fisheries and Food (MAFF) is the sponsoring department for the UK alcohol industry. This involves its Alcoholic Drinks Division in identifying the interests of the industry and representing them within government, assisting the industry with scientific matters and formulating regulatory policies, such as controls over the composition of alcoholic drinks. The Alcoholic Drinks Division is concerned with information policy through its interest in the law on labelling drinks containers, particularly wine bottles. There is a large corpus of European legislation on wine labelling which is enforced, in the UK, by the Wine Standards Board. The Wine Standards Board, which is funded by MAFF and the Vintners Company, has inspectors who visit wine wholesalers and English vineyards to check the authenticity and accuracy of wine labels. MAFF's Standards Division is also involved in the labelling of alcoholic drinks. To conform with recent EC regulations, the UK has been obliged to amend its food legislation so that the labels of all alcoholic drinks declare the percentage alcohol by volume. MAFF's Standards Division drafted the legislation for England and Wales. The British Medical Association has suggested that all alcoholic drinks labels should also include a health warning analogous to those found on cigarette packets: in responding to such suggestions ministers are advised by MAFF's Standards and Alcoholic Drinks Divisions.

The Sport and Recreation Division (SARD) of the Department of the Environment is concerned with the sponsorship of sport by the alcohol and tobacco industries. Since the mid-1970s there has been increasing concern that the tobacco companies, in particular, are evading advertising restrictions through the sponsorship of sport. Snooker championships and other televised events provide the industry with an effective way to gain publicity for their products. In 1977 a Code of Practice was introduced to regulate tobacco industry sponsorship. The Code, which sets limits on sponsorship expenditure and provides for health warnings to be included on all promotional signs and advertisements for events, is agreed between SARD, for the Department of the Environment, the Department of Health and the Tobacco Advisory Council. There is no equivalent code governing sponsorship by the alcohol industry, but any change of policy would involve SARD, one of whose primary concerns is the encouragement of industrial sponsorship to ensure an adequate supply of funding for British sport.

The Home Office is involved in information policy through its responsibilities for broadcasting. The Home Office Broadcasting Department is not directly involved in drawing up the codes of practice governing alcohol and tobacco advertising on television; this is the responsibility of the Independent Broadcasting Authority and the Cable Authority. But the Home Secretary does have the power to ban a specific class of advertisement, and this power was used to end the television advertising of cigarettes and cigarette tobacco in 1965. The Home Secretary may also ask the broadcasting authorities to review their codes of practice governing alcohol advertising and their guidelines on the presentation of smoking or drinking on television programmes. He did so in 1988. The Home Secretary has, therefore, the power to eliminate alcohol and tobacco advertising from what are currently the most influential media – radio and television – or at least to encourage the authorities to introduce further restrictions.

Finally, the Department of Trade and Industry (DTI). The DTI has interests in information policy because it was, until 1988, the sponsor for both the tobacco and the advertising industries. The term 'sponsor' has gone out of favour at the DTI, because it was felt that it implied too cosy a relationship between government and industry. Nevertheless, the department maintains a close relationship with both industries, and its Consumer Affairs Division has intervened in the debate over tobacco advertising, arranging meetings between the DHSS and the Advertising Association, so that advertisers could put the case for the right to advertise tobacco products.

There are a number of consequences that flow from the fragment-ation of information policy between these eleven departments. First, the policies adopted by departments that are primarily interested in trade or advertising, form a set of constraints which limit the way the government can respond to alcohol and tobacco-related problems. Demands for a total ban on tobacco and alcohol advertising, for example, have been resisted because of the implications for the self-regulation of the advertising industry. This is in line with the policy of the DTI and the Office of Fair Trading, which was established partly to promote industrial self-regulation, and with the Enterprise and Deregulation Unit's brief, which is to oppose any further regulation of British business. The Enterprise and Deregula-tion Unit is a central task force, currently based at the DTI, with staff drawn from a number of government departments and business organisations. They have to be informed of any proposals likely to impose costs on business, like advertising regulations, and would need to be convinced that all alternatives to regulation, like voluntary agreements, have been tried and have clearly failed. It is unlikely that the DTI, which is responsible for monitoring the regulation of non-broadcast advertising, would agree that there was a need for statutory controls. The DTI is committeed to the principle of advertising self-regulation – indeed the British Government has just spent ten years resisting a draft directive from the European Commis-sion which would have resulted in the introduction of statutory controls over advertising. The Home Office is also opposed to further regulation, and has just declared itself against statutory controls over viewdata services.

A second consequence of dividing responsibility between eleven departments is that it is extremely difficult to ensure that all departments are delivering consistent messages on prevention and health, or are pursuing similar educational strategies. This results in different departments adopting quite different positions on such things as the value of mass advertising. Some departments have made frequent use of mass media campaigns, even when this has been against professional advice and has involved by-passing traditional channels of communication – like the Central Office of Information or the health education agencies – and dealing directly with advertising agencies. The Department of Health, in particular, has made increasing use of mass advertising as a means of health communication. Last year it spent over £24 million on advertising, more than the entire British government in 1984 (House of Commons, 1988b). Over £9 million went on television and radio advertising (House of Commons, 1988b). This was in addition to the £1.5 million spent by the HEA and SHEG.

This is not a recent development. Every reorganisation of health education in England since the Second World War has involved a greater emphasis on mass advertising, the provision of an enhanced budget, and the imposition of closer central government control. When the Health Education Council replaced the Central Council for Health Education it was given a budget of £248 085 in 1969, its first full year – five times the sum awarded to its predecessor. The increased funding was intended to enable the HEC to make more use of mass advertising campaigns. And despite all the criticism of government funding of health education, Table 11.4 shows that the HEC budget increased substantially, in real terms, between 1969/70 and 1986/87. Central government spending on the HEC increased from nearly £900 000 in 1969, in constant 1980 prices, to nearly £7 million in 1985.

In its evidence to the House of Commons Expenditure Committee in 1977, the HEC contrasted its own budget with the advertising budgets of the alcohol and tobacco industries and called for a 'modest quintuplication' (Expenditure Committee, 1977). The Expenditure Committee supported the HEC demands, as did the Royal Commission on the NHS two years later. Yet although the budget was increased incrementally, it did not lead to proportionately greater expenditure on alcohol education. Money for the tobacco programme was earmarked by government after 1981, but spending on alcohol, which was controlled by the HEC, fluctuated quite a bit. It is difficult to estimate alcohol or tobacco education expenditure precisely because some expenditure is concealed in the budgets for other programmes, but in 1987 the HEC was spending about the same amount on its alcohol programme, in real terms, as it had in 1974.

Table 11.4   Central government expenditure on the Health Education
Council, 1968 to 1986

Year	Central Government funding, current prices (1) (£)	Funding in constant 1980 prices (2) (£)
1968–69	94 237	361 061
1969–70	248 085	895 614
1970–71	342 494	1 130 343
1971–72	607 290	1 868 585
1972–73	836 226	2 355 566
1973–74	1 609 372	3 915 747
1974–75	1 033 438	2 022 384
1975–76	1 738 731	2 917 334
1976–77	1 539 230	2 230 768
1977–78	3 068 187	4 107 345
1978–79	3 693 131	4 355 107
1979–80	4 541 667	4 541 667
1980–81	5 046 553	4 509 878
1981–82	6 519 149	5 365 555
1982–83	8 571 992	6 744 290
1983–84	9 323 473	6 989 110
1984–85	9 645 000	6 816 254
1985–86	10 229 285	6 991 992

Source: (1) HEC Annual Reports, 1969–86, (2) G. Hardman, *Addiction
Research Centre Data Base*, York, Addiction Research Centre, University of
York, 1988.

The 1974 figure was about £213 000 in 1980 prices, the 1987 figure
about £286 000 (Hardman, 1988). The total HEC budget has increased by more than 300 per cent over the same period.

One of the attractions of directly funding an advertising campaign
is that governments can obtain an immediate and highly visible
response to the problems of the day. But is advertising an effective
way to communicate health information to mass audiences? Health
ministers take the view that it is. One of the reasons given by Health
ministers for replacing the HEC with a Special Health Authority was
that the proportion of its budget spent on advertising had declined
substantially over the years. Given the substantial increase in govern-

ment advertising expenditure referred to earlier, it might appear that the Department of Health's increasing use of mass media advertising was part of the Government's information policy, but this is not the case. The Department of Transport intends to phase out the use of advertising over the next three or four years (*Sunday Times*, 23 August 1987, p.8). A Department of Transport review of the drink-driving campaigns conducted since 1976 concluded that they were not demonstrably cost-effective. One life a year can be saved for every £10 000 (at 1976 prices) spent on road improvement; the same amount spent on advertising produces no measurable result. So the two departments responsible for the greatest expenditure on alcohol education – Transport and the Department of Health – take diametrically opposed views on the effectiveness of advertising. There is no coherent government policy on these aspects of public education; just a series of inconsistent departmental policies.

THE EUROPEAN DIMENSION

The compartmentalisation of Whitehall and the division of responsibility for information policies between eleven government departments represent impediments to the development of the UK's prevention strategy, because, as indicated earlier, no progress is possible in the absence of a well-informed public. But a further barrier has emerged in recent years, resulting from the introduction of satellite broadcasting and from the fact that policy-making competence in areas like advertising control has passed to the European Community. Satellite broadcasting enables advertisers to circumvent national laws and advertising regulations. This has already happened in Denmark, where laws governing the advertising of children's toys have been ignored by satellite television companies. Similarly, Scansat, a British satellite broadcasting company, has decided to ignore Swedish laws against naming defendants in criminal cases before a court reaches a finding of guilt. As Scansat's chief news editor explained, they are 'a British company and do not have to follow Scandinavian law' (*Guardian*, 8 August, p.23). The evidence from countries which have always been able to receive foreign television programmes suggests that some sections of the alcohol industry are prepared to use transnational broadcasting to evade national advertising restrictions. Austria does not permit the advertising of wine on

television, for example, but cannot prevent Bavarian stations trans-
mitting wine advertisements with the prices quoted) in Austrian
schillings (*Sunday Times*, 12 December 1982, p. 15).

This problem is likely to become more acute because of the way in
which the transnational corporations are developing global marketing
strategies, and achieving economies of scale from the production and
marketing of products throughout the world. Kentucky Fried Chick-
en eaten in Peking is substantially the same as in Peckham High
Street or Dayton, Ohio and the product is marketed in the same way,
right down to the packaging; the brand image of Marlborough
cigarettes is recognised all over the world. Traditionally, some sectors
of the alcohol industry, like the brewing and cider-making companies, concentrated their advertising on local and regional audiences,
but this is already changing with the promotion of Australian and
American lagers on British television. The new satellite technology
provides an opportunity for the transnational corporations to extend
their influence.

The regulation of satellite broadcasting is a matter for the European Community. The European Commission has recommended that
all member states adopt a common approach to controls over tobacco
and alcohol advertising (European Commission, 1984). This has
different implications for tobacco and alcohol policy. As the majority
of member states ban tobacco advertising on television, the Commission argues that it would be 'consistent with the health policies of the
Community' to make this prohibition general in all member states
(European Commission, 1984, para 32). This means that the European regulations on tobacco will be stricter than those currently in
force in the UK, where the television advertising of cigars and pipe
tobacco is still permitted.

The situation is rather different in relation to alcohol advertising
because it is only prohibited by a minority of Community members.
The Commission has argued that a ban on alcohol advertising is not
the best approach for the Community. It favours a European code of
practice, and a draft directive was placed before the Council of
Ministers in 1980 (European Commission, 1988). The rules governing
alcohol advertising are less extensive than those enforced by the IBA,
containing six clauses against the IBA's eleven. Member states will be
free to impose stricter standards than this, or even to ban alcohol
advertising, but only in relation to broadcasts originating on their
own territories. They will not be allowed to exclude advertising on
satellite channels.

This means that it may become impossible for individual member states to continue with restrictions on alcohol advertising once satellite broadcasting becomes established. Restricting advertising on domestic television will place national stations at a competitive disadvantage, and there could be problems of import penetration if a national alcohol industry was not permitted to advertise while foreign competitors invested in massive promotional campaigns on satellite television. British advertisers would find this totally unacceptable, and would probably fight any national prohibition in the European Court, as a restriction on their commercial freedom of expression.

By and large, the European Commission's proposals reinforce current UK policy on alcohol and tobacco advertising, but effectively rule out the possibility of a future British Government banning alcohol advertising totally. The Commission has therefore introduced a major constraint on future information policy. Those public health campaigners who have sought a ban on alcohol advertisements are not only faced with resistance from British government departments like the DTI, they now have to convince the majority of EC members of the desirability of such a step. Given the fact that the EC is primarily an economic organisation, with important wine producing interests, it seems unlikely that they will succeed.

CONCLUSION

There are two aspects to information policy: the provision of information and the regulation of information. In both of these areas technological, economic and political developments have changed the nature of the prevention debate. The arguments about advertising that have rumbled on for two decades need to be reassessed. Even if the empirical evidence is interpreted as supporting a ban on the promotion of both products, there is a limit to the action that national governments can take. Pressures for the deregulation of broadcasting and the transfer of policy-making competence to the EC have limited the options for policy makers at a national level. Those who wish to see alcohol advertising banned will have to unite with pressure groups in other European countries, because they need to persuade the majority of member states. In a sense this could be a tremendous challenge, rather than an impediment, because national governments are barely able to match the resources of transnational corporations, which need to be fought at a supra-national level. The unified market may present the opportunity to do this. The task is more difficult, but the benefits of European co-operation are correspondingly greater.

Where policy remains largely a matter for the UK government, as in public education, the fragmentation of the policy-making process has resulted in many educational opportunities being under-utilised. It is hard to see how government departments can continue to take the easy option of funding highly visible television advertising campaigns – a practice that has been criticised by the Public Accounts Committee and is to be investigated by the National Audit Office – in the absence of clear evidence for the effectiveness of this form of advertising. A fundamental reassessment of government information policy is, therefore, long overdue.

References

Campaign (1988) *The Top Ten Holding Companies' Advertising Expenditure*, 18 April.

Department of Education and Science (1985) *Better Schools*, Cmnd 9469 (London: HMSO).

Department of Trade (1980) *The Self Regulatory System of Advertising Control*, Report of the Working Party (London: Department of Trade).

European Commission (1984) *Television Without Frontiers*, Green Paper on the establishment of a common market for broadcasting, COM 84, 300 final/2 (Brussels: European Commission).

European Commission, Directorate General for Information (1986) *Television and the Audio-visual Sector: towards a European policy*, 14/86 (Brussels: European Commission).

European Commission (1988) *Proposals for a Council Directive . . . concerning the pursuit of broadcasting activities*, COM 85, 154 final (Brussels: European Commission).

Expenditure Committee (1977) *Preventive Medicine*, First report from the Expenditure Committee, Social Services and Employment Sub-committee (London: HMSO).

Harrison, L. and Tether, P. (1989) 'Information: the Policy Networks', in C. Godfrey and D. Robinson (eds) *Manipulating Consumption: Information, Law and Voluntary Controls* (Aldershot: Avebury).

Harrison, L. and Tether, P. (1987) 'The Coordination of the UK's Policy on Alcohol and Tobacco: the Significance of Organisational Networks', *Policy and Politics*, vol. 15, pp. 77–90.

Hardman, G. (1988) *Addiction Research Centre Data Base*, York, Addiction Research Centre, University of York.

House of Commons (1988a) *Parliamentary Debates 1987–88*, Weekly Hansard, 3 May, Vol. 1448, Col. 398 (London: HMSO).

House of Commons (1988b) *Parliamentary Debates 1987–88*, Weekly Hansard, 14 January, Vol. 1443, Col. 401–2 (London: HMSO).

Scottish Health Education Coordinating Committee (SHECC) (1983) *Health Education in the Prevention of Smoking-Related Diseases* (Edinburgh: SHECC).

Scottish Health Education Coordinating Committee (SHECC) (1985) *Health Education and the Prevention of Alcohol-Related Problems* (Edinburgh: SHECC).

Tether, P. and Harrison, L. (1988) *Alcohol Policies: Responsibilities and Relationships in British Government*, Addiction Research Centre Occasional Paper, York, Universities of York and Hull, 122 pp.

The Times (1987) *The Times 1000: Leading Companies in Britain and Overseas* (London: Times Newspapers Ltd).

Waterson, M. (ed.) (1987) *Advertising Statistics Yearbook 1987* (London: Advertising Association).

12 Legal Controls and Voluntary Agreements

Philip Tether

The core task of the ESRC Addiction Research Centre has been to identify the impediments – structural, procedural and attitudinal – to the development of co-ordinated prevention strategies in respect of alcohol and tobacco-related problems. This task has involved identifying the content of current prevention policies and analysing prevention policy processes. The alternative to this detailed task is, as David Robinson emphasises in Chapter 1, simply more exhortatory calls to 'do something' which both ignore where we are now and the complex realities of the policy process which places constraints on where we may go.

This chapter seeks to illuminate these realities through a discussion of two important prevention policy instruments – law and self-regulatory agreements. Policy instruments are vehicles for announcing and delineating policy and defining attendant duties, rights and responsibilities in relation to its implementation. The issue of which is the most appropriate policy instrument lies close to the surface of a number of prevention debates. Many of the calls to 'do something' are, implicitly or explicitly, calls for more laws. This issue is, of course, particularly prominent where the advertising of tobacco is concerned. The British Medical Association (BMA) advocates an outright ban on the advertising and promotion of tobacco (*Sunday Times*, 14 October 1984, p.7). as does Action on Smoking and Health (ASH) whose Director claims 'legislation works' (Simpson, 1987, p.6).

The demand for more regulation, i.e. more laws, raise important questions which are seldom explored. Laws and voluntary agreements may appear to be very different policy instruments but how different are they? Are laws always a preferable policy instrument? Are they always, in fact, so successful? Are voluntary agreements so unsuccessful? These questions are important because they have implications for the shape and content of co-ordinated prevention strategies and each is examined in turn below.

HOW DIFFERENT ARE LAWS AND VOLUNTARY AGREEMENTS?

The Addiction Research Centre's programme of work involved identifying the content of current alcohol and tobacco prevention policies. This was no easy task given the specialist nature of much policy in both these areas. For instance, only a handful of civil servants are concerned with the medical standards of UK sea-going personnel and are familiar with the contents of the International Labour Organisations (ILO) Convention No. 147, 'Minimum Standards in Merchant Shipping', the Merchant Shipping (Medical Examination) Regulations 1983 and the Department of Transport's Merchant Shipping Notices No. M1121 and M1141. However, such obscure and specialist issues are not unimportant. Seafarers are a 'high risk' group where alcohol is concerned and the existing regulations provide both the opportunity for, and a constraint on, the introduction of alcohol and work policies in shipping companies.

The 'mapping' exercise was also complicated by the constantly shifting patterns of organisational relationships in central government. The allocation and reallocation of functions between departments has been charted in some detail (Pollitt, 1984) but within departments the allocation of functions is equally fluid. Organisational responsibility for aspects of alcohol and tobacco policy shifted in a number of departments during the mapping exercise. Thus, one of the main foci for the DHSS's wide-ranging interests in alcohol use and abuse was a section of Branch 2 in the Community Services Division. In December 1986, the section was relocated in the Children, Maternity and Prevention Division, a move which underlined a commitment to the development of prevention policies (Tether and Harrison, 1988).

Difficult though this mapping process turned out to be, it revealed the two key features of the prevention policy-making process: the existence of organisational networks centred around government departments, each providing the focus for different aspects of prevention policy; and the consensual and hence incremental nature of all prevention policy making.

An organisational network consists of organisations having a significant amount of interaction with each other, sometimes based on mutual benefit and exchange of resources and at other times on conflict and hostility (Benson, 1975). The concept of organisational networks is important since it helps to bring order into what at first sight appears as a bewildering collection of administrative units, groups and organisations and to highlight the role of boundary personnel who provide inter-organisational links. It also draws attention to the distribution and use of power and other resources in shaping policy outputs. Alcohol prevention policy is, in the broadest view, the property of five organisational networks concerned with law and order; health and safety; advertising and the media; employment; and education.

Policy making proceeds incrementally because of the need to bargain, adjust and negotiate. Organisational co-ordination is achieved through the process of 'partisan mutual adjustment' (Lindblom, 1965). In other words groups and organisations concerned with aspects of prevention policy are 'partisan' in pursuit of their own interests and concerns but, nevertheless, they are capable of 'mutual adjustment' in that they adapt to decisions made by other agencies which they seek to influence through bargaining and negotiation. As a result, existing prevention policy is well co-ordinated within networks. The real co-ordination problem arises between networks when policies which policy makers regard as independent but which have implications for each other are developed in isolation.

The process of bargaining, adjustment and negotiation is rooted in the practicalities of the situation. In an increasingly complex society, group co-operation in the formulation and implementation of policy is indispensable and has led to the development of 'sectorisation' (Jordan and Richardson, 1982). Policy is fashioned out of consultations between groups in the many policy sectors and civil servants and 'once agreement has been reached the policy is then "sold" to the rest of government' (Norton, 1987, p.51). As Jordan and Richardson (1982) emphasise, this process is encouraged by both functional and political needs since departments and groups need each other. The legitimacy of this process is fostered by our political culture which is consensual and conflict avoiding. As Sir Ivor Jennings observed, it is virtually a convention of the constitution that in framing legislation, the appropriate department must consult the appropriate interests (Jennings, 1959).

The formulation of alcohol and tobacco-related policies is not exempt from the values, perspectives and procedures rooted in the consensual political culture. Consultation with affected interests can be extensive even on minor issues. Thus, negotiations preceding the introduction of regulations labelling all retail alcohol with its alcohol content by volume, were preceded by consultations with about 150 different groups. These included the Health Education Authority (HEA), the King's Fund Institute, the Medical Council on Alcoholism, the Hops Marketing Board, the Campaign for Real Ale Ltd and the British Oat and Barley Millers Association (MAFF, 1988). On another occasion, the Department of Trade and Industry (DTI) acted to bring the Advertising Association (AA) into direct contact with the DHSS in order that the AA could present its views on the content of the regularly renegotiated voluntary agreements which govern the advertising and promotion of tobacco products. Until the DTI intervened on behalf of the AA, the DHSS had never had any contact with representatives of the advertising industry.

Recognition of the need to ensure that laws, both major and minor, reflect a consensus of opinion, is found at the heart of the law and order network – the Home Office. This is frequently depicted as the regulatory department *par excellence* (Griffith, 1966). However, the Home Office (which is, in effect, a cross between a Ministry of Justice and a Ministry of the Interior) is not an automatic departmental advocate of more laws. Indeed, Home Office officials spend a great deal of their time fending off demands from other parts of government for more laws. In the words of one senior official 'everyone has a law they think will solve everything. We can't have that. The law must reflect a consensus which it is our job to identify and defend'.

From this perspective, the apparent differences between law and self-regulation begin to look less radical. To be effective, to be 'doable', laws – like self-regulation – have to be largely self-enforcing. Recent New York anti-smoking laws are only working because according to a recent Gallup Poll 77 per cent of people agreed that smokers should refrain in the presence of a non-smoker (*Independent*, 28 July 1985, p.3). In this particular case, the law does – in Chief Justice Weddell Holme's words – 'encapsulate the felt necessity of the time'.

New York's successful anti-smoking regulations reflect supportive social attitudes which, in turn, they reinforce and buttress. They have not created those changed attitudes. Any attempt to reverse this process and use law to promote attitudinal and behavioural change when a supportive consensus is lacking, is fraught with difficulties and dangers. A unilateral declaration by public authorities that some aspect or other of what has, hitherto, been regarded as private behaviour is, in fact, a matter for pubic concern, is likely to generate resentment and not only among those directly affected or targeted.

The law is a very blunt instrument indeed for breaking down the walls between the private and public spheres. Governments which attempt to use it for this purpose are likely to be seen as effecting a forced entry.

ARE LAWS ALWAYS SUCCESSFUL?

As a policy instrument, laws have strengths and weaknesses. Their strength lies in the fact that they are a highly visible and authoritative way of sanctioning and legitimating policy. So visible are they that policy is frequently identified with the products of the formal processes which authorises laws, i.e. with specific Acts of Parliament or the statutory instruments which, when activated under delegated legislation, require or permit things to be done or not done. But authoritative though law may be this does not insure against implementation problems. Usually implementation problems result from the exercise of permissive or deliberately discretionary areas of legislation or the unintended but inevitable gaps, inconsistencies and ambiguities resulting from the conflicting interests which influence the formulation of policy in a consensual policy culture (Rhodes, 1979).

The implementation of current drink driving laws varies widely from locality to locality because of the exercise of discretionary and interpretative powers by the police. When the 'breathalyser' was introduced by the Road Traffic Act, 1967 the government proposed (Department of Transport, 1965), that the police should be given unfettered discretion to test motorists.

The proposal to test without, necessarily, any suspicion of impairment, created fierce opposition and charges that the police would engage in random testing thus harrying an innocent motoring majority. The most vociferous opposition in 1967 to conferring unfettered discretion on the police came from the motoring organisations although they had reluctantly accepted the need for a legal limit. It was argued by them and others that testing without evidence of impairment was an unacceptable infringement of civil liberties. This claim found support in the Conservative Party principally among members of its Transport Backbench Committee. The 'civil liberties' issue introduced an ideological, party political element into what had been hitherto an essentially cross-party consensus that 'something must be done'. In addition to the motorists' defence organisations, the police too had doubts. However, their objections arose mainly from a concern for the resource implications of unfettered discretion. Their caution was particularly important since they had been, until then, an important group in the coalition pressing for legislative action on drinking and driving. The final group to throw its weight against the Government's proposals was the licensed trade itself. The National Union of Licensing Victuallers (NULV) and the Wine Trade Defence Committee feared that discretionary or random testing would frighten away customers and damage business. However, the objections of the licensed trade were muted since it was difficult for them to adopt a 'high profile' position on the issue without appearing to be a self-interested group prepared to put up with death on the roads in the interest of profits.

Because neither all affected interests nor public opinion would accept the principle of unfettered discretion a 'stop and test' formula was negotiated which allows police officers to breath test a motorist (i) who commits a moving traffic offence, (ii) who is involved in an accident or, (iii) if they have 'reasonable cause' to believe the motorist has alcohol in their body. Different forces interpret these powers in different ways. Some, by interpreting the current stop and test powers as widely as possible, have approached very closely indeed to random breath testing. In the so-called 'Cheshire Blitz' the police administered ten times the usual number of tests. The result was a doubling of convictions and a 60 per cent reduction in the number of accidents as a consequence of increased driver awareness and, hence, care.

The climate for a law permitting random breath testing may now be right. The consensus may exist. But the issue of police discretion and implementation practice will remain even if the present stop and test powers are swept away and replaced by unfettered discretion. Indeed, the issue is likely to become more acute since effective random breath testing requires considerable resources. Breath tests have to be carried out at a frequency that produces deterrence and we know from the experience of other countries that this is approximately one in three drivers per year. If the introduction of random breath testing is not properly funded by the Home Office, we can expect that implementation patterns will vary considerably around the country as different police forces take different decisions on the resources they can afford, or thinks desirable, to commit to this activity. The Association of Chief Police Officers (ACPO) is now strongly in favour of discretionary or random testing. However, its conversion may owe something to the desire to avoid a law which not only removed existing limitations on police powers to test but which also determined how they would carry out random breath testing operationally. Such a law, to which they are firmly opposed, would be a constitutional departure in that it would remove operational decisions on implementation from Chief Constables.

If gaps, inconsistencies and ambiguities can create implementation problems so can the permanence of laws. This is part of their visibility and authority. But people and their needs change as the social and political climates change. Case law can provide a means of adaptation but this is not always adequate. Liquor licensing is a good example of a policy area in which the purpose and operation of laws have become progressively more uncertain and erratic because of accumulated pressures, especially commercial.

Some form of licensing designed to regulate the retailing of alcohol is a feature of control policies in most countries (Davies and Walsh, 1983). The licensing controls implemented in the First World War included the setting up of a Liquor Control Board with sweeping powers which it did not hesitate to exercise. These powers included imposing a ban on the sale of spirits, ensuring the provision of food in public houses, regulating opening hours, improving the standard of premises and closing down unwanted premises or running them itself. After the war, many of these controls were lifted although the main provisions concerning 'permitted hours' were embodied in the Licensing Act, 1921.

During the first part of the twentieth century *per capita* alcohol consumption in the UK remained low and only began to rise sharply in the 1950s. Since 1960 consumption has doubled and this has been accompanied by a parallel rise in various indicators of harm:

> The recent sharp increase in misuse as measured by a variety of indicators, seems clearly to be linked with the equally marked rise in overall consumption of alcohol that has occurred in the United Kingdom in recent years and the changes in people's drinking habits which underline it. (DHSS, 1981b, p.64)

The 1988 liberalisation of the licensing law, which increased the number of permitted hours premises can open, generated heated controversy. Opponents claimed the reform would usher in a new cycle of harms and was a reckless gamble with the nation's health and well-being.

Licensing justices are responsible for granting a variety of liquor licences and they are appointed annually from among the magistrates of the local bench. Subject to the suitability of the premises and the suitability of the applicant, justices have virtually absolute discretion over the granting of 'on' and 'off' licences. Licensing laws are designed to control the number, type and distribution of licensed premises in a locality and who may drink in such premises and when. Case law confers on justices the right (and indeed the duty) to consider the 'needs' of a neighbourhood when processing applications for a liquor licence. But 'need' is a difficult concept to measure, define and defend.

Who is to say that a neighbourhood does not 'need' one more liquor outlet? Any licensing committee which tries to argue such a case will, very likely, find its decision overturned on appeal especially when, as is often the case, the plaintiff is a determined commercial interest which can afford the best representation. However, justices are discouraged from even trying to 'measure' an application against some pre-determined licensing plan or policy which incorporates strategic ideas on the desirable number, type and distribution of outlets in their area because they are bound to take their decisions 'judicially' that is to say 'according to the rules of reason and justice and not private opinion. It must not be arbitrary, vague or fanciful but legal and regular' (The Justices' Clerks' Society, 1983; p.27). The result is a 'case by case' approach by licensing committees to each application for the grant of a licence which means that appeals are often upheld if there is any suggestion that the justices are making their decisions in terms of some broad policy about the 'needs' of locality rather than in relation to the merits of the particular case under consideration (Tether and Robinson, 1986).

Thus, while the corpus of liquor licensing law lays down many important rules and regulations both procedural and substantive, it suffers from fundamental implementation problems. The law has proved incapable of meeting the key challenge it now faces and, indeed, framing legislation capable of meeting the challenge would be no simple task since no single definition of need could cover every locality and situation. The interesting feature of the recent debates over 'permitted hours' was that practically nothing was heard of this all-important central question of 'need'. This is perhaps not surprising since problems with the implementation of law are often hidden from view at the policy periphery.

The fundamental problem appears to be an uncertainty as to the purpose of licensing law. Is its purpose the short-term maintenance of public order or the long-term promotion of public health or both? Perhaps the prevailing viewpoint can be gauged by the fact that departmental responsibility for licensing issues is lodged in the Home Office.

ARE VOLUNTARY AGREEMENTS SO UNSUCCESSFUL?

Many of the problems associated with the implementation of law are not found with voluntary agreements and this means that such agreements have a number of positive attractions for policy-makers. They are informal and hence easy to amend in situations where movement, adaptation, change and adjustment is desired or anticipated (Baggott and Harrison, 1986).

They are also cheap. The costs of implementing and policing agreements is frequently imposed upon the regulated. This is the case with the advertising industry, where a levy on turnover is collected by the Advertising Standards Board of Finance (ASBOF) in order to fund the operations of the Advertising Standards Authority (ASA). Agreements of this kind do not, of course, preclude parallel government monitoring of self-regulation. A Committee for Monitoring Agreements on Tobacco Advertising and Sponsorship was established by the Right Hon. Norman Fowler MP, Secretary of State for Social Services in October 1986 to oversee the workings of the agreements affecting tobacco advertising in all its non-broadcast forms and its first report was published one-and-a-half years later (DHSS, 1988).

The self-regulation of tobacco advertising has been fiercely criticised as an inadequate policy instrument which amounts to no more than a sell-out to vested interests. This is too crude a judgement. The system is both complex and subtle with some real achievements to its credit.

It has seven separate elements embodied in four codes of practice in three voluntary agreements. These components are:

(1) The Independent Broadcasting Authority (IBA) Code of Advertising Standards and Practice.
(2) The Cable Authority Code.

(3) The Videotext Industry Code.
(4) The British Code of Advertising Practice (BCAP) which governs advertising in the non-broadcast media.
(5) A series of regularly, renegotiated voluntary agreements between the tobacco industry and government on the advertising and promotion of tobacco products.
(6) A separate though interlocking series of agreements on product modifications overseen by the Independent Scientific Committee on Smoking and Health (ISCSH).
(7) A series of voluntary agreements on the sponsorship of sport by tobacco companies in the UK.

One component has a statutory basis since the IBA has a responsibility, reaffirmed in the Broadcasting Act 1981, to maintain and enforce a Code of Practice covering all advertising on commercial television and independent radio. However, although the code has a statutory basis it can be regarded as essentially voluntary since interference by government is rare and the various bodies and committees which administer the code have effective, self-regulatory oversight of its contents. However, government has used the code's statutory basis to enforce a complete ban on the televised advertising of cigarettes.

The first voluntary agreement was negotiated by Sir Keith Joseph in 1971. The agreement was reached against a background of well-publicised Parliamentary agitation over two Private Members' Bills which sought to restrict tobacco advertising. Sir Keith Joseph, Secretary of State for Health and Social Services was, like Enoch Powell, before him, ideologically averse to legislation in this area but, under pressure to act, he was not above using the threat of legislation including (after initial opposition) the tabling of amendments to one of the Private Members' Bills sponsored by Sir Gerald Nabarro (Conservative, Kidderminster) as a lever with the companies. Although the Bill was lost, thanks to what Nabarro called 'a malignant minority' of MPs representing constituencies with tobacco interests, the Secretary of State's ploy was successful. A key feature of serious industry/Government negotiations over the self-regulatory system has been, and remains still, firm evidence that the Government will, if necessary, resort to legislation. Dr David Owen has pointed out that 'A Minister needs to know it too that he has the power to legislate. Then you can have a serious discussion. Though experience tells us that all Governments back off legislation. And the record is true. They do.' (Taylor, 1985, p.87).

The first agreement has subsequently been revised in 1977, 1980, 1982 and 1986. Over this period these successive agreements have developed and elaborated the provisions concerning health warnings (which are known as the 'labelling code'). They have grown larger and more varied. The first message on cigarette packets read: WARNING by HM Government: SMOKING CAN DAMAGE YOUR HEALTH (House of Commons, 1971). In 1977, health warnings were extended to hand-rolling tobacco, leaflets, brochures, coupons, catalogues and circulars (DHSS, 1978). In 1980, two further health warnings were introduced and the space for warnings was increased by 50 per cent (DHSS, 1981). In 1982, the size of the warning was increased again by 15 per cent and extended to material at retail sales points (DHSS, 1983). In 1986, six new health warnings were introduced and the size of the warning was increased to 17.5 per cent of the total advertisement space (DHSS, 1986).

The development of health warnings has been paralleled in other areas. In 1980 the companies represented by the Tobacco Advisory Council (TAC) agreed to limit their expenditure on cigarettes' poster advertising to 70 per cent of the previous year's expenditure subject to allowance for inflation agreed with the DHSS (DHSS, 1981a). By 1986 agreed expenditure on cigarette poster advertising was fixed at 50 per cent of the previous year's expenditure subject to an agreed inflation allowance (DHSS, 1986). Tobacco advertising in cinemas has been phased out (DHSS, 1983). One tobacco product, cigarillos, which survived the ban on televised cigarette advertising imposed in 1965, has now been included (DHSS, 1978).

Two supplementary Codes of Conduct have been instituted under the umbrella of the voluntary agreements between the tobacco industry and government, the first governing the televised advertising of cigars and pipe-tobacco and the second, promotional campaigns of all kinds. The BCAP's 'Cigarette Code' has been refined and an emphasis on young people and women has led to the tobacco industry setting funds aside to promote compliance with the law on tobacco sales to minors and to restrictions on advertising in magazines with a large, predominantly female readership.

Tar levels are monitored by the Laboratory of the Government Chemist and official tar tables have been published since 1973. Government and industry have concluded a series of tar yield agreements based on recommendations by the Scientific Committee which is an important component of the self-regulatory system. The agreement has reduced maximum tar yields. The first tar table contained five tar bands. One of the categories has since been eliminated and the 'high tar' category has been reduced from 29 mg tar and over per cigarette to 18 mg tar and over per cigarette. Since 1977, the 'tar banding' agreed with the tobacco industry has been incorporated into the 'labelling code' thus ensuring that tar categories are displayed on all cigarette packaging and (optionally) on advertisements.

The most striking feature of the self-regulatory tobacco advertising system is the progressive nature of its core agreements pushed on, it would seem, largely by civil servants rather than by politicians. Each agreement is more complex and more detailed than its predecessor. Each tightens existing controls and introduces new ones, thus underlining the adaptability of self-regulation as a policy instrument and the ease with which it can be amended, unlike a law which once passed, cannot be easily or cheaply changed. Moreover, this battery of controls has been assembled in a non-confrontational way which has bought industry co-operation and compliance as well as providing industries with time to diversify.

This complex, self-regulatory system is the product of bargaining processes involving a variety of groups and organisations with conflicting concerns and interests in tobacco advertising. Each component of the self-regulatory system has developed as, and is the current product of, these competing interests and points of view. The policy which emerges from this essentially 'political' process may not be the 'best' judged in terms of some external standard but it will be agreed and hence 'do-able'. The incremental, negotiated and agreed development of the self-regulatory system is not a vehicle for the government's 'advertising policy' in respect of tobacco products. Rather, it is the policy. The system is the result of conflicting pressures and forces rather than any detailed 'rational' plan in the minds of policy makers. In other words, the medium really is the message and as in other policy areas characterised by incrementalism, government has no hidden agenda or 'plan'. A broad tobacco 'policy' has indeed been articulated which is to discourage the uptake of smoking, to encourage those who have started to stop and to limit the hazards for those who do start and cannot stop (DHSS, 1980). Elements of the self-regulatory system such as health warnings and product modifications clearly 'fit' this broad statement. However, the statement did not precede the self-regulatory system. It merely sums up what has happened and to mistake the statement for the policy is to confuse the shadow with the substance.

The system is not satisfactory if you believe, as many do, that the only desirable tobacco advertising policy is a law which completely bans such advertising. However, the evidence for the effects of advertising on tobacco consumption is mixed and inconclusive (Tether and Godfrey,1989). While health lobbyists can certainly claim that there is no evidence that tobacco advertising has no effect on consumption levels, the industry can, with equal validity, turn this statement around and say that there is no evidence that it does encourage consumption. In these inconclusive circumstances, is a law either justified or worthwhile in terms of the relationships it would sacrifice not to mention the encouragement of competition by price which might draw in tobacco imports and reduce the costs of the product?

Some would say 'yes' and emphasise the 'symbolic' value of such a meaure claiming that it would have an important effect on attitudes by underlining, once again, that tobacco is a dangerous product. Claims for the 'symbolic' value of prevention laws are not uncommon. Similar claims are sometimes advanced for the liquor licensing laws. However, laws are far too 'expensive' a policy instrument to be seen solely in symbolic terms divorced from their practical impact. Indeed, it could be argued that whatever symbolic importance laws have, is closely tied up with their effectiveness and practical consequences.

One further point must be made. In recent years, the number of smokers has declined sharply. In 1972, 52 per cent of males and 41 per cent of females smoked. By 1986 this had declined to 35 per cent of males and 31 per cent of females (OPCS, 1988). This has been achieved without a complete ban on advertising. Nor is it solely or even largely attributable to the increased cost of tobacco (see the contribution by Godfrey in this volume). Rather, it is due to a host of factors including, most importantly, the constant barrage of messages from Royal Colleges, the media and innumerable groups and organisations which, between them, have 'got the message across'. The decline in smoking is, in fact, one of the unsung triumphs of health education. The self-regulatory system has, principally, through its 'labelling code' played a part in this programme.

CONCLUSION

Because of our consensual and evolutionary political culture, the difference between laws and voluntary agreements can be overstated since the content of both, contrary to first appearances, is usually shaped by the lowest common denominator. We should recognise that, because of this culture, policy makers will be more than reluctant to impose laws which create major conflicts and confrontations and which lack the support of public opinion. Laws do have a role to play in prevention policy but we must remember that only those which are largely self-enforcing are enforceable at all. We must also remember that, if some current prevention laws are any guide, there may be and probably will be, unforeseen implementation problems. Unfortunately, the advocates of more laws tend to ignore implementation issues in their enthusiasm for authoritative, legislative actions.

Those concerned with the legal addictions should seek to build on and develop existing prevention policies (such as the self-regulatory tobacco advertising system) in a way which systematically recognises and exploits the nature of the policy process and the existence of organisational networks. Networks can be manipulated in a number of ways by means of incentives and sanctions, persuasion and the dissemination of information (Etzioni, 1968; Sharpf *et al.*, 1978). Funding organisations can amend contracts or devise performance incentives and resource allocation criteria to promote co-ordination as well as manipulating networks by increasing or decreasing the total flow of resources or the channels through which they flow (Benson, 1975). Governments can alter the composition of committees to ensure that certain topics regularly reach committee agendas and provoke debate.

Strategies such as these seek to manipulate the complex, incremental and consensual policy-making process in appropriate and helpful directions. One possible example which comes to mind concerns the departmental responsibility for liquor licensing issues which was discussed earlier. If the 'health potential' of liquor licensing law is to be identified, developed and exploited then network adjustment which shifted liquor licensing responsibilities from the Home Office to the DHSS would be an appropriate strategy. Exactly the same kind of network adjustment occurred in 1971 when it was decided to make the rehabilitation of the habitual drunken offender a health issue. As a result, responsibility for this policy area was transferred from the Home Office to the DHSS.

A similar move might well be appropriate in the case of the alcohol industry which is sponsored by MAFF. Sponsorship is the formalisation and institutionalisation of group–department relationships in which the department assumes specific responsibility for articulating a group's views and interests, for acting as the industry's 'friend at court' and for providing a two-way channel of communication with the black box of government decision making. Sponsorship does not automatically turn a department into an uncritical advocate of a group's interests when policy is being made, but it does confer on a department a general duty to watch over, guard and defend the welfare of its clients. The doctrine applies most commonly to groups producing goods and services, but the services need not be commercial. The Home Office is the sponsor for the police service in the UK.

The MAFF is a relatively small department with a narrow range of responsibilities. Departments of this kind can be 'captured' by client groups (Peters, 1978) and it is sometimes alleged that the National Farmers Union has come to dominate policy making in the MAFF (Davies, 1985). Farming interests are closely entwined with those of the drinks industry and its transfer to the DTI might have practical as well as symbolic consequences. The DTI was formerly the departmental sponsor for many producer groups including the tobacco industry. However sponsorship was ended early in 1987 since it was felt to be inimical to the development of an entrepreneurial culture. The effect of the DTI's decision on the department's relationship with groups is unclear. It may have the effect of strengthening the industries which it intends should be more self-reliant. However, the policy is designed to promote the interests of consumers, in a way which it is believed was not done when the department simply provided industries with a voice in government. Clearly, the interests of consumers should involve a consideration of the health consequences of industrial and employment policies. In addition, the DTI has an important cluster of alcohol concerns including consumer safety, weights and measures and sickness and absenteeism. If it took responsibility for the alcohol industry it would be in a position to co-ordinate production and consumption issues.

Other network adjustment strategies are possible. Some departments including the Home Office, the Department of Health and the Scottish Office have an alcohol policy co-ordinator because their interests are fragmented among a variety of internal administrative units. Co-ordinated policy making within departments and across organisational networks would be facilitated and promoted if all had similar co-ordinators to promote communication, disseminate views, identify problems and help shape common goals. A start in this direction has been made with the establishment of the Ministerial Group on Alcohol Misuse but much more could be done to facilitate linkages between networks and expose insulated policy-making processes to wider considerations. A committee has been established to monitor the various tobacco advertising agreements. Should a similar committee be created to watch over the various codes governing the advertising of alcohol?

The list of possible network adjustments which could be made with a view to promoting more co-ordinated alcohol and tobacco prevention policies is long. But identifying such strategies hinges upon developing a keen appreciation of the structures and processes through which prevention policy is made and the attitudes of policy participants and, hence, the specific impediments which currently militate against the making of more effective policy. It means acknowledging the complex, piecemeal nature of prevention issues and tackling these with the range of policy instruments available as opportunities for doing something sensible present themselves instead of reaching for hand-me-down slogans and calls for 'big bang' solutions. This means learning to live with untidy and partial outcomes and recognising that, while the policy culture and policy process can be a source of frustration, it is also a source of opportunity if we understand, in detail, how policy is made and who makes it. Better a self-regulatory agreement which works than a more ambitious law which does not. Better to have knowledge of the many detailed aspects of the self-regulatory tobacco advertising system, and a realistic view of how it should be developed, than to indulge in rhetorical calls for more laws.

The ESRC Addiction Research Centre's brief was to identify the impediments to a co-ordinated prevention strategy in relation to alcohol and tobacco. We found co-ordinated strategies already in place within the networks. The nature of the policy process which pivots around intra-departmental, inter-departmental and departmental–group consultations sees to that. However, this is not to deny that in many areas policy is implicit and under-developed, nor that policies in different networks are sometimes poorly co-ordinated and take little account of each other. If the self-regulatory system is being developed it is unhelpful for instance to find that at the same time, budget decisions or non-decisions make tobacco cheaper. The task is to make prevention policy more explicit and more developed by removing or neutralising the specific impediments which inhibit its growth and by encouraging co-ordination across networks. These impediments come in various shapes and sizes. But perhaps the most important, in that it diverts attention away from these important detailed tasks, is the very call for a co-ordinated prevention strategy.

References

Baggott, R. and Harrison, L. (1986) 'The Politics of Self-Regulation: the Case of Advertising Control', *Policy and Politics*, vol 14(2) pp. 143–59.

Benson, J. K. (1975) 'The Interorganisational Network as Political Economy', *Administrative Science Quarterly*, vol. 20, pp. 229–49.

Davies, M. (1985) *The Politics of Pressure* (London: British Broadcasting Corporation).

Davies, P. and Walsh, D. (1983) *Alcohol Problems and Alcohol Control in Europe* (Beckenham: Croom Helm).

Department of Health and Social Security (DHSS) (1978) *Tobacco Products Advertising Promotion and Health Warnings*, T8055 (London: DHSS).

Department of Health and Social Security (DHSS) (1980) *On the State of the Public Health for the Year 1978* (London: HMSO).

Department of Health and Social Security (DHSS) (1981a) *Tobacco Products Advertising Promotion and Health Warnings*, TC 143 (London: DHSS).

Department of Health and Social Security (1981b) *Drinking Sensibly*, a discussion document prepared by the Health Departments of Great Britain and Northern Ireland (London: HMSO).

Department of Health and Social Security (DHSS) (1983) *Tobacco Products Advertising Promotion and Health Warnings*, TE 439 (London: DHSS).

Department of Health and Social Security (DHSS) (1986) *Voluntary Agreement on Tobacco Advertising and Promotion and Health Warnings*, TH 575 (London: DHSS).

Department of Health and Social Security (DHSS) (1988) *First Report of the Committee for Monitoring Agreements on Tobacco Advertising and Sponsorship*, TC 143 (London: DHSS).

Department of Transport (1965) *Road Safety Legislation*, Cmnd 2859 (London: HMSO).

Etzioni, A. (1968) *The Active Society* (London: Macmillan).

Griffith, J. A. G. (1966) *Central Departments and Local Authorities* (London: George Allen & Unwin).

House of Commons (1971) *Parliamentary Debates 1970–71*, 24 June, Vol. 819, Cols 340–4 (London: HMSO).

Jennings, I. (1959) *The Law and the Constitution* (London: University of London Press).

Jordan, A. G. and Richardson, J. J. (1982) 'The British Policy Style or the Logic of Negotiation?', in Richardson, J. J. (ed.), *Policy in Western Europe* (London: George Allen & Unwin).

Lindblom, C. (1965) *The Intelligence of Democracy* (New York: Free Press).

Ministry of Agriculture, Fisheries and Food (MAFF) (1988) *News Release: Alcoholic Strength Labelling Proposals*, 49/88 (London: MAFF).

Norton, P. (1987) 'Parliament and Policy in Britain: The House of Commons as a Policy Influencer', in Robins, L. (ed.), *Topics in British Politics* 2 (London: Political Education Press).

Office of Population Censuses and Surveys (OPCS) (1988) *Cigarette Smoking 1972 to 1986*, Monitor SS88/1 (London: Government Statistical Service).

Peters, G. (1978) *The Politics of Bureaucracy* (New York and London: Longman).

Pollitt, C. (1984) *Manipulating the Machine* (London: George Allen & Unwin).

Rhodes, R. A. W. (1979) 'Research into Central-Local Relations in Britain', in ESRC, *Central-Local Government Relationships*, a Panel Report to the Initiatives Research Board, London.

Sharpf, F., Reissert, B. and Schnabel, F. (1978) 'Policy Effectiveness and Conflict Avoidance in Intergovernmental Policy Formation', in Hauf, K. and Scharpf, F., *Interorganisational Policy Making* (London: Sage).

Simpson, D. (1987) 'Tobacco Advertising', *Health and Hygiene*, vol. 8, pp. 1–6.

Taylor, P. (1985) *Smoke Ring* (London: The Bodley Head).

Tether, P. and Godfrey, C. (1989) 'Liquor Licensing', in Godfrey, C. and Robinson, D. (eds), *Manipulating Consumption: Information Law and Voluntary Controls* (Aldershot: Avebury).

Tether, P. and Harrison, L. (1988) *Alcohol Policies: Responsibilities and Relationships in British Government*, Universities of Hull and York, Addiction Research Centre.

Tether, P. and Robinson, D. (1986) *Preventing Alcohol Problems: A Guide to Local Action* (London: Tavistock).

The Justices' Clerks' Society (1983) *Licensing Law in the Eighties* (Bristol: The Justices' Clerks' Society).

Index